Details in Architecture

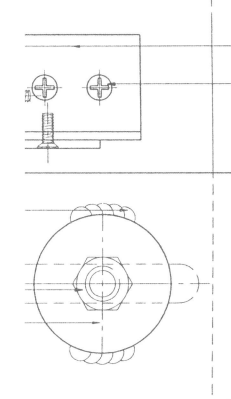

Details in Architecture

Creative Detailing

by some of the World's

Leading Architects

150

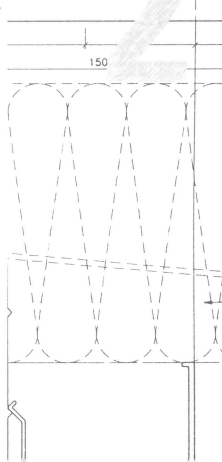

First published in Australia in 2000 by
The Images Publishing Group Pty Ltd
ACN 059 734 431
6 Bastow Place, Mulgrave, Victoria 3107, Australia
Telephone: (613) 9561 5544 Facsimile: (613) 561 4860
email: books@images.com.au
website: www.imagespublishing.com.au

Details in architecture: creative detailing by some of the
world's leading architects.

Includes index.
ISBN 1 86470 038 6 (vol. 2)

1. Decoration and ornament, Architectural. 2. Architecture
– Details.

721

Designed by The Graphic Image Studio Pty Ltd
Melbourne, Australia

Printed in China

CONTENTS

CONTENTS

GLASS DIMENSION

INSULATION RETAINER

6mm THK GLASS PANEL
W/ OPACIFIER CERAMIC FRIT

5mm FILLET WELD
(25mm LONG)

M12x150mm S.S. BOLT & NUT

ø50x6mm THK. C.M.S. WASHER

75mm THK. INSULATION

ø14x75mm SLOT HOLE

1
DE12

OUTSIDE

DOUBLE SIDES
ADHESIVE TAPE

STRUCTURAL SEALANT

SETTING BLOCK

SILICONE SEALANT
WITH BACKER ROD

6 + 12 + 6mm THK.
DOUBLE GLAZING GLASS

GLASS DIMENSION

40

150

100

40

70

40

40

150

1.5

10

15

15

16

15

10

1.5

Any discussion about details in architecture brings
Mies van der Rohe's statement to mind:
'God is in the details.'

Architecture is all about details. How we choose materials
and put them together becomes the life of architecture.
Traditional materials like wood, brick, concrete, steel and
metals required the know-how and capacities of the
craftsman, an accepted discipline and logic. New materials
like structural glass, textiles and plastics require the
knowledge of specialists in engineering, physics, chemistry
and biology. Without this assistance, architecture becomes
merely a formalist and a stylist endeavour, not able to
achieve technological efficiency and advancement. This is
not to say technological expression (like hi-tech) should be
the result of this process. The result is rather to make
technology and details invisible.

In a time fascinated by theory and with the image, the
detail is more important than ever in producing real and
lasting architecture. Real danger exists that the possibilities
of the computer to produce seductive images will alter our
perceptions of time and space through application of
software technology. However, this should not and cannot
distract architects from attention to detail.

—Helmut Jahn (Murphy/Jahn Inc. Architects)

ROOF
SHANGHAI PUDONG INTERNATIONAL AIRPORT, SHANGHAI, CHINA
ADP Architects/Paul Andreu

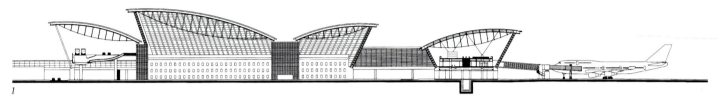

1

2

3

4

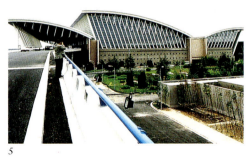

5

1   *Transversal section row 26*
2&4 *Checking hall*
3   *Departures level, near façade*
5   *Access road to airport*
6   *Transversal section row 34*
7   *Roof plan general view*
Photography: Le Scour (2,3,5),
Xu Zhi Gang (4)

The construction comprises two contrasting but complementary elements: light steel roofs and a heavy concrete base containing all of the engineering and electronic equipment for baggage, airconditioning, electricity and so on. There is nothing particularly novel about this method of construction. A stone base is traditionally associated with a light roof framing, and the two are symbolically related to the earth and the sky. Modern construction techniques make it possible to express this symbol even more forcefully by building roofs that appear extremely light.

The roofs of the Shanghai terminal are simple, economic and discrete despite their size. They seem to stretch out in a movement that recalls the petals of a flower, the wings of a bird, or the widening ripples formed by a breeze in water.

The direction of the curves in the roofs changes in the four zones. Two swing upward to indicate the opening on the landside, while the others curve up towards the planes and the sky.

Here and there are large openings in the roof that provide passengers with a view of the sky. The upper parts of the façades are tilted in such a way as to make them brighter and also to control the solar energy input.

The Shanghai project pursues earlier research on the relationship between structure and light. The metal frame of the roofs is prestressed, with

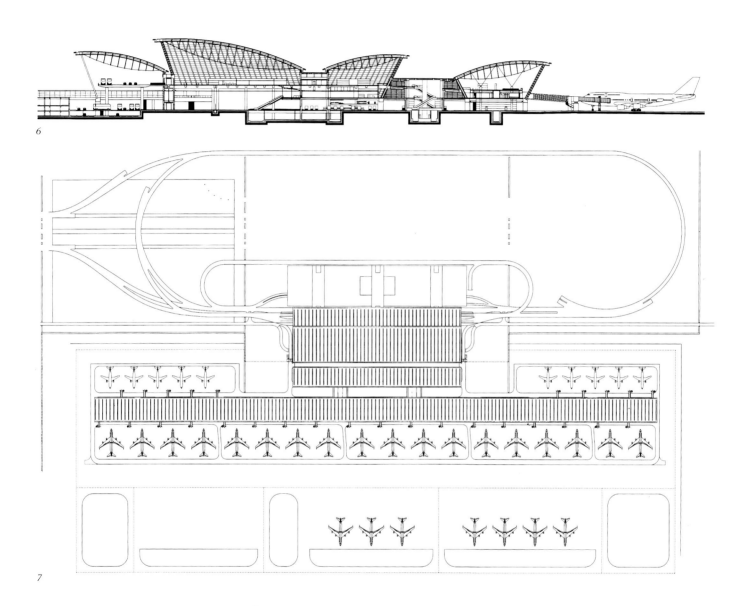

6

7

no diagonal bars. All of the vertical bars vanish
into bright holes pierced in the deep blue ceiling.
These tubes let the sunlight penetrate into the
heart of the public zones while highlighting the
vertical quality of the space. At night, when they
are lit, they look like a shower of comets falling
from the sky.

EXPOSED STEEL CONSTRUCTION
MANN MUSIC CENTRE, PHILADELPHIA, PENNSYLVANIA, USA
Alfredo De Vido Architects

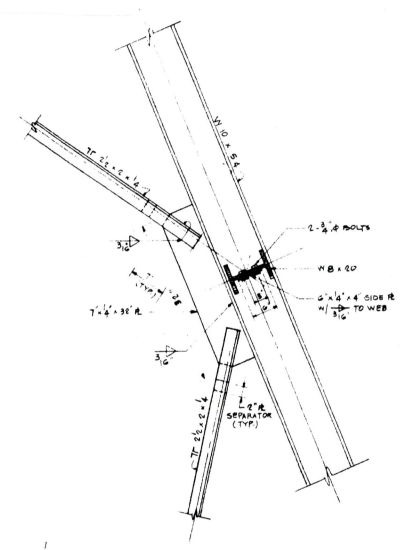

1

2

3

1   Detail of structural bracing for side
    walls
2   Interior view from balcony
3   Interior view of auditorium
4   Bracing of bar joists
5&6 Exposed steel details
7   View of stagehouse inside building
8   View of hung acoustical cloud
Photography: Ed Stoecklein
Structural Engineers: Charles Thornton, Paul
Gossen

The structure was conceived as a series of lightweight queen post trusses with spans in between filled with stock bar joists. The pattern of the beams became important and the spacing was varied at little additional cost to allow exposed joints to line up. The whole roof is covered with heavy decking, providing a structural diaphragm as well as excellent acoustical reflection.

In general, with an exposed structure, it is important to discuss the concept early with the engineers to find out what is the most economical and aesthetically pleasing solution.

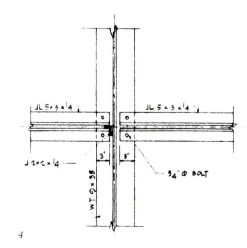

4

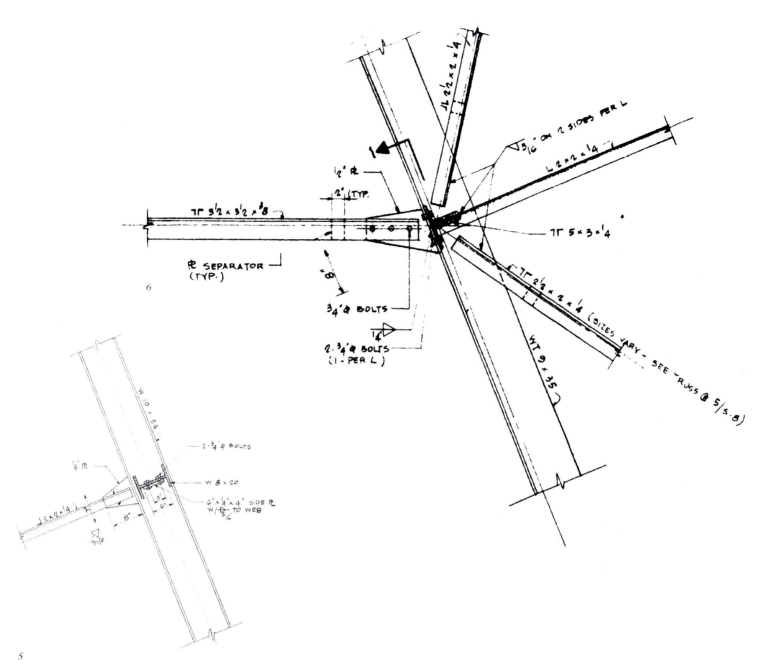

6

5

7

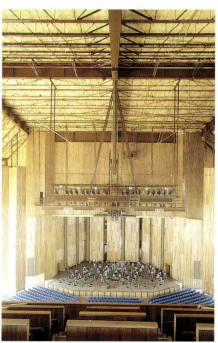

8

CANTILEVERED GLASS FAÇADE

SYDNEY CONVENTION AND EXHIBITION CENTRE SOUTH, DARLING HARBOUR, SYDNEY, AUSTRALIA
Ancher Mortlock Woolley Pty Ltd

1

1 *Eastern entry terrace and sloping glass wall
   to pre-function area*
2 *Detail of pre-function area*
3 *Glass wall*

This building links the original large conference centre and the exhibition centre – both important buildings by other architects. It completes the arrangement and provides central registration and management together with a 1,000-seat auditorium, a 1,000-seat banquet hall and 2,220 square metres of conjoined exhibition space, plus a variety of conference rooms.

The site is beneath a complex of elevated freeways whose massive concrete columns penetrate, but cannot be utilised to support the new building. The height limitations imposed by the roadways, which rise, tilt and interweave above the

conference centre, severely limit the arrangement of the larger building spaces and the lines of columns affect the planning opportunities.

A new elevated entrance for taxis and coaches is provided on the west, linked by the main foyer to the east waterfront entrance, which intersects the original north/south linkage of the conference centre and exhibition halls.

Where the new building asserts itself and faces the waterfront, the huge freeway structures are so visually dominant and dynamic that the response was to refine the design into large gestures – such

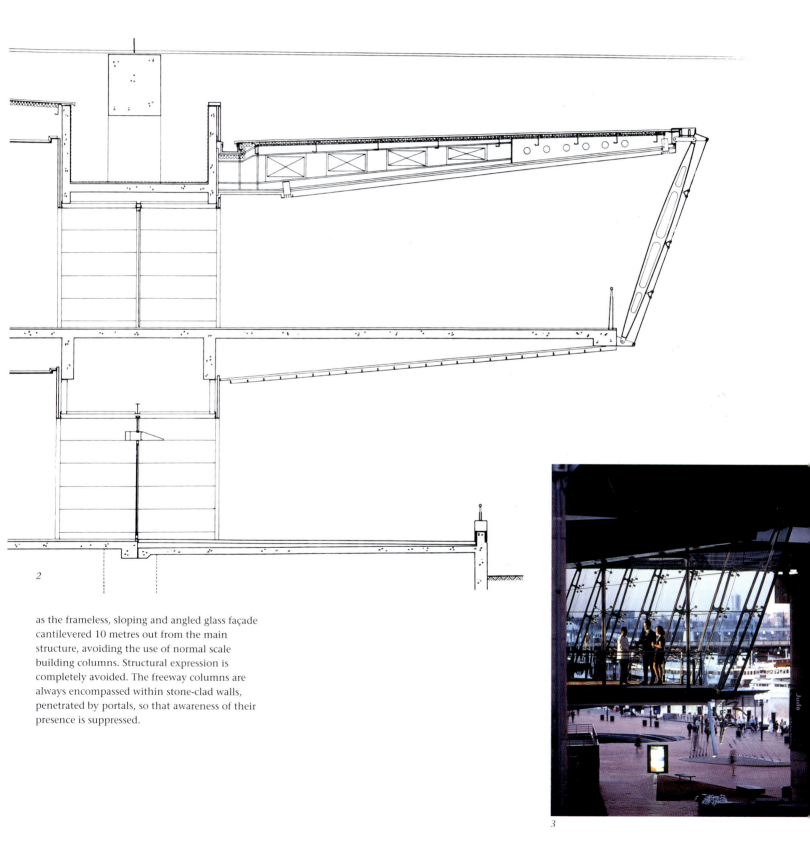

2

as the frameless, sloping and angled glass façade cantilevered 10 metres out from the main structure, avoiding the use of normal scale building columns. Structural expression is completely avoided. The freeway columns are always encompassed within stone-clad walls, penetrated by portals, so that awareness of their presence is suppressed.

3

4   Eastern entrance and terrace
5   Cross section through auditorium and
    western entry
6   Longitudinal section through auditorium,
    meeting rooms, ballroom and pre-function
    area
7   Detail concept drawing by Ken Woolley
8   Ballroom pre-function area and glass wall
Photography: Eric Sierins (1,4,8), The Sydney
Convention & Exhibition Centre (3)

4

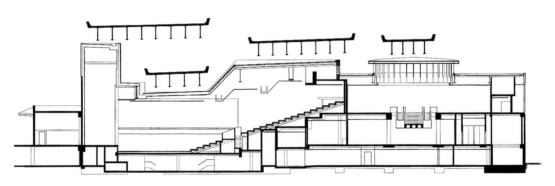

5

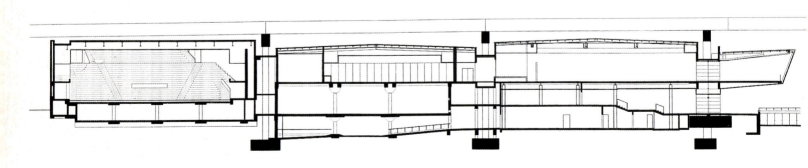

6

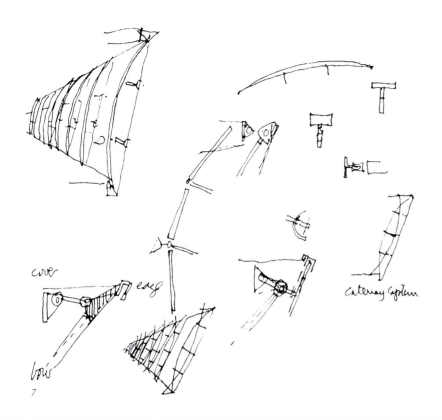

cover

edge

bois

catenary system

7

8

ROLL-UP DOOR AND ROOF
HOUSE AT TORO CANYON, MONTECITO, CALIFORNIA, USA
Barton Myers Associates, Inc.

1

2

4

3

The house at Toro Canyon is sited in a picturesque mountain canyon in Montecito, with panoramic views of the Channel Islands to the south and mountain peaks to the north. A creek runs the length of the site, and native oaks and rich ochre sandstone form a serene Southern Californian landscape. The siting strategy was to make a series of smaller, discrete interventions, thus preserving and enhancing the natural landscape of the site.

The house is comprised of a procession of four steel loft buildings positioned on three terraces that ascend the length of the site. A 500 square foot garage and 1,000 square foot guest house are located on the lower terrace, the 2,800 square foot main residence on the intermediate terrace, and a 1,400 square foot ancillary/archives building on the upper terrace. The sequence of these structures utilises the site contours to minimise the impact upon the landscape, while its north/south orientation takes maximum advantage of the southern exposure and beautiful views.

A recirculating pool system is incorporated into the rooftops, transforming the structures into a series of terraced reflecting ponds. Spilling from one pool to another, the water cascades down the

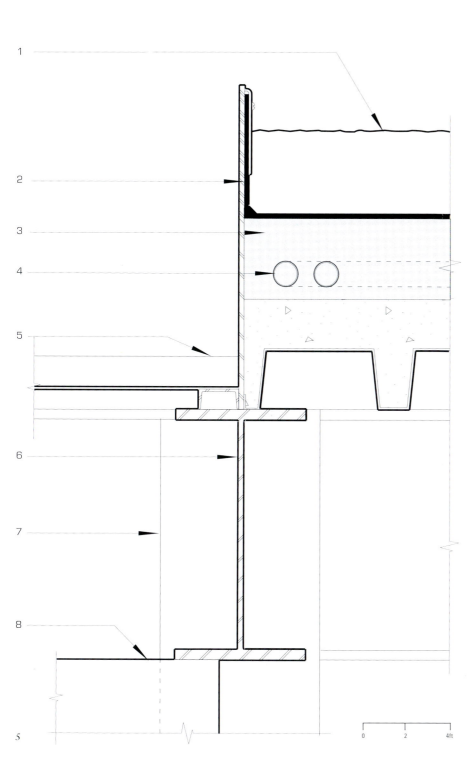

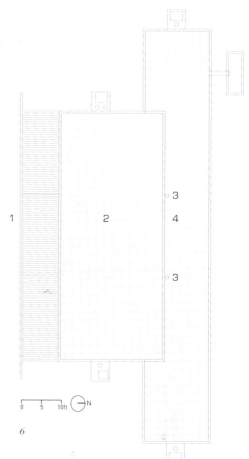

1 Metal decking
2 Upper reflection pool
3 Spillways
4 Lower reflecting pool

6

7

procession of rooftops. The pools serve as a fire-resistant roof assembly and insulation, and the pool atop the guest house is used as a lap pool. The sight and sound of the moving water mimics the continuously flowing creek native to the site.

Each building is an exposed structural steel frame, with a metal deck framing and concrete retaining walls and floors. The structures are open loft spaces enclosed by glazed aluminium sectional doors, which can be opened and closed to varying degrees. North-facing clerestory windows provide panoramic views to the mountains and ample natural ventilation by taking advantage of the ocean breezes that rise up the hillside.

1 Water line
2 Waterproof membrane
3 Foam insulation
4 Conduit for building services
5 Steel decking (seal to fascia)
6 Beam
7 Column
8 Roll-up door hood

1 *Main residence: rear façade of roof reflecting pools at dusk*
2 *Main residence: side elevation and garden*
3 *Main residence: exterior terrace with sectional doors open*
4 *Main residence*
5 *Detail of roof*
6 *Roof plan of main residence*
7 *Main residence: rear façade of bedroom and roof spillway*

8

9

Galvanised rolling fire shutters above every
opening protect the house from brush fires
indigenous to the area and create a secondary
envelope that provides additional insulation and
sun control.

The house at Toro Canyon is an 'elegant warehouse' in the tradition of Eames' and early Barton
Myers' houses. It builds upon the Southern
Californian tradition of seamless spatial integra-
tion of indoors and out, and continues Barton
Myers' explorations in steel housing in which
industrial materials are used out of context; an
emphasis first developed with the Wolf House,
and the earlier Myers' residence in Toronto.

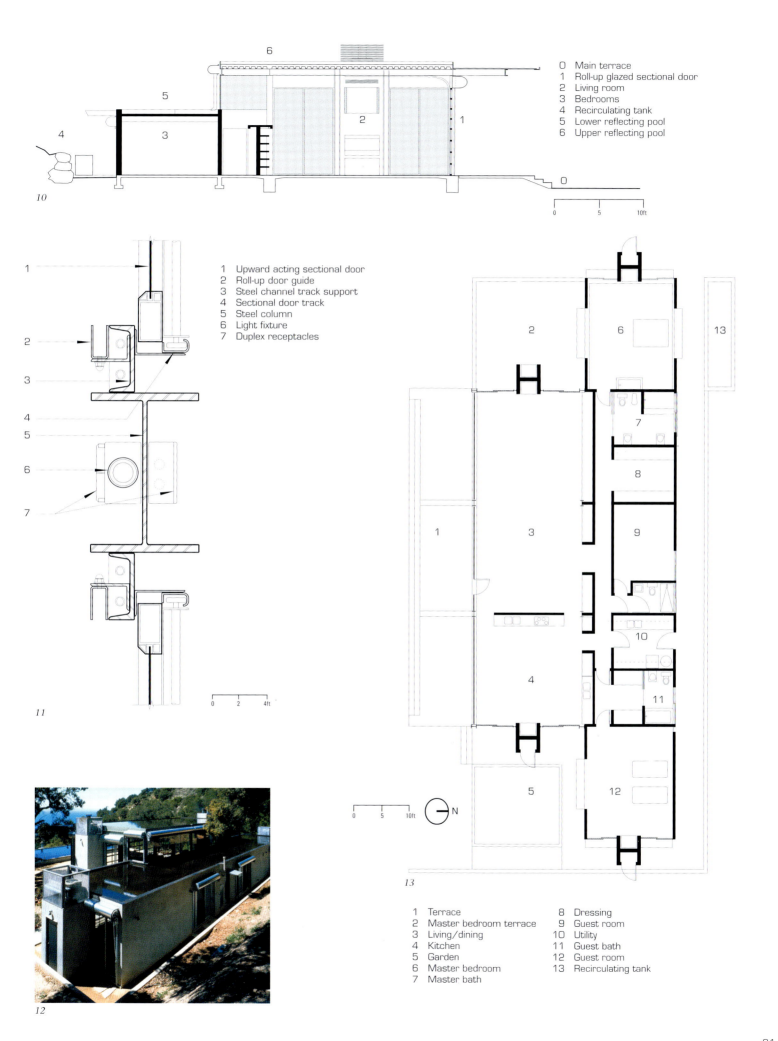

0 Main terrace
1 Roll-up glazed sectional door
2 Living room
3 Bedrooms
4 Recirculating tank
5 Lower reflecting pool
6 Upper reflecting pool

10

0   5   10ft

1 Upward acting sectional door
2 Roll-up door guide
3 Steel channel track support
4 Sectional door track
5 Steel column
6 Light fixture
7 Duplex receptacles

0   2   4ft

11

12

13

0   5   10ft   N

1 Terrace   8   Dressing
2 Master bedroom terrace   9   Guest room
3 Living/dining   10 Utility
4 Kitchen   11 Guest bath
5 Garden   12 Guest room
6 Master bedroom   13 Recirculating tank
7 Master bath

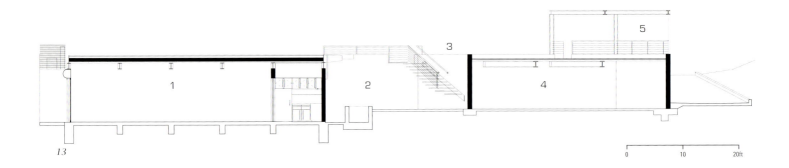

13

0   10   20ft

1   Guest house
2   Recirculating pool
3   Entry stair
4   Garage
5   Roof terrace and trellis

14

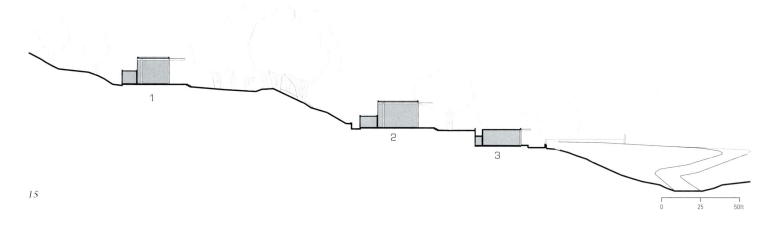

15

1 Studio
2 Residence
3 Guest house

16

17

13 Guest house/garage cross section
14 Guest house: detail of exterior terrace and fireplace
15 Site section
16 Guest house
17 Guest house: south façade
Photography: Grant Mudford

STRUCTURAL STEELWORK
NSW TENNIS CENTRE, HOMEBUSH, NEW SOUTH WALES, AUSTRALIA
Bligh Voller Nield Pty Ltd

2

3

1

The NSW Tennis Centre is the tennis venue for the Olympic tennis and subsequently will be the headquarters of Tennis NSW.

Concrete and galvanised steel are used – matter-of-fact and appropriate for this type of building. This suits both the Centre Court and the Players' Building, which are the two major structures in the Tennis Centre. In the Player's Building, a light steel and glass structure containing the Player's Lounge, Function Rooms and TNSW Offices sits over a concrete base that holds the future Tennis Museum, venue and tournament management offices, Proshop and Locker Rooms. It is linked by a tunnel to the Centre Court and other match courts. The materiality of the concrete links to retain walls to the other service buildings, and

the 'lighter' office buildings and amenity areas, sit on top. The relationship of this building to the No. 2 Court is recognised by the shading structures to the Player's Terrace that lift up and acknowledge the centre line of the court.

The materiality of the concrete base to this building provides a continuous link to the Services Building, retaining walls and paving details that define the Public Domain, and to the structural elements of the Centre Court. The use of galvanised steel for the structural frame is consistent between both the Player's Building an the Centre Court. The Player's Building and Centre Court are strong and robust buildings where the variety of materials is kept to a minimum.

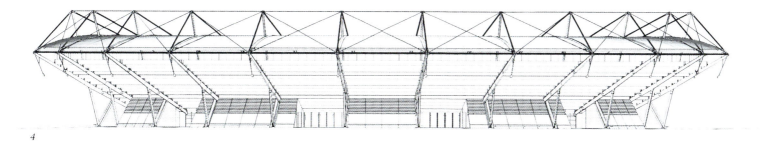

4

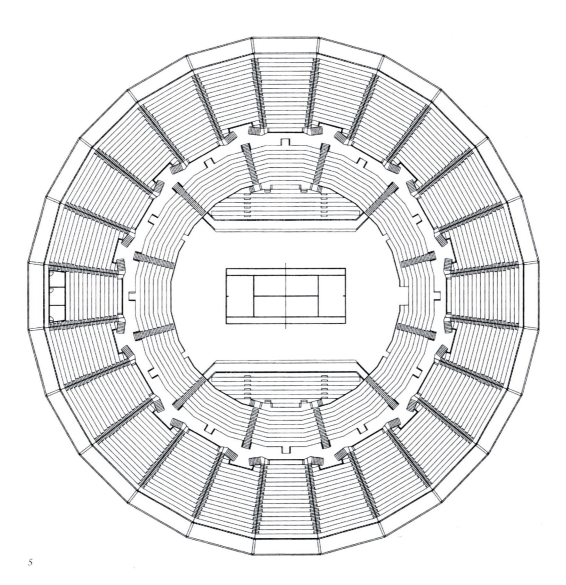

5

The Centre Court is circular, or more exactly, a 24-sided figure. This plan allows a precise, geometric and lineal structure. The super-structure supporting the seats above the cross-aisle involves tier beams, masts and three-ring beams. The ring beams are in fact the cause of the minimal structure. They, in a sense, allow less vertical support to the tier beams, that is, less columns. The precast plats, the structure that supports the seating, simply span between the tier beams. The use of a regular circular figure is unusual in both tennis centres and open sporting venues in general. Its use however, allows a simple and more efficient structure than a less regular shape.

6

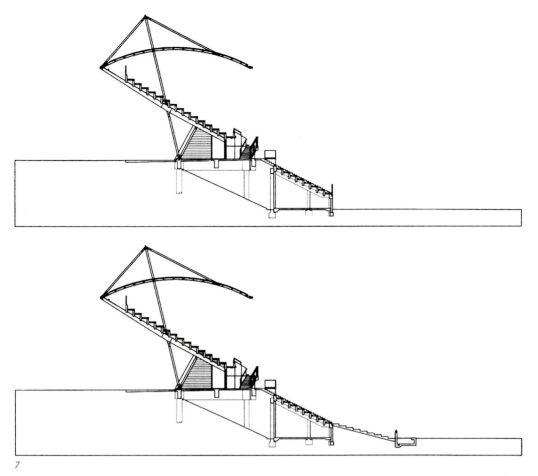

7

8

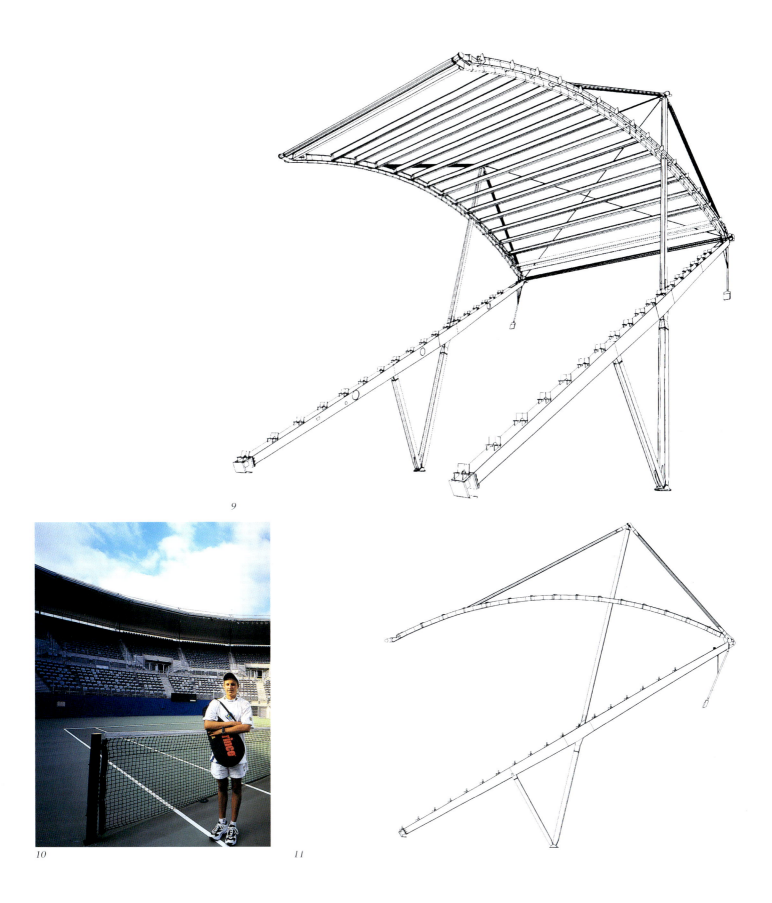

7   Centre Court bowl sections
8&10   NSW Tennis Centre
9   Centre Court bowl structural steelwork three-
    dimensional drawing
11   Centre Court bowl structural steelwork typical
     section
Photography: John Gollings, Southline Drafting Pty Ltd
for three-dimensional model of structural steel

GLASS FAÇADE

CENTRO BRITÂNICO BRASILEIRO, BRITISH BRAZILIAN CENTER, SÃO PAULO, BRAZIL

Botti Rubin Arquitetos Associados

1

2

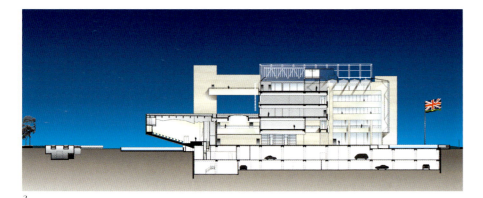

3

4

1   Frontal view
2   External general view during
    construction
3   Longitudinal section of building
4   Façade
5   General façade
6   Section of façade
7   Plan of façade steel structure
8   Detail A – sliding door track box
9   Detail B – section
10 Detail C – track box moulded on glass
    mullion

This building, built by the Cultura Inglesa for its own use in São Paulo, also houses British organisations including the British Consulate General, the British Council, the Energy Commission, in addition to a small theatre, conference and exposition rooms, a library and a restaurant. The entrance hall (19 metres high) is covered by a sky roof; this 32 millimetre structural insulate glass façade is 360 square metres wide and hangs on three-dimensional tubular beams. The lower panels, 4 metres high with 12 millimetre tempered glass, rest on 1 metre high stainless steel vertical pipes immersed into a water mirror that extends around the building.

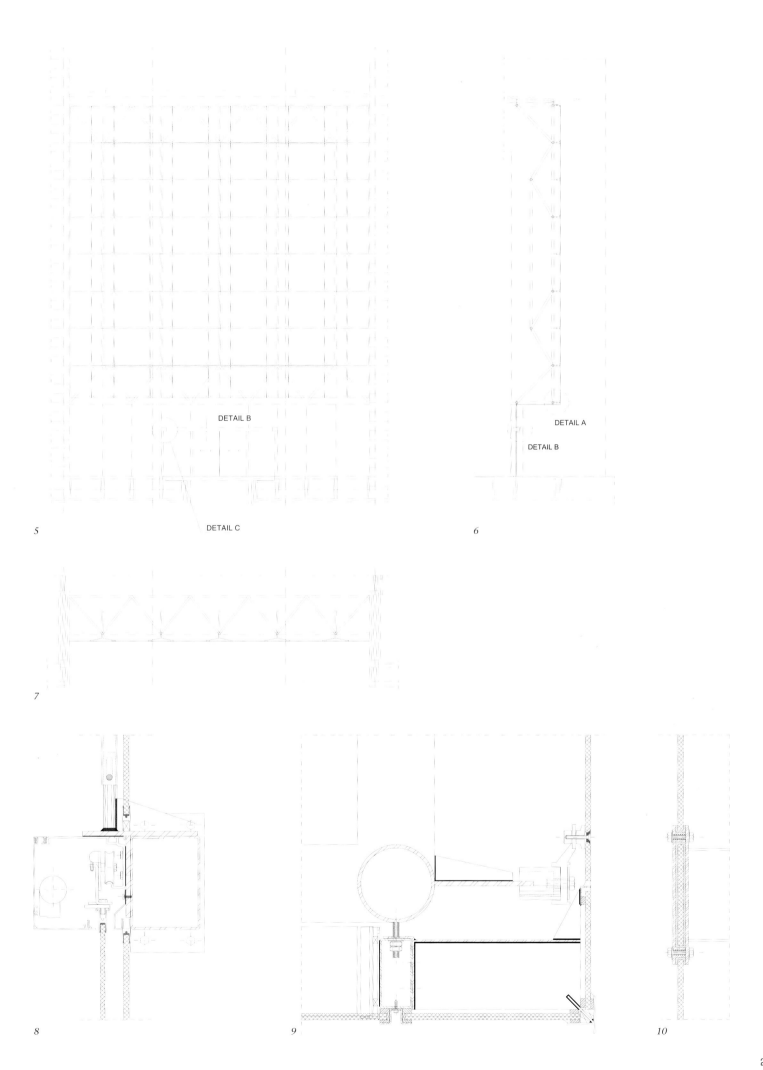

5

DETAIL B

DETAIL C

6

DETAIL A

DETAIL B

7

8

9

10

11

12

13

Opposite:
    Frontal view at night
11 13 Details
14 Section
15 Section details
Photography: Gerson Bilezikjian

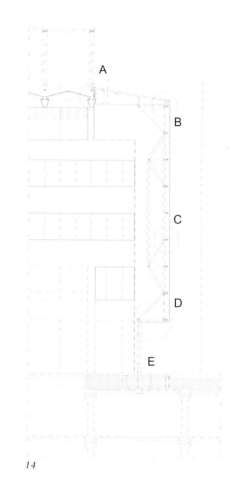

14

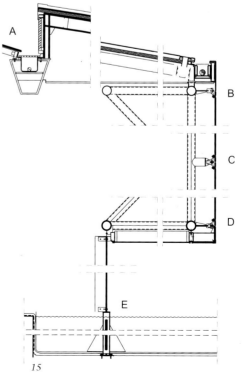

15

FAÇADE GLAZING
VILAR FLORAL HALL, ROYAL OPERA HOUSE, COVENT GARDEN, LONDON, UK
Building Design Partnership

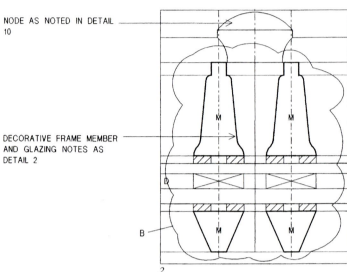

NODE AS NOTED IN DETAIL 10

DECORATIVE FRAME MEMBER AND GLAZING NOTES AS DETAIL 2

2

1

3

The refurbishment and restoration of the Royal Opera House project has been designed to preserve the 140-year-old theatre and redevelop the backstage facilities, so that it can continue as the home of the nation's premier opera and ballet companies.

The Grade I listed 2,267-seat auditorium has been faithfully refurbished to preserve its essential character. Extensive interventions and repairs have improved sightlines, acoustical performance, audience comfort and facilities, access, seating capacity and theatrical lighting. In addition there is the 420-seat Linbury Studio Theatre, and the sky-lit Clore Studio. The rebuilt galleried fly tower,

accommodating scenery, flying sets and lighting bars, is now large enough for six production sets to be erected, retained and moved on automatic stage wagons.

The centrepiece of the whole redevelopment, forming a spectacular new public space, is the reconstructed Vilar Floral Hall. Destroyed by a fire in 1956, four bays have been restored; a mirrored wall giving the illusion of the original eight bays, while making room for the new stage areas behind. The barrel-vaulted roof and fan elevation to Bow Street have been historically reconstructed using a cast iron and glazed structure; however, all new elements are explicitly modern. The wall on

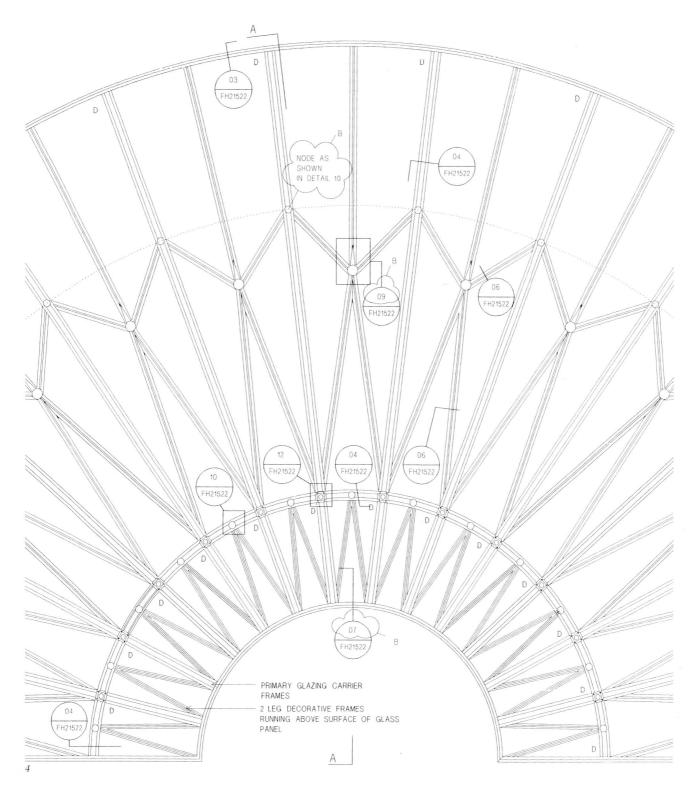

A

D

03
FH21522

D

D

D

B
NODE AS
SHOWN
IN DETAIL 10

04
FH21522

B

09
FH21522

06
FH21522

12
FH21522

04
FH21522

06
FH21522

10
FH21522

D

D

D

D

D

D

D

07
FH21522

B

D

D

D

D

PRIMARY GLAZING CARRIER
FRAMES

2 LEG DECORATIVE FRAMES
RUNNING ABOVE SURFACE OF GLASS
PANEL

04
FH21522

D

D

D

D

A

4

one side of the hall is the external enclosure to the historic auditorium while the other is the structural glass wall separating the hall from the escalator. The escalator, which is believed to be the longest in London, leads up to the amphitheatre bar. Inset into the Floral Hall mirror and accessed via the amphitheatre bar is a window that overlooks the hall. Lit up at night this appears from below as a box floating within the mirror. As the focus of front-of-house activities, an evening-only champagne bar is at the centre of the hall with restaurants at mezzanine levels along each side.

1 Exterior of Floral Hall at night
2 Detail of façade glazing
3 View across Floral Hall at mezzanine level
4 Elevation of inner fanlight frame (window into new cast steel structure)

CAST OR FABRICATED
DECORATIVE NODE AT JUNCTION
OF FRAME MEMBERS

LINE OF U/S OF FRAME MEMBERS
AT INTERSECTION BELOW
SHOWN DOTTED

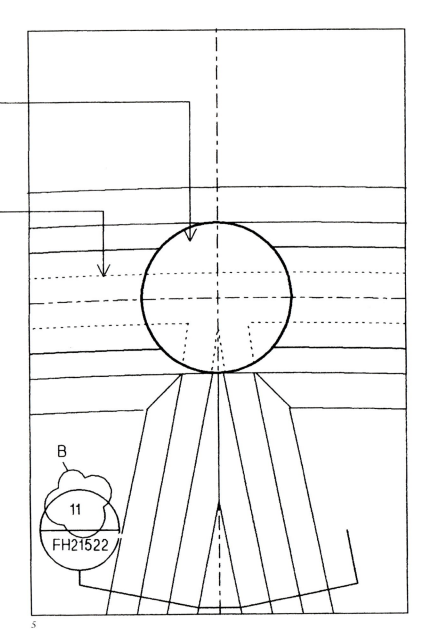

B

11
FH21522

5

6

7

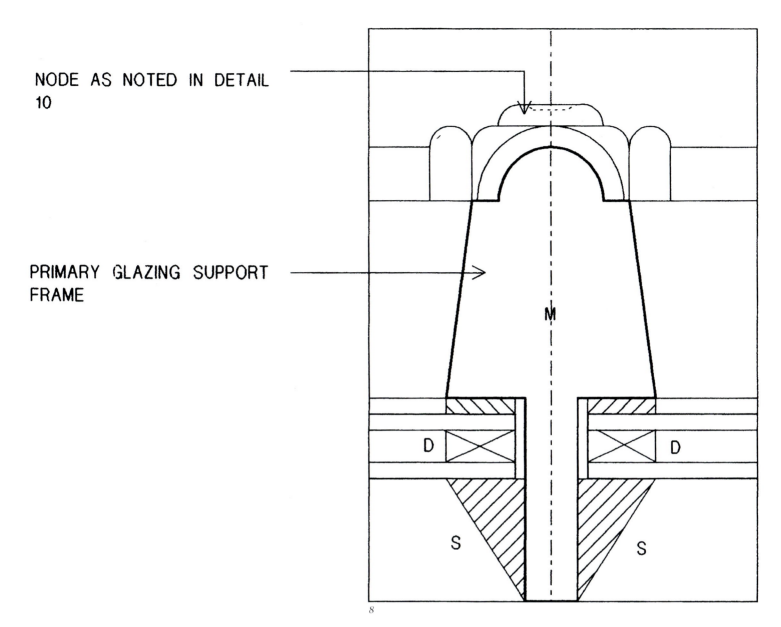

NODE AS NOTED IN DETAIL
10

PRIMARY GLAZING SUPPORT
FRAME

8

9

Shaded areas indicate cast steel or cast iron structural elements.

S Denotes Sika Ltd Sikaflex 11 FC sealant or equal used as sealant and glazing compound
D Denotes sealed double-glazed unit comprising 4mm outer pane, 6mm air gap, 6mm inner pane with low
E Coating to cavity face and inner pane (build up of double-glazed unit to be confirmed)
M Denotes metal window frame member drilled, tapped and counter sunk screw fixed to cast steel structural opening.

5 Detail drawing of façade glazing
6 Mirrored wall and window of amphitheatre bar overlooking the hall
7 Cast iron column structure
8 Façade glazing detail, fanlight inner frame
9 Structural glass wall separating hall from the escalator
Photography: Dennis Gilbert

GLAZED ROOF

NEPTUNE COURT, NATIONAL MARITIME MUSEUM, GREENWICH, LONDON, UK
Building Design Partnership

1

1   Ticket desk at ground level
2   Cross sectional view
3   Key section A – A; typical detail section
    through roof; original parapet detail; key
    roof plan of structure and glazing
4   View of Neptune Court from Greenwich
    Observatory

BDP's master plan of the National Maritime Museum includes the redevelopment and roofing of the Neptune Court, designed to provide a radical reconfiguration of the museum galleries.

The redesign of the courtyard and surrounding wings provides eleven new gallery spaces, including the spectacular indoor glazed courtyard. It returns the courtyard to the original nineteenth century scheme by removing poor twentieth century additions and refurbishing all the original façades based on original drawings. Modern components inserted into the courtyard, such as the podium, the bridges at various levels linked

to the wings, and the all-glass roof improve circulation and exhibition space, while respecting the original architecture.

The primary engineering issue was the creation of the dramatic new clear-span, glazed roof covering the courtyard, an area 52 x 44 metres – one of the largest glass roofs in Europe. Detailed structural investigation proved that the masonry walls could be reinforced and substantially underpinned to take the 240 tonne load of a glazed roof structure. The roof now covering the courtyard is supported on the existing nineteenth century surrounding façades, leaving the vast internal exhibition space column free.

2

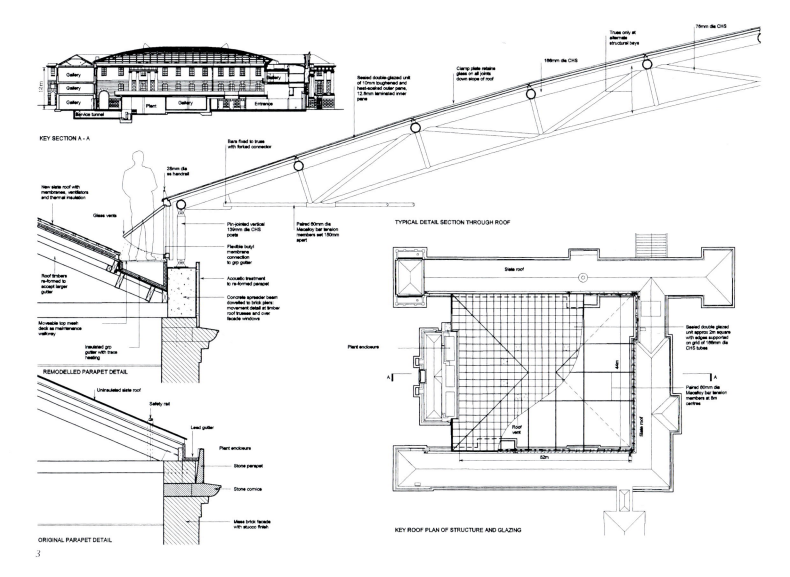

KEY SECTION A - A

12 m

Gallery | Gallery | Gallery | Gallery | Plant | Gallery | Entrance | Service tunnel

Truss only at alternate structural bays

76mm dia CHS

166mm dia CHS

Clamp plate retains glass on all joints down slope of roof

Sealed double-glazed unit of 10mm toughened and heat-soaked outer pane, 12.8mm laminated inner pane

Bars fixed to truss with forked connector

28mm dia ss handrail

New slate roof with membranes, ventilators and thermal insulation

Glass vents

Roof timbers re-formed to accept larger gutter

Moveable top mesh deck as maintenance walkway

Insulated grp gutter with trace heating

Pin-jointed vertical 139mm dia CHS posts

Flexible butyl membrane connection to grp gutter

Acoustic treatment to re-formed parapet

Concrete spreader beam dowelled to brick piers; movement detail at timber roof trusses and over facade windows

Paired 60mm dia Macalloy bar tension members set 150mm apart

TYPICAL DETAIL SECTION THROUGH ROOF

REMODELLED PARAPET DETAIL

Uninsulated slate roof

Safety rail

Lead gutter

Plant enclosure

Stone parapet

Stone cornice

Mass brick facade with stucco finish

ORIGINAL PARAPET DETAIL

Slate roof

Plant enclosure

Roof vent

Sealed double glazed unit approx 2m square with edges supported on grid of 166mm dia CHS tubes

Paired 60mm dia Macalloy bar tension members at 8m centres

44m

52m

A

A

KEY ROOF PLAN OF STRUCTURE AND GLAZING

3

The structure is restrained against buckling by fins, varying from 500 to 750 millimetres in depth. The roof is stabilised by the existing walls in their longitudinal directions; no forces transverse to the walls are transmitted to them, while all horizontal arch thrusts are resisted by seven pairs of cables. The glass panes are tough enough to withstand anticipated loading, including the weight of maintenance workers, snow and wind loads.

4

5   Glazed roof over mezzanine podium
6   Cross section
7   Long section
Photography: Andy Borzyskowksi (4), Dennis
Gilbert (1, 5)

5

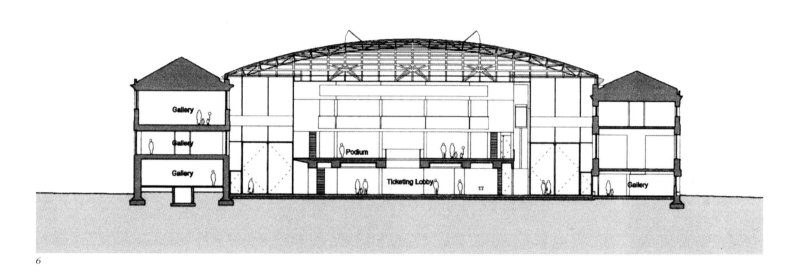

6

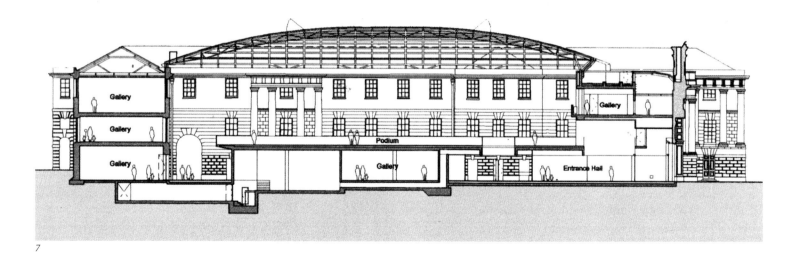

7

39

TILTED GLAZED WALL

THE BIG IDEA, ARDEER PENINSULA, AYRSHIRE, SCOTLAND
Building Design Partnership

1

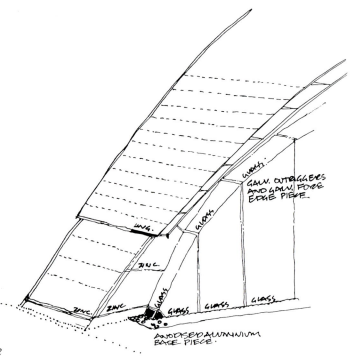

2

1 *Detail of tilted glazed east elevation*
2 *Sketch of zinc/glass wall junction at base*
3 *Diagramatic elevation of sloping glass wall*
4 *Section through glazed gable and roof edge*
5 *Detail of glazing*
Photography: Keith Huner (1,5)

Located on the tip of the Ardeer peninsula in Ayrshire, Scotland, The Big Idea is an exhibition and visitor attraction that celebrates 1,000 years of invention and discovery, the history of explosives and 100 years of Nobel Prizes and Laureates. It also features the life and achievements of Alfred Nobel and commemorates Nobel's big idea – the Nobel Prizes – through an interactive experience.

The 4,000 square metre building takes its form from the natural topography of the site: a vast area of sea grass and heather-covered sand dunes. It shows a deliberate reference to the bunker-type building form, which is traditional on a site where explosives are manufactured. The 60 metre span arched concrete shell is covered in earth and local turf, completely reinstating the building's green footprint, and creating an energy-efficient structure with high thermal mass.

The fully glazed east elevation, at over 500 square metres and 12 metres high, affords panoramic views over the nearby bird sanctuary and the Scottish Maritime Museum at Irvine Harbour. It is tilted outward at an angle of 10 degrees removing sky reflection to maximise transparency and to settle environmental concerns about the morning sunlight reflecting and disturbing the wildfowl breeding grounds. It is one of the largest tilted glass walls in Europe.

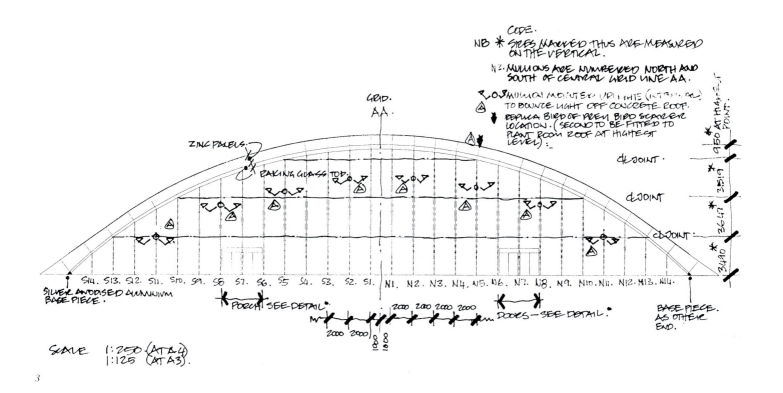

CODE.

NB * SIZES MARKED THUS ARE MEASURED ON THE VERTICAL.

N2. MULLIONS ARE NUMBERED NORTH AND SOUTH OF CENTRAL GRID LINE AA.

A MULLION MOUNTED UPLIGHTS (INTERNAL) TO BOUNCE LIGHT OFF CONCRETE ROOF.

↓ REPLICA BIRD OF PREY BIRD SCARER LOCATION. (SECOND TO BE FITTED TO PLANT ROOM ROOF AT HIGHEST LEVEL):-

GRID. AA.

ZINC PANELS.

RAKING GLASS TOP.

950 AT M14 HIGH POINT.

CL JOINT.

CL JOINT.

3517

CL JOINT.

3647

3440

S14. S13. S12. S11. S10. S9. S8 S7. S6. S5 S4. S3. S2. S1. N1. N2. N3. N4. N5. N6. N7. N8. N9. N10. N11. N12. N13. N14.

SILVER ANODISED ALUMINIUM BASE PIECE.

PORCH - SEE DETAIL.

2000 2000 2000 2000

1800

1000

DOORS - SEE DETAIL.

BASE PIECE AS OTHER END.

2000 2000

SCALE 1:250 (AT A4)
1:125 (AT A3).

3

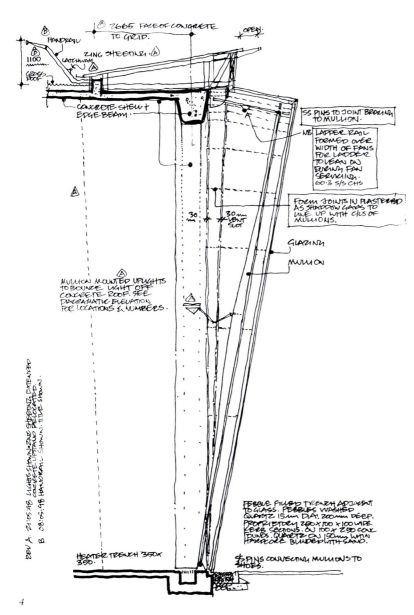

2665 FACE OF CONCRETE TO GRID. OPEN.

HANDRAIL

ZINC SHEETING. A

1100

LATCHWAY

GLASS ROOF.

CONCRETE SHELL + EDGE BEAM.

SS PINS TO JOINT BRACING TO MULLION.

NB LADDER RAIL FORMED OVER WIDTH OF FANS FOR LADDER TO LEAN ON DURING FAN SERVICING. 60.3 S/S CHS

FORM JOINTS IN PLASTERBD AS SHADOW GAPS TO LINE UP WITH CLS OF MULLIONS.

30

30mm VENT SLOT

GLAZING

MULLION

MULLION MOUNTED UPLIGHTS TO BOUNCE LIGHT OFF CONCRETE ROOF. SEE DIAGRAMATIC ELEVATION FOR LOCATIONS & NUMBERS.

REV A. 21.05.98 LIGHTS SHOWN, ZINC EXTENDED, CONCRETE UPSTAND RELOCATED.
B. 08.06.98 HANDRAIL SHOWN. TILES SHOWN.

PEBBLE FILLED TRENCH ADJACENT TO GLASS. PEBBLES WASHED QUARTZ. 15mm DIA. 200mm DEEP. PROPRIETORY 260 x 100 x 100 WIDE KERB SECTIONS ON 100 x 250 CONC FDNS. QUARTZ ON 150mm WITH HARDCORE BLINDED WITH SAND.

HEATER TRENCH 350 x 350.

SS PINS CONNECTING MULLION TO SHOES.

4

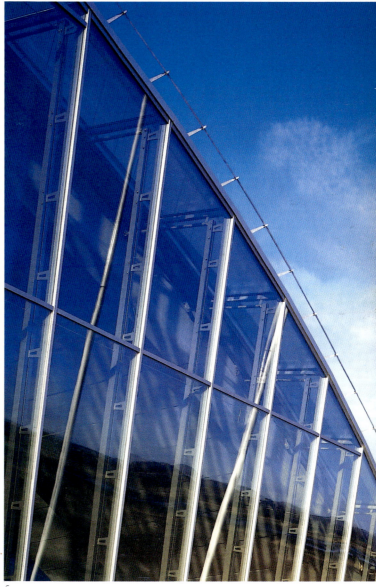

5

41

CANOPY AND WALL
TERMINAL AT WASHINGTON NATIONAL AIRPORT, WASHINGTON DC, USA
Cesar Pelli & Associates Inc

1

2

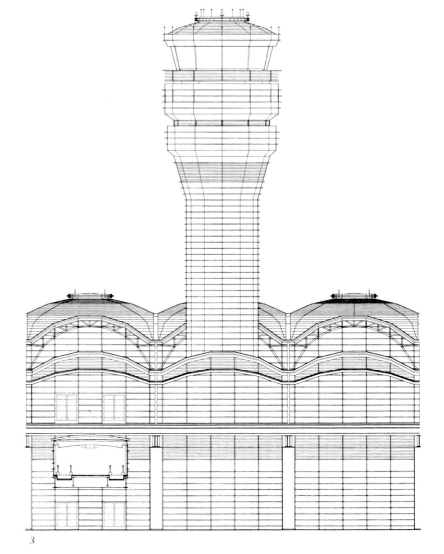

3

1 Detail of airside curtain wall
2 Detail of air traffic control tower
3 Tower elevation
4 East wall section
5 Detail of east wall
6 Details of air in-take and drop-off canopy
7 Transverse section
Photography: Jeff Goldberg/ESTO (1),
Eric Taylor/MWAA (2,5)

Located north of the original 1941 terminal, the new terminal comprises approximately 1 million square feet, including a 1,600 foot concourse that maximises views of the airfield, the Federal Core and the mall, and is designed to accommodate approximately 16 million passengers per year.

The new terminal has a ticket lobby parallel to the metro line and three perpendicular piers containing 35 airline gates. The enplane (departure) curb and ticket counters are located on the uppermost level and the main concourse is on the middle level. This middle concourse level links the metro/garage bridges with the piers and the south

terminal connector, providing direct access to the piers for those arriving from metro stations and parking garages. The lowest level contains baggage claim areas and the deplane (arrival) curb.

The design is based on a 45x45 inch repetitive structural steel bay that establishes scale, flexibility and architectural proportions. Interior public spaces feature exposed painted steel columns and vaulted roof dome trusses. Exterior cladding consists of clear, patterned and spandrel glass with a painted aluminium mullion system.

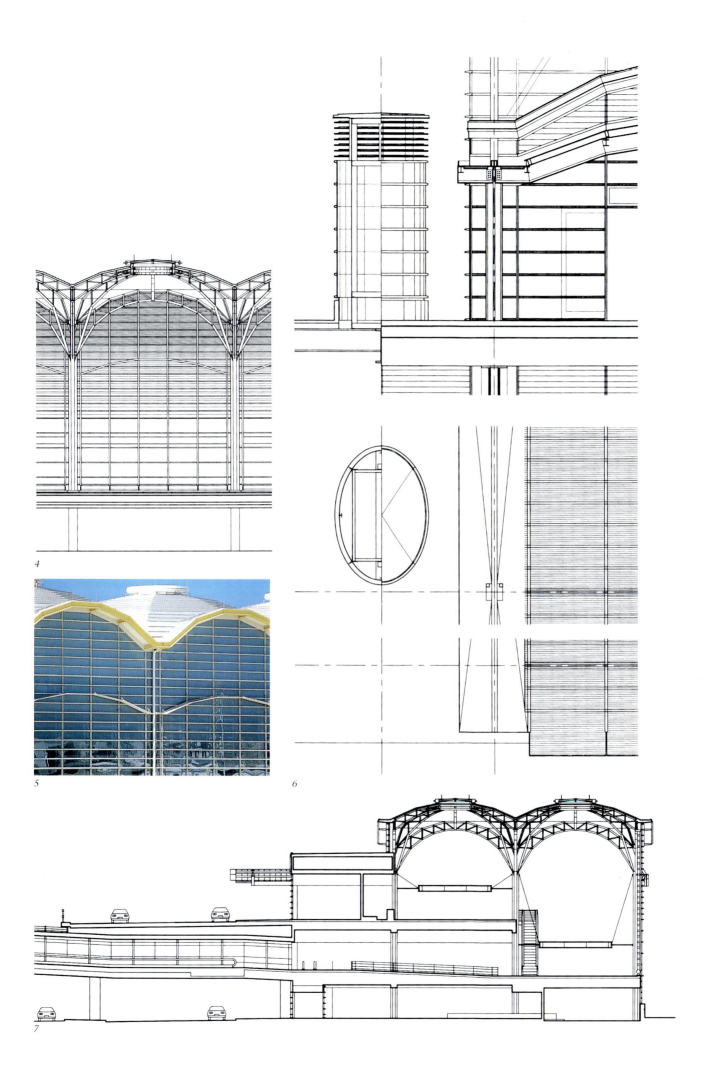

4

5

6

7

CURTAIN WALL
KUALA LUMPUR CITY CENTRE PHASE ONE, KUALA LUMPUR, MALAYSIA
Cesar Pelli & Associates Inc

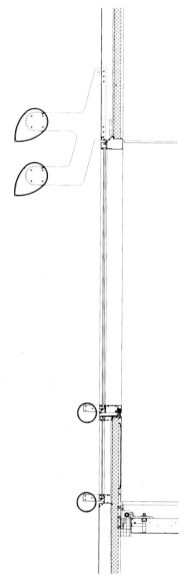

2

3

4

1

1   *Curtain wall section*
2   *Detail of sunshade*
3   *View up Tower # 2*
4   *Detail of column cover at tower base*
5   *Skybridge*
6   *Base podium link front elevation*
7   *Axonometric of tower pinnacle*

Malaysia is among the fastest emerging industrial-ised countries in the Pacific Basin. To meet the demands of urban growth in its federal capital, Kuala Lumpur, the Malaysian Government allowed the Selangor Turf Club and its surrounding land, which is strategically located in the Golden Triangle commercial district, to be developed as a new 'city-within-a-city'. Cesar Pelli & Associates was selected to design Phase One of the Kuala Lumpur City Centre development following an international design competition.

With a site area of 14.15 acres, Phase One comprises more than 10.7 million square feet of mixed-use development, including the twin 88-storey

Petronas Towers of 4.5 million square feet; two additional office towers (designed by others); retail/entertainment facilities; and below-grade parking for 5,000 cars. Public functions within the complex include the Petroleum Discovery Centre, an art gallery, the 850-seat Dewan Petronas Filharmonik concert hall, and a state-of-the-art multimedia conference centre. A multi-story shopping and entertainment galleria connects the office towers at the base, integrating the entire complex.

Designed as the corporate headquarters for the national petroleum company, Petronas, the two stainless steel-clad towers are connected at the Sky

5

6   7

Lobby levels (forty-first and forty-second floors) by a skybridge, facilitating inter-tower communication and traffic. Organised around this circulation system are shared Petronas facilities such as the conference centre, the upper *surau* (prayer room) and the executive dining room.

Malaysian colours, patterns, traditions and crafts have been incorporated throughout the buildings so that they appear not as foreign elements but as new and exuberant citizens of Malaysia. The geometry of the twin towers is based on Islamic traditions as is the development from simple to complex forms. The lobby core walls are finished with light-coloured Malaysian woods within

a stainless steel grid. The pattern of the marble lobby floor derives from popular regional Pandan weavings and bertam palm wall mattings. Reinforcing a sense of the tropical locale and optimising the use of Malaysian crafts, a continuous wooden screen wall shields the perimeter of the lobby wall to minimise the contrast of brightness between the exterior and interior.

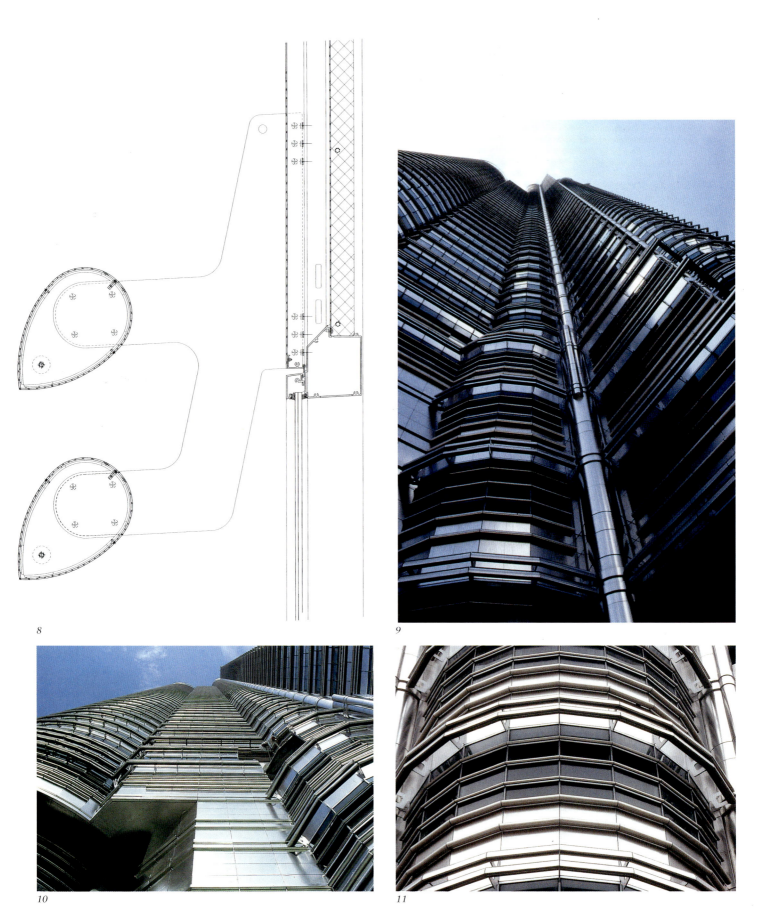

8

9

10

11

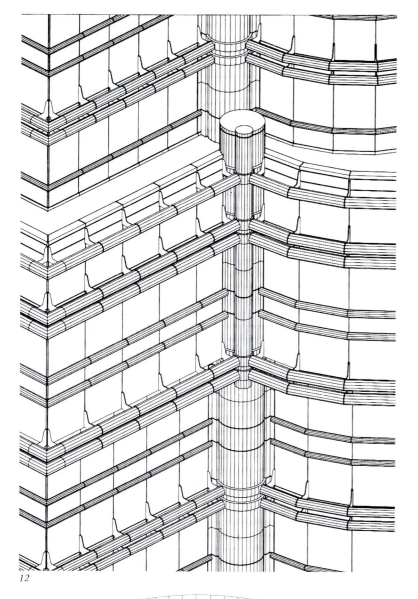

12

8   Detail of curtain wall section
9&10 View up tower
11   Detail of curtain wall at round bay
12   Curtain wall detail at setback floor
     (level 59)
13   Detail of curtain wall at setback floor
14   Perspective view of street-level tower
     entrance
Photography: J. Apicella/CP&A
(2,5,10,11), P. Follett/CP&A (3,9,13),
Jun Mitsui (1)

13

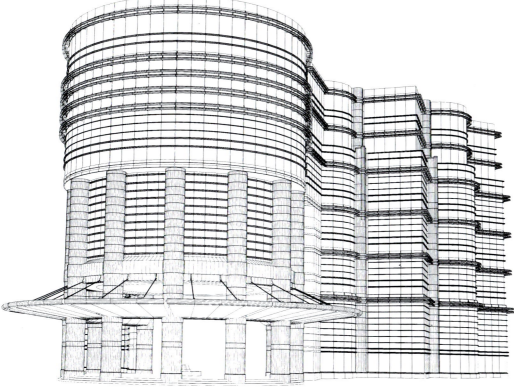

14

EAVES AND FAÇADE

SOKA GAKKAI BUDDHIST CENTRE, HOMEBUSH BAY, SYDNEY, AUSTRALIA
The Cox Group

1

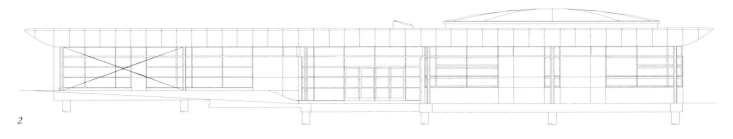

2

3

1   *North-west façade*
2   *South-east elevation*
3   *North façade*
4   *Detail section of main hall and eave soffit*
5   *North façade blade projection*
6   *Façade detail*
Photography: Patrick Bingham-Hall

The Soka Gakkai Buddhist Centre is a horizontal pavilion building, designed to reconcile its religious undertones with its context in a commercial business park. Produced for a lay Buddhist group originating from Japan, the centre serves a rapidly growing membership in Australia. The client's brief mandated against a 'stand-out' building, preferring harmonious inclusion in its environment and a contemporary character.

The simple design consists of a broad protective roof, imparting physical and symbolic shelter, while the rich colours of monastic robes are reflected in the wall treatments. Entry is defined on both sides by a continuous 'blade' separating the 600-seat cultural centre from administrative areas. Other facilities include conference and meeting rooms, a guest lounge, library and bookshop. Height is gained for the cultural centre by a level change responding to external topography, and enhanced by an elliptical roof dome.

All walls in the building are kept short of the ceiling plane, symbolising openness and allowing daylight to penetrate across the interior spaces. Various other symbolic references, particularly to contemporary Japanese architecture, are created and extended into the landscape.

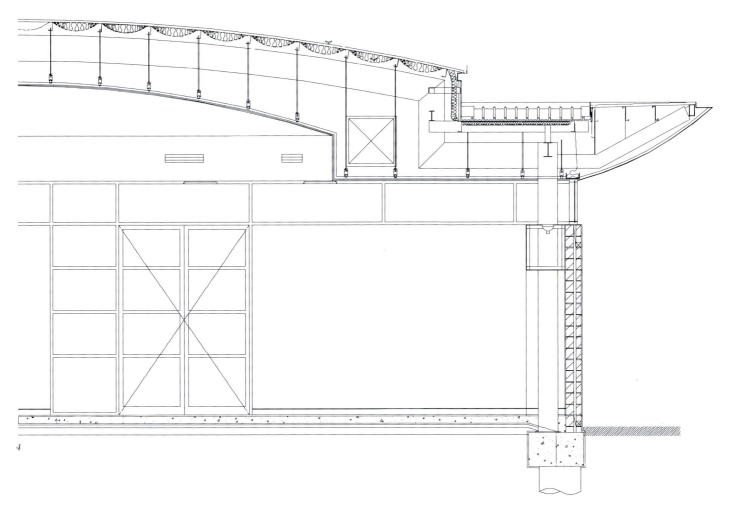

4

5

6

ROOF

CAIRNS CONVENTION CENTRE, QUEENSLAND, AUSTRALIA
The Cox Group

1

1 *Front entrance*
2 *South-west elevation, 1:1000*
3 *Roof framing study*
4 *Connection details for roof trusses*
5 *Shadow play from struts*

Cairns Convention Centre was undertaken in two stages, the first completed in 1996 for the main plenary hall, foyer and meeting spaces, and the second in 1999 comprising a dual-use performance and indoor sports hall.

The design for the convention centre is based upon three concepts. The first is developed from the influence of the region's industrial vernacular of innovative shed structures, and uses folded plate technology as the primary structure. The second derives from the centre's appeal in ecotourism, for which a comprehensive series of environmental systems were developed. The third is a planning

response to the centre's role as the final ingredient in a master plan, in which the folded plate geometry allows the roof to rotate towards the urban renewal area.

Folded plate structure was determined as the most efficient means for simultaneously spanning the 60 metre width and cantilevering out some 8 metres on either side for tropical climate protection. The roof system is exposed internally, and accentuated by lighting along the bottom chords of each 'rib'. The two halls are inserted within the roof canopy as simple box forms, creating a range of arresting geometries in the concourse and foyer

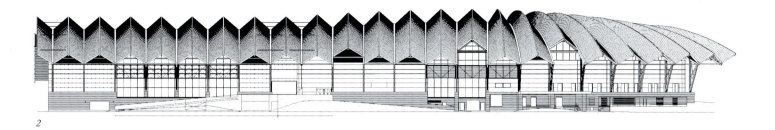

2

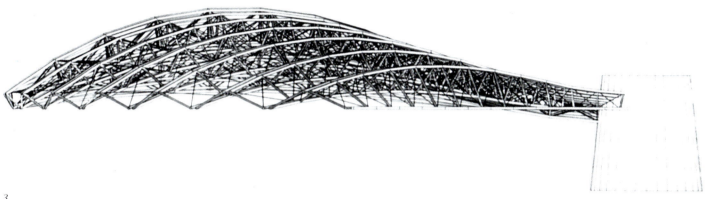

3

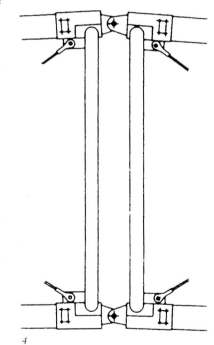

4

spaces. Laminated plantation timber posts externally support the roof, reflecting the many rural structures in the region that served the traditional sugar industry.

The public spaces were developed in collaboration with regional artists from a variety of areas including Thursday Island and the Torres Strait, in works ranging from relief sculpture to contemporary indigenous works.

5

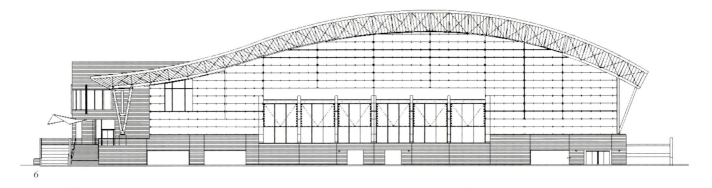

6

6 North-west elevation, 1:1000
7 Details of solar-adjustable screens
8 Section through multipurpose arena,
   1:1000
9 Uplighting dominates the folded-plate
   roof edges
10 Construction details for roof trusses
Photography: Patrick Bingham-Hall

7

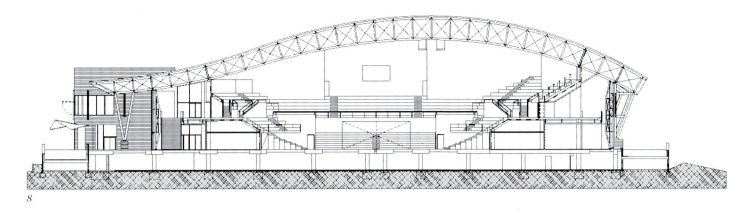

8

9

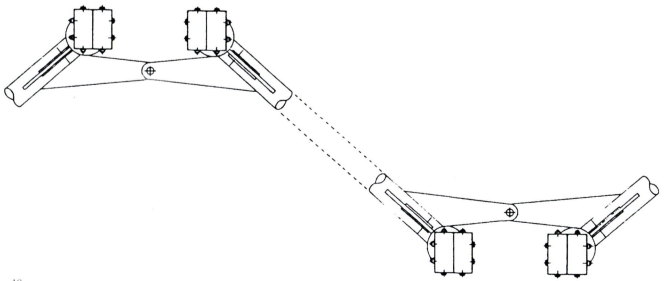

10

ROOF

MUSEUM OF TROPICAL QUEENSLAND, TOWNSVILLE, NORTH QUEENSLAND, AUSTRALIA
The Cox Group

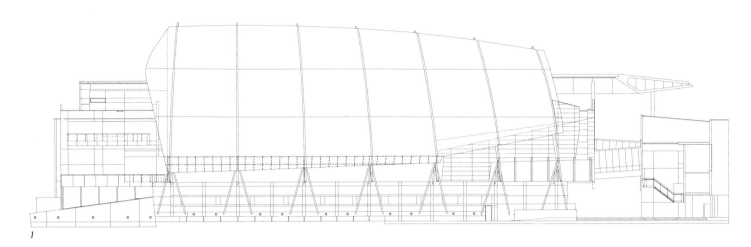

1

2

3

This museum is an extension of the Queensland Museum and focuses upon four primary aspects of north Queensland history: indigenous culture, maritime history, natural history and coral collections.

Its centrepiece is the HMS Pandora, the famous vessel shipwrecked off the far northern tip of Queensland. Pandora relics are being collected in stages and are insufficient to reconstruct the vessel, but the active process of the salvage gives meaning to the concept of a 'living museum'. The bow of the vessel has been replicated at full scale and is housed in a 12 metre high gallery with the

remainder of the plan imprinted across the gallery floor. The gallery is roofed by a continuous three-dimensional curved 'sheet', which carries down over the building podium onto struts. The structure itself is a parody of rigging, inverted hulls and sails, as well as discernible metaphor for the indigenous 'lean-to' or the ribbed cage of prehistoric creatures – all recalling the main themes of the museum.

The building contrasts an internal box (a 'Pandora's box') encassed in 'broken' forms evocative of a shipwreck. The internal box houses the main themed galleries, the more exuberant

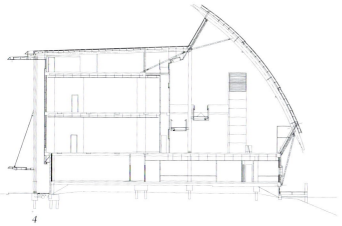

4

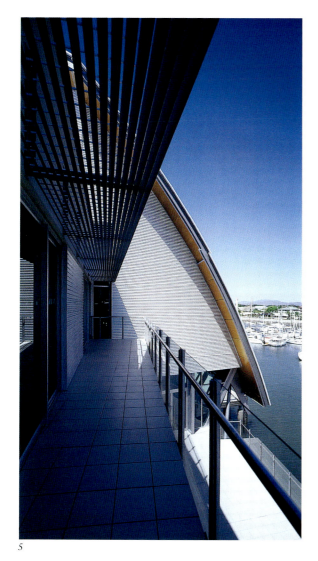

5

spaces accommodating a children's gallery and education areas, public facilities and café. The galleries are elevated above a podium containing the curatorial and storage areas, which can be glimpsed through narrow slots from the wharf side of the museum.

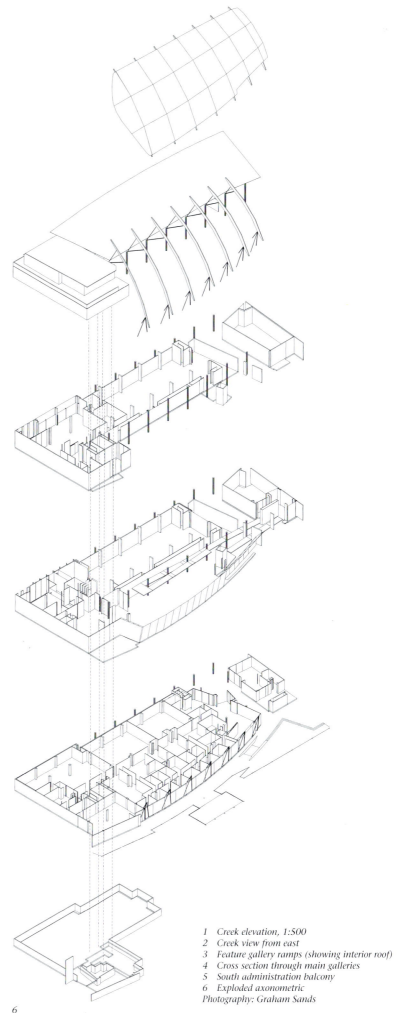

1   Creek elevation, 1:500
2   Creek view from east
3   Feature gallery ramps (showing interior roof)
4   Cross section through main galleries
5   South administration balcony
6   Exploded axonometric
Photography: Graham Sands

6

SYMBOLIC FLAG
EUREKA STOCKADE INTERPRETIVE CENTRE, BALLARAT, VICTORIA, AUSTRALIA
The Cox Group

1

The Eureka Centre commemorates one of the defining moments in Australia's history, the Eureka Stockade, in 1854 the scene of a bloody battle between 500 troops and 400 rebellious goldminers. While the original Stockade Hill location remains uncertain the plan is reminiscent of the mound, using masonry walls encircling an internal contemplation space with a commemorative lawn that spans the mound and reaches up to meet the arching roof. The sunken contemplation space within is a metaphor for both the mines and the protection of the stockade.

The Southern Cross flag soars at an angle over the roof and is aligned on an axis with Ballarat's main street. Its mast pierces the roof as if pinning the museum to the earth, and the flag is dramatically oversized as a commentary on the significance of what was a comparatively small physical event that had major political repercussions throughout the British colonies. Other contrasts further reflect struggle: indigenous and exotic plantings flourish the local landscape, while fragile sunscreens vie with the mass precast panels that symbolise rock cuttings.

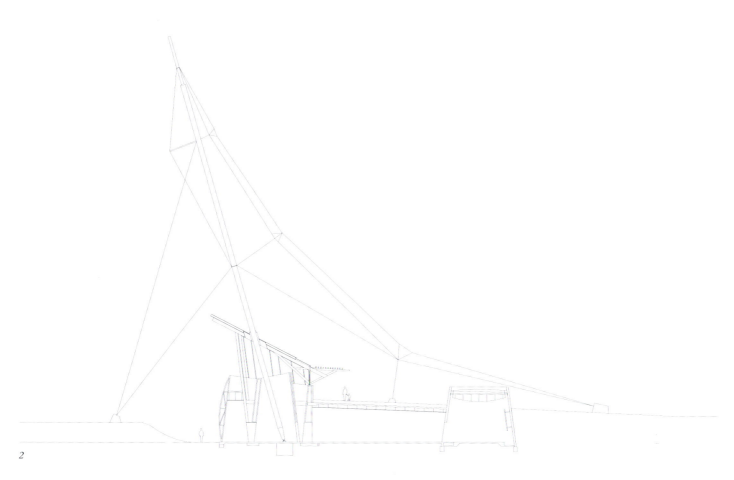

2

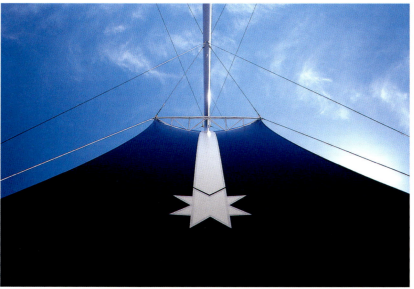

3

4

These treatments perform effective environmental roles – automated louvres induce natural ventilation at high and low levels, masonry walls and earth berm surrounds deliver thermal insulation, and the slatted façade and overhangs screen northern sun such that evaporative cooling dispenses with the need for airconditioning.

1   Sail from internal court
2   Cross section through mast
3   Mast and sail
4   Northern façade

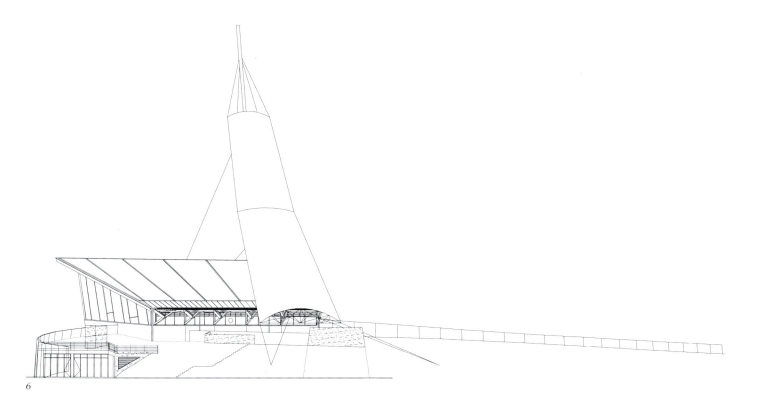

6

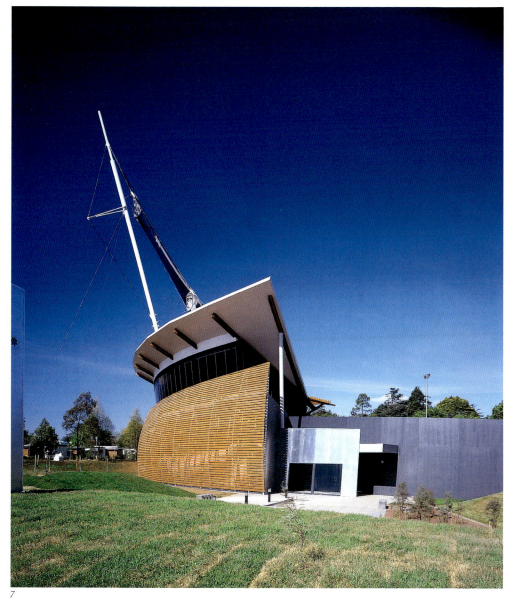

7

Opposite:
  Night view
6   *South elevation*
7   *Entry view*
Photography: Patrick Bingham-Hall

FAÇADE
PIER ONE PARKROYAL HOTEL WALSH BAY, SYDNEY, NEW SOUTH WALES, AUSTRALIA
Crone Associates

1

2

3

4

1 A modern extension has been added to the southern end of the original wharf building
2 New cladding materials have been recessed within the original façade module to provide a rich textural appearance to the building
3 Decorative steel framing and metallic elements together with splashes of bold colour have been used in the modern extension
4 A combination of screens, louvres, glass selection and façade layering has been used to control the exposure to the western orientation
5 Section through new annexe; building façade is behind decorative steel framing
6 Section though existing structure with new façade work recessed

Photography: courtesy of Crone & Associates

Pier One Parkroyal is a low-rise international boutique-style hotel built within an original 1912 Finger Wharf on Sydney Harbour. The heritage-listed building has been adapted, refurbished and extended to provide accommodation for 165 hotel guestrooms and associated facilities including restaurants, bars and café. Four new floor levels have been constructed within the existing building envelope.

The existing timber-framed structure and substructure has been retained to emphasise the historic character of the wharf. A new façade has been recessed within the existing structural module. The western orientation, with exposure of internal areas to the sun and subsequent heat load, has been controlled through the use of high-performance glass, insulation and timber screens. This variety of materials, combined with metal louvres, timber, steel and sheet metal panels, provides a rich textural appearance to the harbourside façade.

The southern end of the building has been extended by the addition of a new four-storey annexe. This modern extension, with a façade of reinforced concrete, sandstone and face brickwork overlaid with decorative steel framing and metallic elements, provides an interesting contrast to the original timber-framed wharf building.

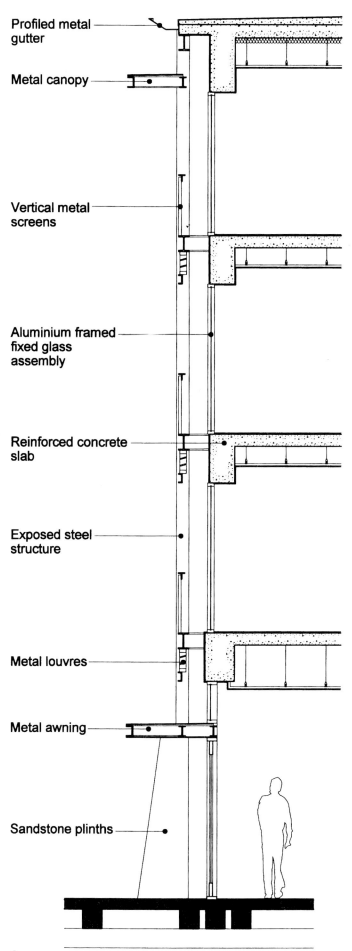

Profiled metal gutter

Metal canopy

Vertical metal screens

Aluminium framed fixed glass assembly

Reinforced concrete slab

Exposed steel structure

Metal louvres

Metal awning

Sandstone plinths

5

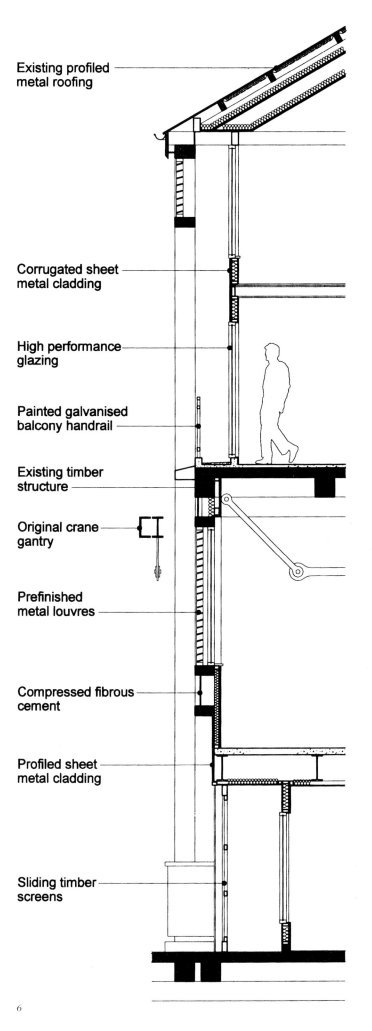

Existing profiled metal roofing

Corrugated sheet metal cladding

High performance glazing

Painted galvanised balcony handrail

Existing timber structure

Original crane gantry

Prefinished metal louvres

Compressed fibrous cement

Profiled sheet metal cladding

Sliding timber screens

6

PODIUM FAÇADE AND ROOF
CITIGROUP CENTRE AND GALERIES VICTORIA, SYDNEY, NEW SOUTH WALES, AUSTRALIA
Crone Associates

1

2

1 *From George Street the three-storey high glass wall enclosing the northern retail laneway of Galeries Victoria divides the sandstone and granite podium into separate buildings*
2 *The Tower of granite glass and aluminium rises above the sandstone and copper roofscape of the Queen Victoria Building*
3 *The George Street façade of the Galeries Victoria clearly shows the three parts of the podium façade*
4 *Elevation of podium façade, arcade entry, George Street*
5 *Section of podium façade, arcade entry, George Street*

The Citigroup Centre is a 41-storey premium-grade office tower (72,000 square NLA) and a four-level basement for carparking, loading docks and storage areas. The Galeries Victoria is a four-level retail podium connected to Town Hall Station and the Darling Harbour Monorail (14,000 sqm NLA). Both buildings are situated on a 8,091 square metre site.

The tower façade is clad in a range of materials including exfoliated and polished granite, pale copper coloured PVF2-coated aluminum panels and window frames with small areas of anodised aluminum highlighting. The use of light coloured

materials reminiscent of Sydney sandstone, together with the stepped corners and chevron plan form of the east and west ends give the building a unique presence.

The Galeries Victoria retail podium occupies the lower ground floor, ground floor and the first two levels of the podium. The podium façades have been designed to reflect the building's prestige and importance while complementing nearby heritage buildings. The materials and modelling are similar to the tower above, but include honed sandstone and polished and exfoliated granite. Bright metal and PVF2-coated or anodised aluminium window

3

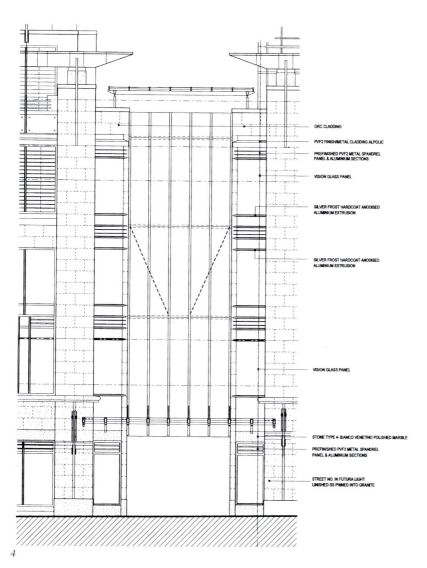

4

GRC CLADDING

PVF2 FINISH/METAL CLADDING ALPOLIC

PREFINISHED PVF2 METAL SPANDREL
PANEL & ALUMINIUM SECTIONS

VISION GLASS PANEL

SILVER FROST HARDCOAT ANODISED
ALUMINIUM EXTRUSION

SILVER FROST HARDCOAT ANODISED
ALUMINIUM EXTRUSION

VISION GLASS PANEL

STONE TYPE 4- BIANCO VENETINO POLISHED MARBLE

PREFINISHED PVF2 METAL SPANDREL
PANEL & ALUMINIUM SECTIONS

STREET NO. IN FUTURA LIGHT
LINISHED SS PINNED INTO GRANITE

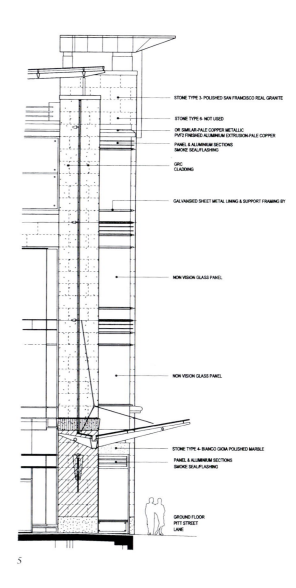

5

STONE TYPE 3- POLISHED SAN FRANCISCO REAL GRANITE

STONE TYPE 6- NOT USED

OR SIMILAR-PALE COPPER METALLIC
PVF2 FINISHED ALUMINIUM EXTRUSION-PALE COPPER

PANEL & ALUMINIUM SECTIONS
SMOKE SEAL/FLASHING

GRC
CLADDING

GALVANSIED SHEET METAL LINING & SUPPORT FRAMING BY

NON VISION GLASS PANEL

NON VISION GLASS PANEL

STONE TYPE 4- BIANCO GIOIA POLISHED MARBLE

PANEL & ALUMINIUM SECTIONS
SMOKE SEAL/FLASHING

GROUND FLOOR
PITT STREET
LANE

frames together with the footpath awnings and entrance canopies provide the building with a user friendly atmosphere.

Within the Galeries Victoria, paired escalators at the eastern and western ends of the four-storey retail complex provide easy access to all levels of the this complex, and to the monorail station. A short pedestrian mall under George Street connects the lower ground floor to Town Hall railway station concourse and the southern end of the Queen Victoria Building.

The Pitt Street side of the podium includes street frontage retail, entrances to the retail avenues (linking through to George Street and Town Hall Station) and the historic School of Arts. This heritage building has been restored and will be adapted to include a new retail facility, or possibly a pub and restaurant.

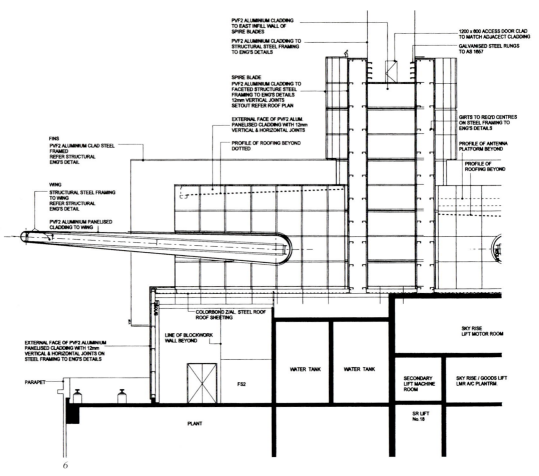

PVF2 ALUMINIUM CLADDING
TO EAST INFILL WALL OF
SPIRE BLADES

PVF2 ALUMINIUM CLADDING TO
STRUCTURAL STEEL FRAMING
TO ENG'S DETAILS

1200 x 600 ACCESS DOOR CLAD
TO MATCH ADJACECT CLADDING

GALVANISED STEEL RUNGS
TO AS 1657

SPIRE BLADE
PVF2 ALUMINIUM CLADDING TO
FACETED STRUCTURE STEEL
FRAMING TO ENG'S DETAILS
12mm VERTICAL JOINTS
SETOUT REFER ROOF PLAN

EXTERNAL FACE OF PVF2 ALUM.
PANELISED CLADDING WITH 12mm
VERTICAL & HORIZONTAL JOINTS

GIRTS TO REQ'D CENTRES
ON STEEL FRAMING TO
ENG'S DETAILS

FINS
PVF2 ALUMINIUM CLAD STEEL
FRAMED
REFER STRUCTURAL
ENG'S DETAIL

PROFILE OF ROOFING BEYOND
DOTTED

PROFILE OF ANTENNA
PLATFORM BEYOND

PROFILE OF
ROOFING BEYOND

WING
STRUCTURAL STEEL FRAMING
TO WING
REFER STRUCTURAL
ENG'S DETAIL

PVF2 ALUMINIUM PANELISED
CLADDING TO WING

COLORBOND Z/AL. STEEL ROOF
ROOF SHEETING

SKY RISE
LIFT MOTOR ROOM

EXTERNAL FACE OF PVF2 ALUMINIUM
PANELISED CLADDING WITH 12mm
VERTICAL & HORIZONTAL JOINTS ON
STEEL FRAMING TO ENG'S DETAILS

LINE OF BLOCKWORK
WALL BEYOND

WATER TANK

WATER TANK

SECONDARY
LIFT MACHINE
ROOM

SKY RISE / GOODS LIFT
LMR A/C PLANTRM.

PARAPET

FS2

SR LIFT
No.18

PLANT

6

7

8

6 Roof section
7 Roof wing
8 Spire
9 Tower viewed from the north-west; George Street
   façade of the Galeries Victoria retail podium in the
   foreground
10 Elevation, podium façade, typical bay
11 Section, podium façade, typical bay
Photography: Courtesy Crone & Associates

9

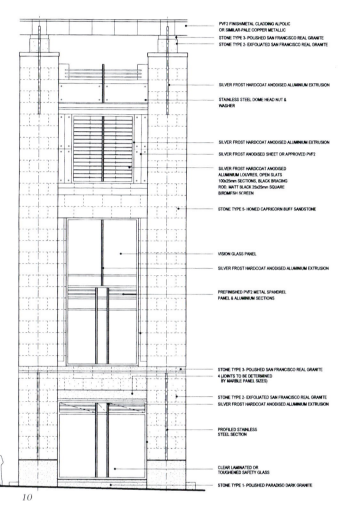

PVF2 FINISH/METAL CLADDING ALPOLIC
OR SIMILAR-PALE COPPER METALLIC

STONE TYPE 3- POLISHED SAN FRANCISCO REAL GRANITE

STONE TYPE 2- EXFOLIATED SAN FRANCISCO REAL GRANITE

SILVER FROST HARDCOAT ANODISED ALUMINIUM EXTRUSION

STAINLESS STEEL DOME HEAD NUT &
WASHER

SILVER FROST HARDCOAT ANODISED ALUMINIUM EXTRUSION

SILVER FROST ANODISED SHEET OR APPROVED PVF2

SILVER FROST HARDCOAT ANODISED
ALUMINIUM LOUVRES, OPEN SLATS
100x25mm SECTIONS, BLACK BRACING
ROD, MATT BLACK 25x25mm SQUARE
BIRDMESH SCREEN

STONE TYPE 5- HONED CAPRICORN BUFF SANDSTONE

VISION GLASS PANEL

SILVER FROST HARDCOAT ANODISED ALUMINIUM EXTRUSION

PREFINISHED PVF2 METAL SPANDREL
PANEL & ALUMINIUM SECTIONS

STONE TYPE 3- POLISHED SAN FRANCISCO REAL GRANITE
4 (JOINTS TO BE DETERMINED
   BY MARBLE PANEL SIZES)

STONE TYPE 2- EXFOLIATED SAN FRANCISCO REAL GRANITE
SILVER FROST HARDCOAT ANODISED ALUMINIUM EXTRUSION

PROFILED STAINLESS
STEEL SECTION

CLEAR LAMINATED OR
TOUGHENED SAFETY GLASS

STONE TYPE 1- POLISHED PARADISO DARK GRANITE

10

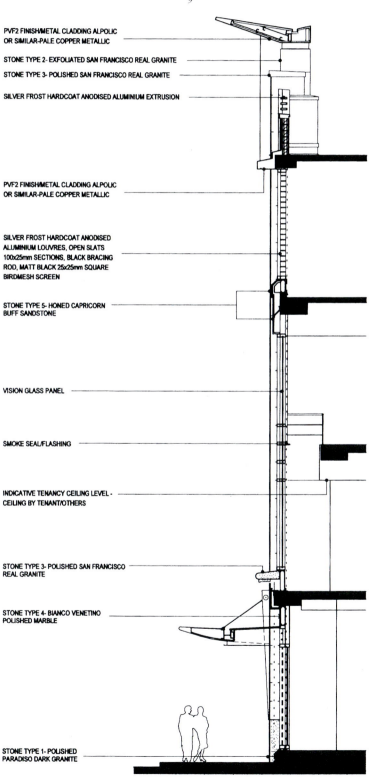

PVF2 FINISH/METAL CLADDING ALPOLIC
OR SIMILAR-PALE COPPER METALLIC

STONE TYPE 2- EXFOLIATED SAN FRANCISCO REAL GRANITE

STONE TYPE 3- POLISHED SAN FRANCISCO REAL GRANITE

SILVER FROST HARDCOAT ANODISED ALUMINIUM EXTRUSION

PVF2 FINISH/METAL CLADDING ALPOLIC
OR SIMILAR-PALE COPPER METALLIC

SILVER FROST HARDCOAT ANODISED
ALUMINIUM LOUVRES, OPEN SLATS
100x25mm SECTIONS, BLACK BRACING
ROD, MATT BLACK 25x25mm SQUARE
BIRDMESH SCREEN

STONE TYPE 5- HONED CAPRICORN
BUFF SANDSTONE

VISION GLASS PANEL

SMOKE SEAL/FLASHING

INDICATIVE TENANCY CEILING LEVEL -
CEILING BY TENANT/OTHERS

STONE TYPE 3- POLISHED SAN FRANCISCO
REAL GRANITE

STONE TYPE 4- BIANCO VENETINO
POLISHED MARBLE

STONE TYPE 1- POLISHED
PARADISO DARK GRANITE

11

STREET AWNING
400 GEORGE STREET, SYDNEY, NEW SOUTH WALES, AUSTRALIA
Crone Associates

1

2

3

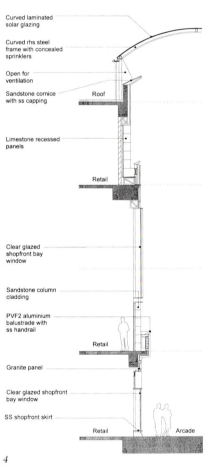

Curved laminated
solar glazing

Curved rhs steel
frame with concealed
sprinklers

Open for
ventilation

Sandstone cornice
with ss capping   Roof

Limestone recessed
panels

Retail

Clear glazed
shopfront bay
window

Sandstone column
cladding

PVF2 aluminium
balustrade with
ss handrail   Retail

Granite panel

Clear glazed shopfront
bay window

SS shopfront skirt

Retail   Arcade

4

400 George Street is a comprehensive development of a major city site, bounded by George, King and Pitt streets with the Strand Arcade to the south.

The development consists of a 33-level commercial office tower and four-storey podium incorporating retail, offices, lobbies and entrances. Total gross floor area is 76,000 square metres.

The building is designed to reinforce the city's historic pattern of development and includes a retail podium that fully integrates the surrounding heritage fabric (including the Strand Arcade, and the corner buildings of Darrel Lea, Bally Shoes and the Tag Heuer Store). It also includes the retention of the former Sydney Arcade façade.

This is a commercial office tower that recognises the corporate importance of the George Street address, its alignment with King Street, and its stepped form protects solar access to the Pitt Street Mall.

The tower has been designed as a 'tenant friendly' building incorporating: maximum natural light; flexible floor plates; internalised core configuration for greater planning efficiencies and secured access to service areas; and large terraces for outdoor activity, which provide for a new workplace lifestyle.

5

6

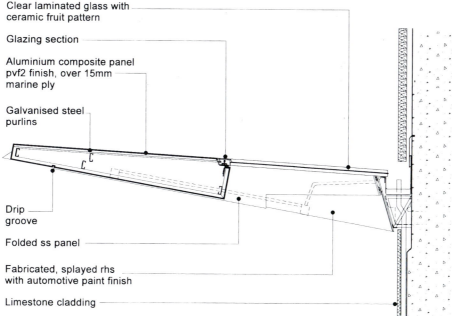

Clear laminated glass with
ceramic fruit pattern

Glazing section

Aluminium composite panel
pvf2 finish, over 15mm
marine ply

Galvanised steel
purlins

Drip
groove

Folded ss panel

Fabricated, splayed rhs
with automotive paint finish

Limestone cladding

7

The tower entrance off George Street is defined by the strong symmetrical modelling of the podium and dominant position of the tower above.

The lobby is a dramatic linear space, connecting the three lift lobbies while providing an interactive business café/lounge as the 'social' focus. Significant artwork and sculpture were commissioned for this space.

The rooftop is used to terminate the tower form, while amplifying the building's address and giving a unique signature to the city's skyline.

A curved, glass-covered laneway, named Sydney Arcade, connects the Pitt Street Mall to King Street; providing a new public street environment that provides access to unique fashion multiple-level retailing.

The tower façade is a composition of punched masonry granite (*conquistador dorato*) with highly profiled glass curtain wall elements. The podium façade is predominantly sandstone (*donnybrook acrogem*) with deep reveals, and large bay windows for retail display. The podium base is polished granite (*paradiso light*) with honed limestone (*villefort ramage*) up to the underside of the partially glazed awning.

1 Detail view of new Sydney Arcade store detailing, feature light fittings, bay windows and metal balconies
2 Office tower viewed from north illustrating podium infill between various adjoining heritage buildings and façades
3 New Sydney Arcade showing glass roof four levels above pavement curved in both plan and section
4 Section through Sydney Arcade
5 Detail view of awning
6 Awning detail adjacent to main office entry in George Street
7 Section through street awning
Photography: courtesy Crone & Associates

CANOPY, STAIR AND RAIL

SONY AUSTRALIA HEAD OFFICE, NORTH RYDE, NEW SOUTH WALES, AUSTRALIA
DEM Design Pty Ltd

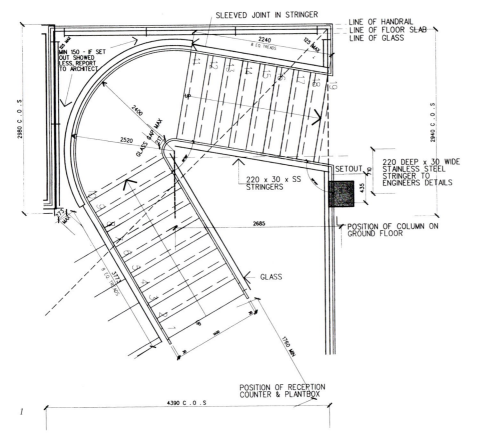

1

2

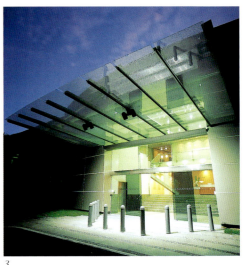

3

1   Stair detail
2   Stairs from level 1
3   Canopy at dusk
4   Reception and entry foyer
5   Stair rail detail
6   New canopy and façade
7   Canopy span
8   Details of canopy
Photography: courtesy DEM Design

Refurbishment was proposed to lift the present building to a standard that would be suitable to accommodate Sony for the next decade. The details featured here are the stairs and canopy from the refurbished public entrance.

Due to the free-standing appearance of the main stairs, they were treated as an artist's sculpture – a thing of great individual beauty in the open foyer area. It was vital to Sony and the DEM designers alike, that the stairs be a feature of visual beauty from any angle, especially when viewed from the foyer. To achieve this, materials were restricted to all stainless steel and laminated glass – evoking a modern and stylish feel. To deaden the footfall of the stairs' expected heavy traffic, the

carpet treads were laid on top of an insulating rubber material. The balustrade detail, in laser-cut stainless steel, follows the theme established throughout the rest of the building – the blending of traditional Japanese interiors with modern Australian influences. An unusual and successful feature of the balustrade is the supports, which are at right angles to the stair instead of the conventional vertical alignment.

The dynamic stairs free-form shape was chosen to enhance the simplistic feel of the foyer and reinforce the natural flow of traffic from the entrance, up the stairs and into the heart of the office space.

4

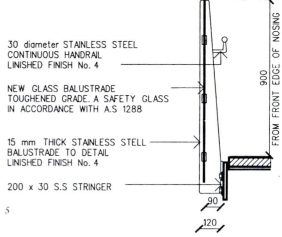

30 diameter STAINLESS STEEL
CONTINUOUS HANDRAIL
LINISHED FINISH No. 4

NEW GLASS BALUSTRADE
TOUGHENED GRADE. A SAFETY GLASS
IN ACCORDANCE WITH A.S 1288

15 mm THICK STAINLESS STELL
BALUSTRADE TO DETAIL
LINISHED FINISH No. 4

200 x 30 S.S STRINGER

FROM FRONT EDGE OF NOSING

900

90

120

5

6

7

8

An important issue in the refurbishment was to strongly define the building's public entrance and the new canopy is an integral part of the curved entry statement. The canopy projects out 6 meters from the building and the use of very slender structural supports 'lightens' the overall appearance of the feature. The glass has an applied pattern that enforces a feeling of semi-enclosure while allowing sunlight to filter through. The canopy is both an aesthetic and functional addition, providing the foyer with shade and rain protection. The canopy's slope back to the building allows for the collection of rainwater in an oversized gutter, discharging into concealed downpipes.

The strategic lighting for the canopy is bracketed onto two of the canopy members and is incorporated as an integral part of the lighting for the entire entrance.

CEILING, COLUMN CAPITAL AND HANDRAIL

LE MERIGOT HOTEL, SANTA MONICA, CALIFORNIA, USA
DiLeonardo International, Inc.

1

1 Fine dining room showing column capitals
   with back lighting
2 Fine dining ceiling detail
3 Fine dining room wall section

As you set foot in the lobby of the Le Merigot Hotel you can immediately sense subtle European influences. Oversized comfortable furniture and fixtures balance soft clean lines, with the neutral background of granite floors, wood-clad columns and Venetiart walls.

From the lobby you are drawn through the open space to a wall of windows. The proportion of these windows allows a subtle transition from the lobby to the outdoor balcony. Other spaces, such as corridors and elevator lobbies, are brought to a more residential scale through the use of giant portals that describe the excellence and quality of this environment.

The public space is equipped with an upscale boardroom, elegant meeting rooms, a casual dining area, a fine dining restaurant and a spa. The boardroom and meeting rooms complement the clean lines of the lobby and provide a comfortable business environment that is outfitted with the latest in modern technology. The two food and beverage outlets suit the needs of any traveller. The fine-dining restaurant is a unique experience and the design ties back to the hotel through warm woods and iron fixtures.

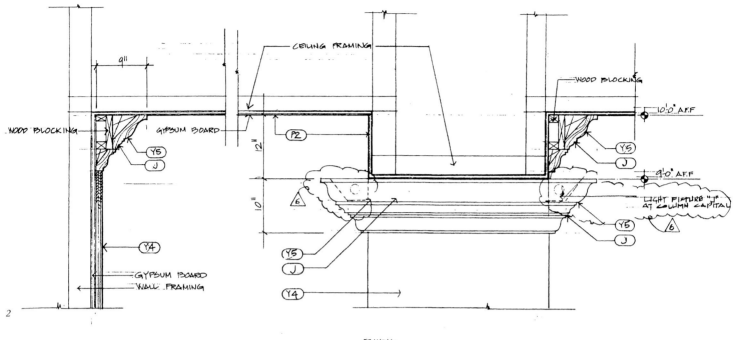

CEILING FRAMING

9"

WOOD BLOCKING

GYPSUM BOARD

Y5

J

WOOD BLOCKING

10'-0" A.F.F

Y5

J

12"

P2

10"

6

9'-0" A.F.F

LIGHT FIXTURE "J" AT COLUMN CAPITAL

6

Y5

J

Y4

Y5

J

GYPSUM BOARD WALL FRAMING

Y4

2

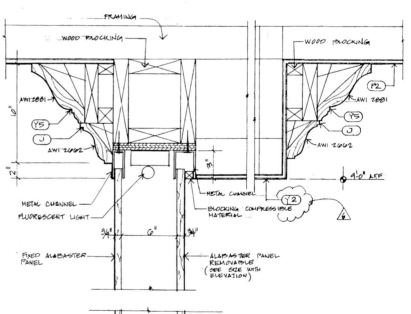

FRAMING

WOOD BLOCKING

WOOD BLOCKING

10"

AWI 2881

AWI 2881

P2

Y5

J

Y5

J

AWI 2662

AWI 2662

3"

2"

9'-0" A.F.F

METAL CHANNEL

Y2

6

METAL CHANNEL

FLUORESCENT LIGHT

BLOCKING COMPRESSIBLE MATERIAL

3/4"

6"

3/4"

FIXED ALABASTER PANEL

ALABASTER PANEL REMOVABLE (SEE SIZE WITH ELEVATION)

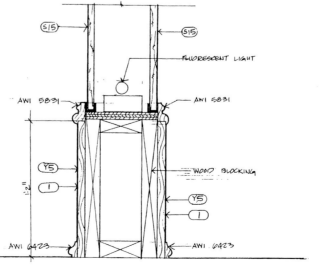

S15

S15

FLUORESCENT LIGHT

AWI 5831

AWI 5831

Y5

J

WOOD BLOCKING

1'-2"

Y5

J

AWI 6423

AWI 6423

3

Floating column capital with back-lighting

The floating column capital with back-lighting increases the perceived height of the ceiling in this gourmet restaurant. The double molding profile introduces a sense of scale to the space. The higher profile is up-lit by the concealed light in the lower molding.

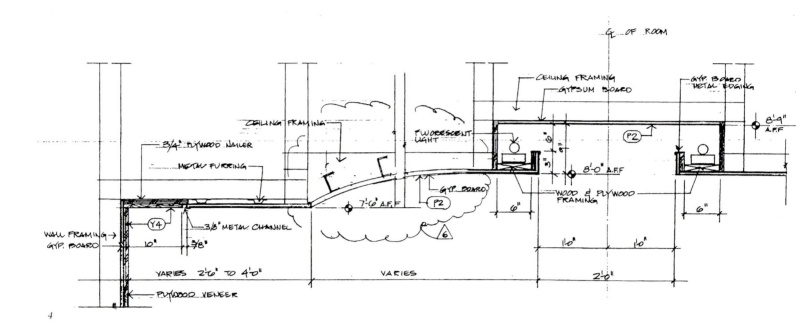

CL OF ROOM

CEILING FRAMING

3/4" PLYWOOD NAILER

METAL FURRING

CEILING FRAMING
GYPSUM BOARD

GYP. BOARD
METAL EDGING

FLUORESCENT
LIGHT

8'-9"
A.F.F

P2

P2

GYP. BOARD

WALL FRAMING
GYP. BOARD

Y4

7'-6" A.F.F

8'-0" A.F.F

WOOD & PLYWOOD
FRAMING

3/8" METAL CHANNEL

10"

3/8"

6

6"

1'-0"

6"

1'-0"

VARIES 2'-6" TO 4'-0"

VARIES

2'-0"

PLYWOOD VENEER

4

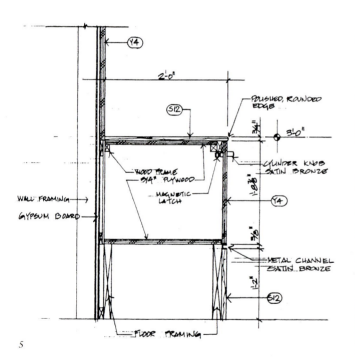

Y4

2'-0"

S12

POLISHED, ROUNDED
EDGE

3/4"

3'-0"

CYLINDER KNOB
SATIN BRONZE

WOOD FRAME
3/4" PLYWOOD

MAGNETIC
LATCH

Y4

WALL FRAMING

GYPSUM BOARD

METAL CHANNEL
SATIN BRONZE

1'-2"

S12

FLOOR FRAMING

5

Boardroom ceiling detail

The intent of this detail was to provide interest
through form and lighting in an economical way.
Using simple plywood framing and gypsum board,
the relatively small linear space is broken. This
highlights the function of the room as well as
capturing a sense of day lighting.

6

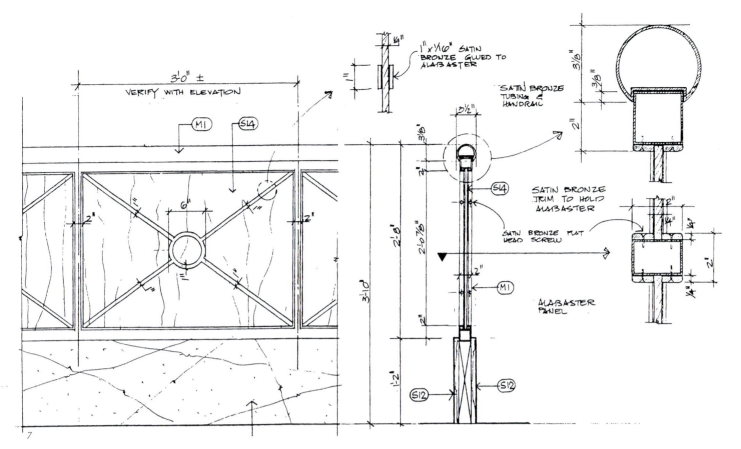

4   *Boardroom ceiling section*
5   *Section*
6   *Boardroom showing ceiling detail*
7   *Handrail detail*
8   *Handrail*
Photography: Warren Jagger

Handrail

The focus of this rail detail is the variation in the alabaster. The detailing on the rail is kept to very thin profiles and proportions allowing light to transmit freely through the stone. A 14 inch stone base was used to co-ordinate with the available size of alabaster at 24 x 36 inches. This eliminates joints in the stone and dictates the rhythm of the rail.

COFFER AND MOULDINGS

AN AMERICAN PLACE RESTAURANT, NEW YORK, NEW YORK, USA
DiLeonardo International, Inc.

1

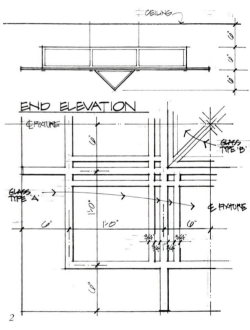

END ELEVATION

2

1 Interior showing coffer and mouldings
2 Plan detail of coffer and mouldings
3 Section
4 Reflected plan view
Photography: Warren Jagger

Renowned chef Larry Forgione relocated his restaurant, one of New York's most distinctive, to this hotel. The restaurant provides room service and catering for the hotel's meeting and banquet facilities. The new location continues to spotlight Forgione's award-winning American cuisine in a setting described as one of 'modern elegance'. While creating a new image for this restaurant, the décor also captures many of the signature design accents of the previous restaurant.

This 2,800 square foot space contains an open kitchen; a dining room for up to 16 people; a dining room for 80 people, and a dining lounge

bar area for 50 people. The existing columns, grids, stairwells, elevator shafts, hotel mechanical rooms and utility locations have all been retained.

The restaurant has a clean, crisp contemporary look, accented with splashes of colour. The dining room features mahogany panels, vibrant persimmon painted walls, large window panels with semi-sheer curtains, custom-made decorative light fixtures, black leather and mahogany furnishings, and a signature hand-knotted, multi-primary-coloured carpet. The restaurant also features a sleek bar area. The bar itself, along with the floor, is granite with a mahogany ceiling. A granite drink

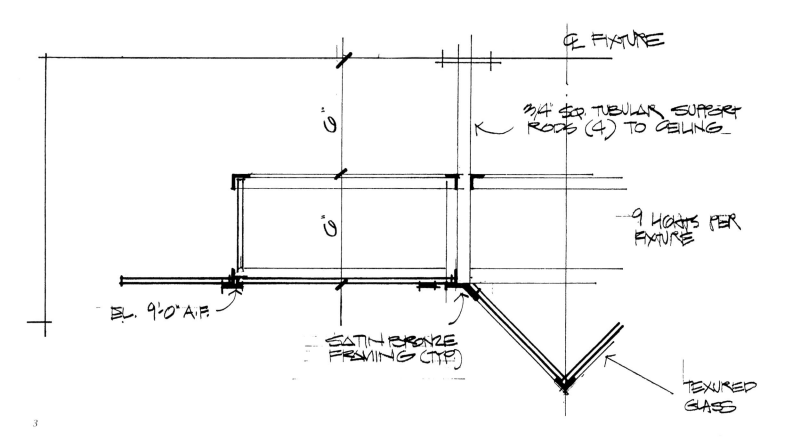

℄ FIXTURE

3/4" SQ. TUBULAR SUPPORT RODS (4) TO CEILING

9 LIGHTS PER FIXTURE

EL. 9'-0" A.F.F.

SATIN BRONZE FRAMING (TYP)

TEXTURED GLASS

3

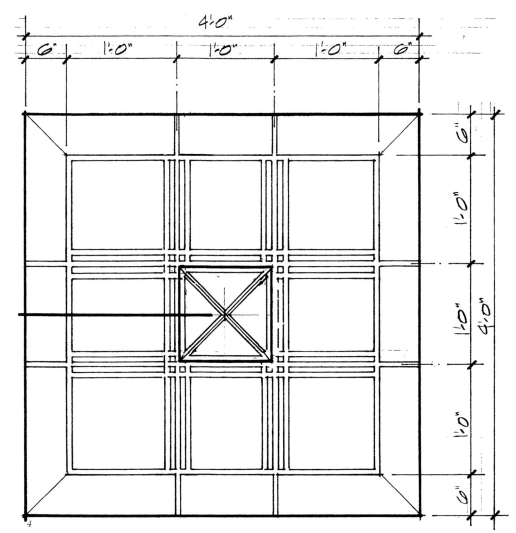

4'-0"

6" 1'-0" 1'-0" 1'-0" 6"

6"

1'-0"

1'-0" 4'-0"

1'-0"

6"

4

rail runs along 50th Street accommodating eight seats with street-side views; a bronze screen separates the bar area from the main restaurant. In addition, a private dining room features sliding wood door panels with frosted glass, original stained glass window and a wall of wines in a temperature-controlled enclosure.

Coffer and mouldings were used to conceal the linear diffusers. Half rounds are set against the orthogonal geometry of the light fixture creating subtle shadow lines in the ceilings.

OLYMPIC VELODROME ROOF

LANDSBERGER ALLEE, BERLIN, GERMANY
Dominique Perrault Architect and APP Berlin

1

1　General view of metal mesh covering
　　velodrome's roof
2&4　Joint detail between metal mesh mats,
　　specially designed for this project by
　　Dominique Perrault
3　Overhang of metal mesh roof
5　Section and plans of exterior edge of
　　roof

The site is at the intersection of two important urban elements: a major axis that goes from the city centre, a wide avenue that subsequently meets a second element, and a peripheral one, namely a short metro line that has since linked east and west and which enables a tour of the city to be made.

There is an intersection of different networks and fabrics. The concave part of the system contains an ensemble of fabrics typical of the standard Berliner block, plus the presence of the former Berlin abattoirs. On the other hand, on the far side of the railway track, there are 20 kilometres of extended, slab-type blocks of flats – a completely different type of urbanism. In order to resolve the conjunction of these two systems, it was decided, in a somewhat obvious experiment, to cause the two buildings that house the Olympic swimming pool and velodrome to vanish from sight.

The concept here is limited to the considerations of a rectangular, quadrilateral territory on which two forms are inscribed: a round shape for the velodrome and a rectangular one for the swimming pool. The question of the form being thus resolved, other issues were able to be addressed. There were many things to stitch back together in this neighbourhood; many things to link up, and neither the time nor the place appeared to lend

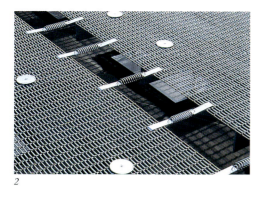

2

3

4

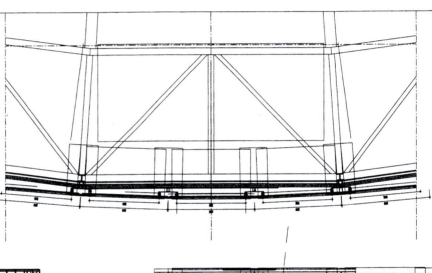

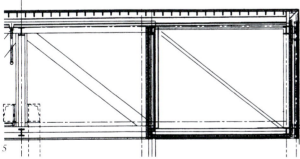

5

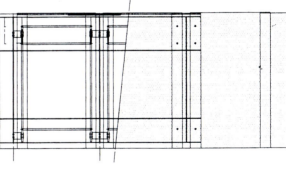

itself to the reception, the welcoming of a volume (or two volumes, the swimming pool is just beside the Velodrome) of this size, which would have curtailed exchanges between the different areas, rather than uniting and developing them.

The urban concept behind this project is the creation of a green space on a handsome scale (approximately 200 x 500 metres), and at the centre to implant buildings. The idea was to create an orchard, namely, to plant apple trees. The idea is that when you approach on foot through this orchard you discover, set into the ground and protrudes at a height of about a metre, two tables: one round and the other rectangular, covered with

a wire gauze. These two metal surfaces shimmer in the sunlight and appear, at first sight, to be stretches of water rather than buildings – like lakes at the centre of the orchard. Over 400 apple trees were planted, and they bear the traces of their past so that there is the feeling that this orchard has existed for a certain time.

6

7

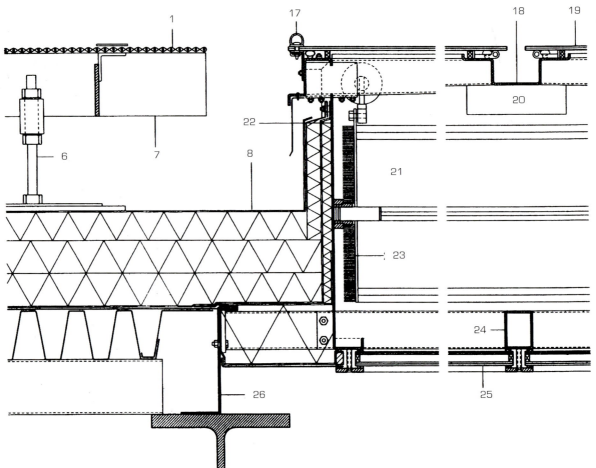

8

Figure 8
The 3.555 tonne roof, with a diameter of
142 metres has a clear span of 115
metres and is supported by 16 concrete
columns. The main load-bearing elements
of the construction are the 48 trussed
girders laid out in radial form. They are
anchored to tension members at the ends
and bear either directly on the concrete
columns or on the main ring beam, which
has a diameter of 115.2 metres. At the
centre of the roof is a large skylight,
supported by an inner trussed ring beam.

1	Stainless steel rod mesh
6	Metal support, adjustable in height
7	130/8 mm steel flat bearers
8	Moisture-proof membrane three-layer insulation vapour barrier 0.63 mm sheet metal trapezoidal-section ribbed sheeting
17	Quarter-turn locking device for cleaning
18	3 mm sheet steel gutter with 2% falls
19	8 mm single glazing in partially tensioned safety glass
20	2 steel flats 60/10 mm
21	Sunscreen louvre
22	3 mm steel casting
23	Brush steel
24	80/60/3 mm steel RHS
25	Double-glazing with 8 mm laminated safety glass lower pane
26	4 mm steel casting

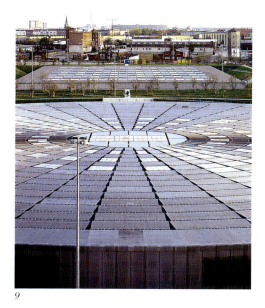

9

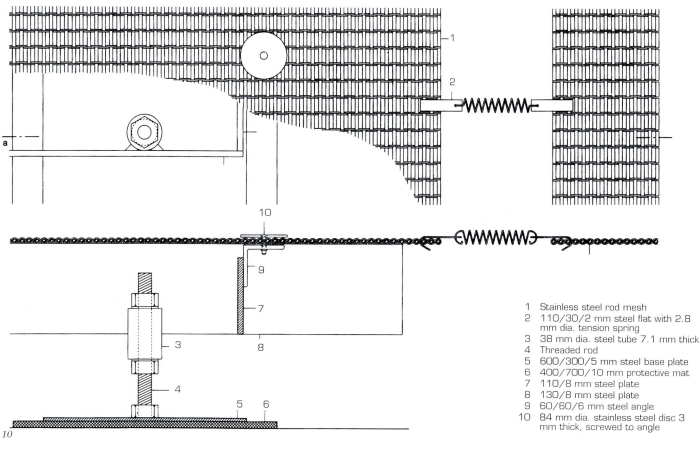

10

1   Stainless steel rod mesh
2   110/30/2 mm steel flat with 2.8
    mm dia. tension spring
3   38 mm dia. steel tube 7.1 mm thick
4   Threaded rod
5   600/300/5 mm steel base plate
6   400/700/10 mm protective mat
7   110/8 mm steel plate
8   130/8 mm steel plate
9   60/60/6 mm steel angle
10 84 mm dia. stainless steel disc 3
    mm thick, screwed to angle

Figure 10

The metal mesh lies in the same plane as the roof lights, so that, seen from a distance, the entire roof surface appears as a uniform, homogenous structure. The mesh mats are fixed to galvanised steel supports that are adjustable in height. The relatively great dead weight of the individual mesh strips obviates the need for any further fixing to the roof structure. The strips are connected to each other with steel springs. These can be easily opened and the mesh strips rolled back for cleaning purposes. The roof can support foot traffic both at the junctions between elements and on the surface of the rod mesh itself.

6   Inside view of velodrome track
7   Overhang of metal mesh roof
8   Vertical section through roof light, edge
    of roof and façade
9   The two volumes incrusted in the
    ground, the Velodrome in first plan and
    swimming pool in second
10 Details of support for metal mesh plan
    (cross-section, scale 1:5)
Photography: ADAGP, Georges Fessey

SKYLIGHT PLATFORM

IRSID, USINOR-SACILOR CONFERENCE CENTER, PARIS, FRANCE
Dominique Perrault Architect

1

2

3

Vis-à-vis the charm of the 'chateau' and its 'jewel-case of green', the addition or attachment of a new building seems contradictory, complicated and unsightly. In fact, what is called for is the revaluation and restoration of the existing building. In placing the 'chateau' 'on a glass plate', one creates a conspicuous place and a clearly defined landmark.

This conspicuousness results from the tactful insertion of the new extension, which incorporates the lower part of the 'chateau' into a glass volume that is set into the ground. The geometry of this circular base draws to it the many approaches that follow the main axis, the future entrance, and even the walkways at the far end of the park.

The glass disk filters the natural light and plays with the artificial light. This plate will, in effect, be smooth and shiny by day. The 'chateau' will be reflected in it, as in a stretch of water. At nightfall, however, the effect will be the opposite, because the surface will be lit up, illuminating the 'chateau'.

One could describe this project as a 'glass and steel device', the reactions to which testify to the vitality of the building *qua* object, as well as to that of the surroundings. The spatial organisation of the different functions is divided between 'spaces for meeting', located in the 'chateau', and 'spaces for communication', situated in the base. The whole structure is linked together by a stairway set at the centre of the device.

4

5

1 Main view of 'chateau'
2 Metal structure that supports the glass disk;
  photographed during the construction works
3 Reception room under glass disk
4 Entrance footbridge over glass disk
5 View of 'chateau' from under glass disk
6 Detail section through beam that supports glass disk
7 Detail of glass-beam junction
Photography: ADAGP, Michel Denancé and Georges Fessy,
photographers

The communications centre is accessed through
the 'chateau' via a metal footbridge extending over
the glass disk.

Seen in plan, a concentric system extends around
the ancient building. In the central part an area
for services and corridors is located beneath the
'chateau'; then comes a crown, which integrates
the restaurant and auditorium; and finally, a
technical ring groups the service entrances and
emergency exits.

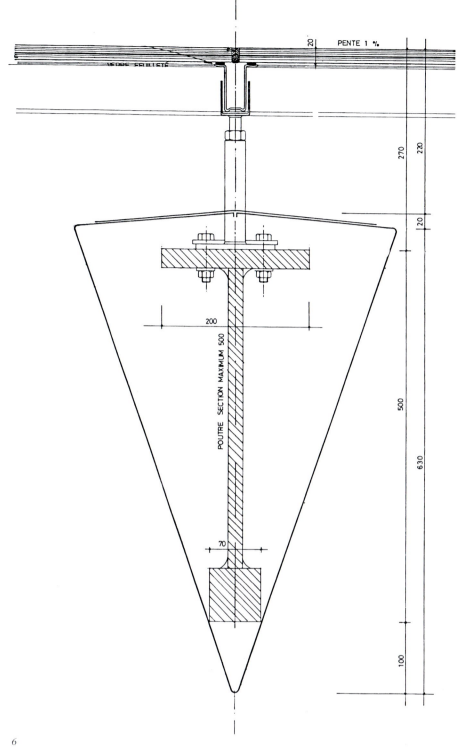

6

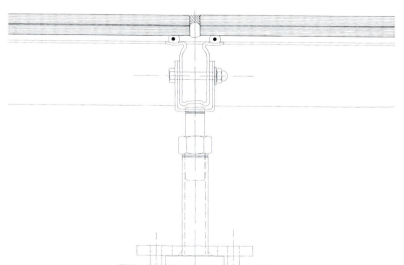

7

WOODEN SUSPENSION BRIDGE
GOSHONO REMAINS, ICHINOHE TOWN, NINOHE COUNTY, IWATE, JAPAN
Environment Design Institute

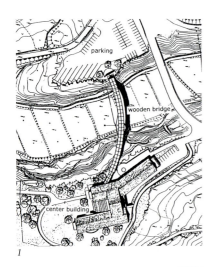

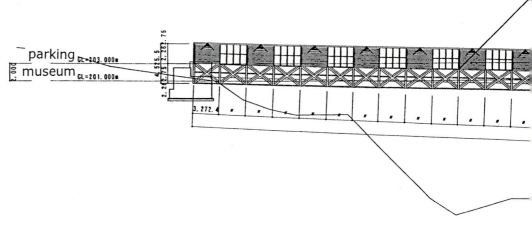

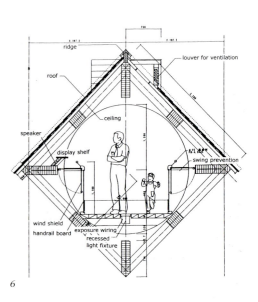

1 Site plan showing bridge connecting
   parking area to centre building
2 Façade
3 View of entire bridge from valley
4 Elevation (the outside curve) with section
   detail
5 Interior view
6 Section showing scale
7 Elevation and section
Photography: courtesy Environment Design
Institute

The bridge is designed as a footbridge to connect the Goshono Remains with its parking area, which is located beyond a valley. The Goshono Remains, occupying a 6.5 hectare site, are preserved as national historical remains, and contain scenery from the Jomon period, which occurred about 4,500 years ago.

The bridge traces a line from the parking area to the centre of the park, and curves at R=100 metres horizontally. Since it is a cold area in winter, the roof is attached to obstruct wind and snow the wind shield is located on outside of the handrail.

Its sectional shape is square and hollowed, and its centre is circular. Its framing is a glued laminated timber truss construction, consisting of code, lattice and frame timbers. It is hung at two points, the outside and the middle, from steel posts located at the side. Two inner sides that hang materials are supports.

The bridge is not only for walking across but also for time-travelling to an ancient scene. Because of its curve, a vista is not provided – this would stimulate expectations and anxieties. The change of light through the bridge arouses a feeling of compressed time. As the glued laminated timber construction consists of slender timbers, to walk across the bridge itself feels very exciting.

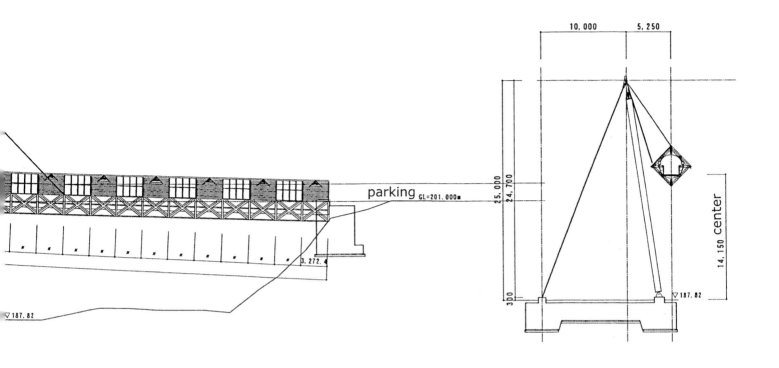

parking GL=201.000m

10,000   5,250

25,000
24,700
300

14,150 center

▽187.82

3,272.4

▽187.82

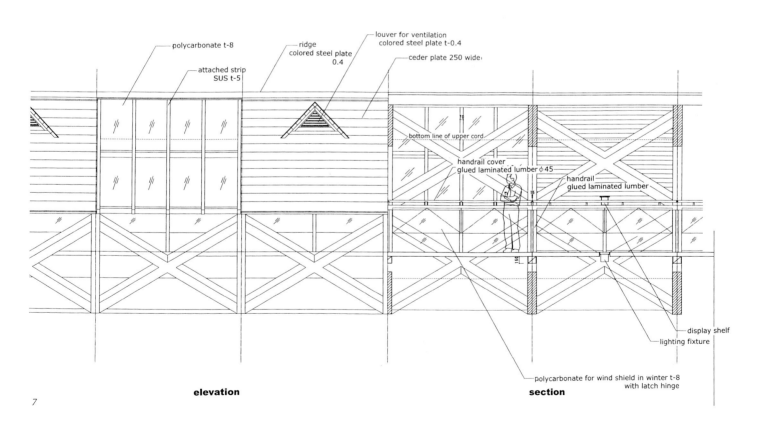

polycarbonate t-8

attached strip
SUS t-5

ridge
colored steel plate
0.4

louver for ventilation
colored steel plate t-0.4

ceder plate 250 wide

bottom line of upper cord

handrail cover
glued laminated lumber φ45

handrail
glued laminated lumber

display shelf

lighting fixture

polycarbonate for wind shield in winter t-8
with latch hinge

elevation

section

7

GLASS ROOF, WALLS AND CANOPY

VUOSAARI METRO STATION, HELSINKI, FINLAND
Arkkitehtitoimisto Esa Piironen Oy

1

2

4

3

5

1–3   Platform area (artwork by Jussi Niva)
4   Façade
5   Stairway to upper level
6   Cross section of glass roof and wall
7   Glass/steel canopy detail
Photography: courtesy Arkkitehtitoimisto
Esa Piironen Oy

The Vuosaari metro station is mostly an over-ground building, with special attention paid to spaciousness and light. The track section between the ticket halls of the station is covered with glass.

The main architectural theme of the station is based on glass roofs. The platform area is asymmetrical. At the platform level, the external walls of the station are made of mesh plate cassettes.

The two main construction materials are as follows: the building frame with reinforced concrete used in load-bearing structures; and the interior with steel and glass used in load-bearing structures.

The site was excellent for foundation works, which were realised using conventional cast-in-structures. The platform level and the spaces built underneath are made of cast-in-situ concrete. The plinths of the external walls, that contained long continuous sections and identical parts, are built with prefabricated concrete units.

The shape of the building and the light skin materials, as well as the traffic requirements specified for the platform level, made it necessary to select a combination of space frames supported on steel mast columns for the stiffening system of the building frame.

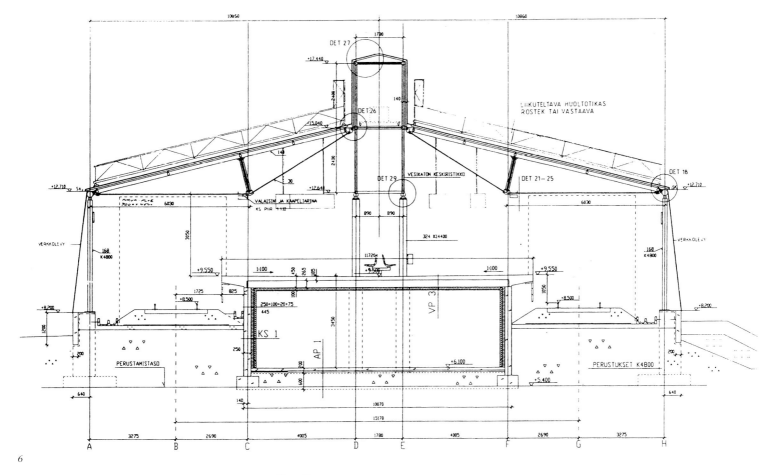

6

Detail

1. circular hollow section, Ø 273x12.5 mm

2. circular hollow section, Ø 219x12.5 mm

3. circular hollow section, Ø 273x12.5 mm

4. circular hollow section, Ø 139x10 mm

5. steel rod, Ø 20 mm

6. insulating glass of single float glass and
   laminated glass

The expansion joints required for the stiffening lattice of the over 200 metre (656 feet) long building, as well as the management of restraint action applied to these joints, were solved by using a 'suspension expansion joint'.

Due to the lightness requirement of the skin structures, annealed double glazing was used. The cooling requirement, on the other hand, led to the use of selective glass and perforated wall boards.

7

SKYLIGHT INSET AND CABLE TRUSS SYSTEM

DENVER INTERNATIONAL AIRPORT PASSENGER TERMINAL COMPLEX, DENVER, COLORADO, USA
Fentress Bradburn Architects Ltd

1

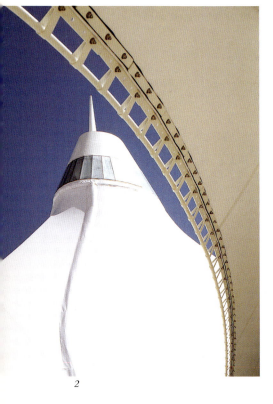

2

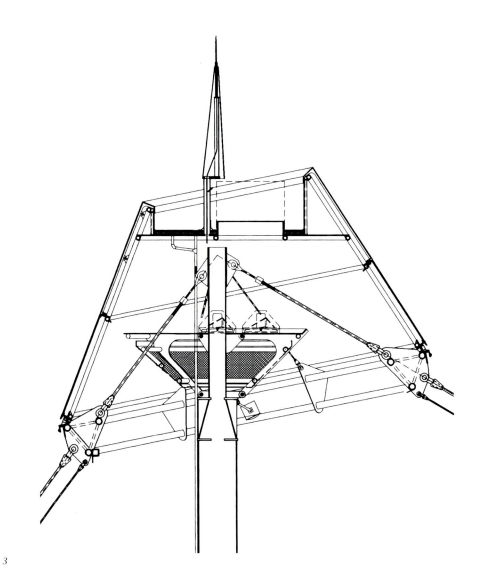

3

Denver International Airport's peaked, white roof is an instantly recognisable landmark in Colorado, inspired by the peaks and valleys of its Rocky Mountain backdrop. On both sunny and overcast days, the enormous interior space is flooded with both direct and diffuse daylight from an abundance of clerestories, large cantilevered glass curtain walls and the translucent roof. This natural daylighting also affords significant energy savings.

The Teflon-coated roof, which is one of the largest structurally integrated tensile-membrane roofs in the world, allows hot air to escape by way of osmosis and minimises the need for artificial lighting, which in turn reduces energy consumption and heat production. Further reduction of heat transfer and build-up is eliminated through the roof's ability to reflect 40 per cent of incident solar radiation. The structure is rated by roofing experts to perform better than conventional roofing systems for spans greater than 100 feet. The fabric roof weighs 2 pounds per square foot less than traditional roofing materials and comes with a warranty 12 years' longer than most conventional roofing systems. It is held in place by 34 masts, eight of which bring direct light into the space through clerestories at the top. The masts, which reach up to 150 feet, can shift up to 2 feet laterally during high wind storms. Because the roof is not rigid, the large glass curtain wall of the terminal had to be cantilevered by way of a cable truss system.

1   A symmetrical double-bowstring cable truss is framed into the wall 37 feet above its base to uniformly distribute the lateral load
2   The higher masts stand at the points in the terminal where bridges cross the space; the greater amount of light at the clerestories helps identify these points and direct passenger flow through the terminal
3   Mast top, longitudinal section; darkened lines along edges of bottom half of truncated cone indicate placement of skylight clerestories

4   South wall cable truss section; drawing shows a north-south cross-section of glass wall and its bow-string cable truss system that runs on both interior and exterior of glass curtain wall
5   Exterior shot of south wall; cable truss system provides lateral stability and rigidity in the 60 foot tall, 220 foot long glass curtain wall
6   Skylight clerestories increase the already abundant natural daylight of the interior

Photography: Nick Merrick (1,3), Ron Johnson (2), Timothy Hursley (6)

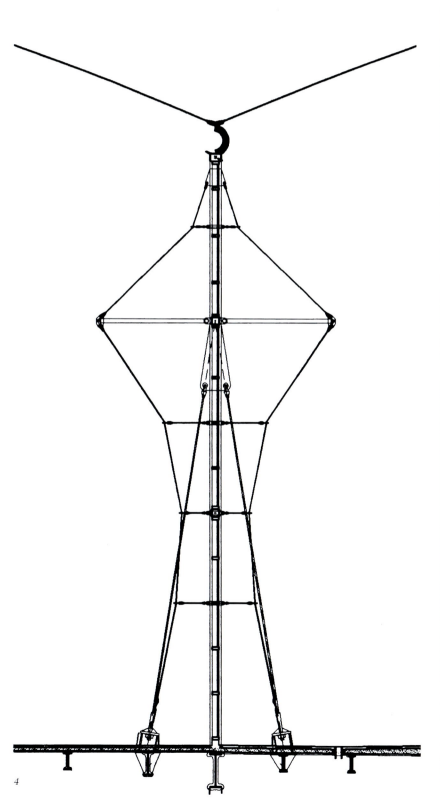

4

5

6

WINDOWS

PHILIPS SEMICONDUCTOR PLANT, LIGHT INDUSTRY AND SCIENCE PARK, CALAMBA, LAGUNA, THE PHILIPPINES
R N Ferrer & Associates, Inc.

1

1 *Production building façade showing wedge-shaped windows and aluminium wall panels*
2 *Architectural bay section*

The production building's aluminium panel skin and recessed wedge-shaped windows are just two of the many features of this project, which is a semiconductor plant that is the first of its kind to showcase the 'Factory 2000' production layout. Its concept entails a layout that allows all functions of production to be on the same floor; one that provides easy expansion and alteration, with minimum work-in-process and handling.

The wedge-shaped, recessed windows were developed through the basic architectural philosophy of 'form follows function'. In this case, the structure's function needed to satisfy the owner's requirements for maximum flexibility

consistent with the 'Factory 2000' concept. Moreover, the design needed high distances between floor levels as required by the mechanical and electrical utilities. Consequently, this required a structural configuration with slender columns and wide spacing. These merged functional and technical requirements, in turn, necessitated the use of heavy structural cross-bracings between columns and beams. The intersections of these bracings fell along the line of the 4.35 metre high mezzanine floor. This resulted in wedge-shaped areas for the windows on the ground floor, and V-shaped aluminum louvre windows in the mezzanine.

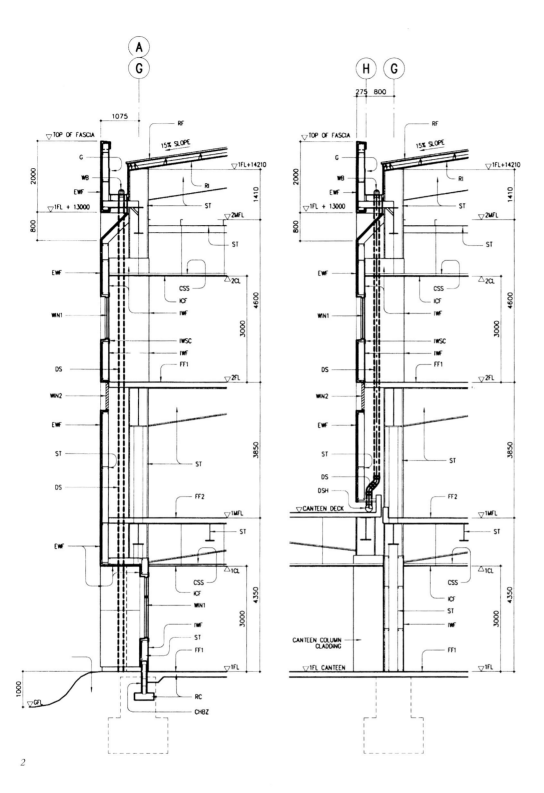

LEGEND :

CHBZ – (CHB ZOCCALO) 6" CONCRETE HOLLOW BLOCKS 300mm HIGH FROM FINISH FLOOR LINE

CSS – (CEILING SUSPENSION SYSTEM) DONN DX GALVANISED STEEL DOUBLE WEB SECTION 40mm HIGH X 25mm EXPOSED FLANGE

DS – (DOWNSPOUT) 150mm ⌀ PVC PIPE

ECF – (EXTERIOR CEILING FINISH) GA24 "SPANDREL" CEILING SHEETS

EWF – (EXTERIOR WALL FINISH) 4mm THK ALUMINIUM COMPOSITE PANELS (ROUT & RETURN FORMED); FLOUROCARBON FINISH

EWFJ – PANEL JOINT SYSTEM BY PANEL SUPPLIER

EWFS – PANEL SUPPORT SYSTEM BY PANEL SUPPLIER

EWI – (EXTERIOR WALL INSULATION) ACI 25mm THK PANEL TYPE(RIGID) GLASSWOLL INSULATION WITH WIRE MESH SUPPORT

FF1 – (FLOOR FINISH 1) ESD FLOORING / CONDUCTIVE FLOOR TILES 10^4 TO 10^9

FF2 – (FLOOR FINISH 2) EPOXY COATED FLOOR SLAB WITH WATERPROOFING FOR ALL MEZZANINE FLOOR SLAB

G – (GUTTER & GUTTER ACCESSORIES) GA20 STAINLESS STEEL SHEETS

ICF – (INTERIOR CEILING FINISH) CAPAUL 10x610x1220 (NON-PERFORATED) CEILING PANELS FOR CLASS 100 ENVIRONMENT

IWF – (INTERIOR WALL FINISH) 12mm THK HIGH PRESURE LAMINATED MINERAL FIBER BD WITH ALUMINUM TRIMMINGS (ROCKWOOL OR CALCIUM SILICATE)

LCS – LIGHT GAUGE STEEL FRAMING (GA18)

MF – 25mm PROFILE METAL FURRING

RC – (REINFORCED CONCRETE) SEE STRUCTURAL DRAWINGS

RF – (ROOFING FINISH) GA24 PREFORMED COLOR BONDED, LONGSPAN ROOFING SHEETS

RI – (ROOF INSULATION) 25mm THK GLASSWOOL PANEL TYPE INSULATION WITH WIREMESH SUPPORT

WB – (WIRE BASKET) 150 ⌀ PAINT COATED STEEL

WIN1 – (WINDOW TYPE NO.1) 6mm THK TEMPERED BLUE GLASS ON ALUMINUM FRAME

WIN2 – (WINDOW TYPE NO. 2) GA20 ALUMINUM LOUVERS

2

These windows are repeated along the perimeter of the building in a rhythmic line, and this pattern is complemented by the busy lines that were created by the aluminium panels' joint scorings on the building skin. In addition, the colour scheme was a forerunner to what later became known as the millennium colours: blue and silver. This scheme is supplemented by the recessed window design, which creates heavy wedge-shaped shadows on the building's base that add a play of light and shadow to the factory building.

Lastly, the ground floor windows are aluminium framed without internal mullions. The butt joints on tempered glass create a continuous colour on the building's base shadow during daytime, while allowing a series of lighting sources from inside the building to shine through. The aluminium composite panels constitute a curtain wall supported by steel channels directly connected to the main structural frame. And the panel terminations are of rout-and-turn joints with black sealant, not just for thermal and moisture protection, but also to define the skin's scoring. The building's main skin is 1.075 metres away from the perimeter grid-line, while the interior face of the wall at the ground floor level is flushed to the interior face of the columns – thus the recessed wedge-shaped windows.

3   Curtain-glass walls and aluminium
     panels highlight the design
4&7 Structural frame elevations
5   South elevation
6   Aerial view of facility
Photography: courtesy of R N Ferrer &
Associates, Inc.

3

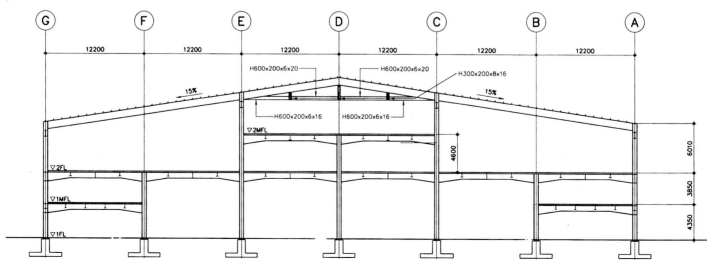

4

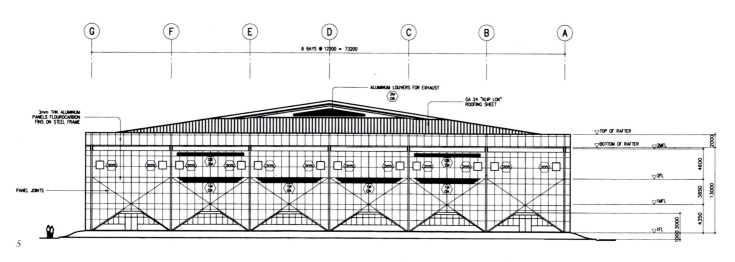

5

6

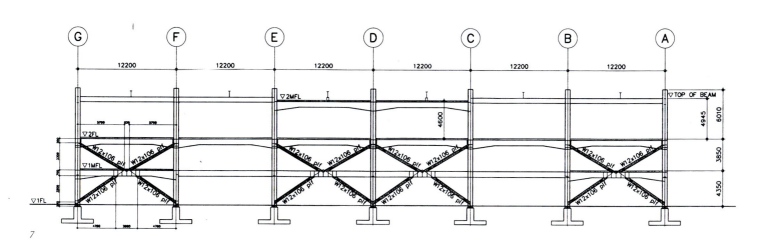

7

GREENHOUSES

UNIVERSITY OF WISCONSIN-MADISON, MADISON, WISCONSIN, USA
Flad & Associates

1

2

At the University of Wisconsin, a greenhouse range marked the western edge of the campus and provided a clear icon for the University's agricultural program for more than a century. In 1992, to create space for a new laboratory facility, the greenhouses were razed.

The University's new instructional greenhouses create a dramatic, western entry to Plant Sciences. Elevated from the street by a few steps, this predominantly glass structure is a transparent jewel among its neighbours.

The greenhouse prominently fronts the major east/ west pedestrian route through the campus. A series of tree-like columns branch up to support curved Glulam beams above the greenhouse entrance, forming a new entry to the previously undistinguished Plant Sciences building. The tree-like columns are found both on the exterior and within the greenhouses, and serve to unify the design scheme.

The new facility provides eleven separate environments for growing a variety of plants, a head house for potting and preparation, and a 1,400 square foot conservatory, which showcases the work of the department.

The vaulted greenhouse units are built from an aluminium frame system that uses insulated polycarbonate roof components and tempered glass sidewalls. The greenhouse glazing system was modified to wrap around the Glulam frame of the conservatory.

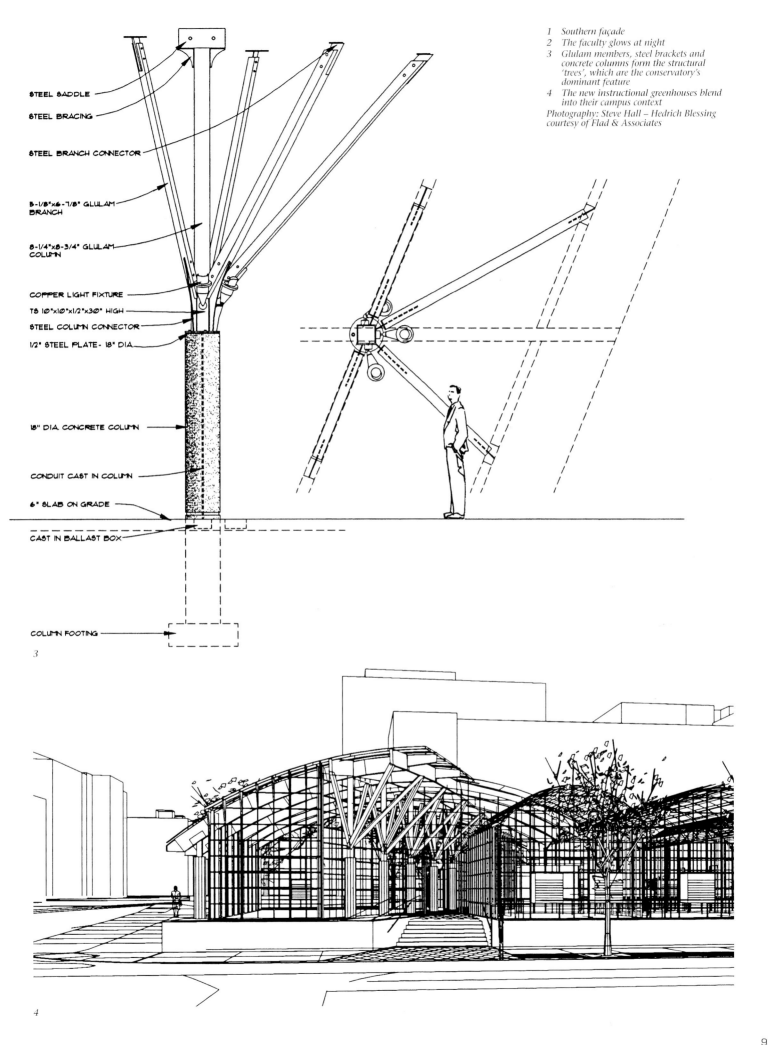

STEEL SADDLE

STEEL BRACING

STEEL BRANCH CONNECTOR

3-1/8"x6-7/8" GLULAM BRANCH

8-1/4"x8-3/4" GLULAM COLUMN

COPPER LIGHT FIXTURE

TS 10"x10"x1/2"x30" HIGH

STEEL COLUMN CONNECTOR

1/2" STEEL PLATE - 18" DIA.

18" DIA CONCRETE COLUMN

CONDUIT CAST IN COLUMN

6" SLAB ON GRADE

CAST IN BALLAST BOX

COLUMN FOOTING

3

4

1   *Southern façade*
2   *The faculty glows at night*
3   *Glulam members, steel brackets and concrete columns form the structural 'trees', which are the conservatory's dominant feature*
4   *The new instructional greenhouses blend into their campus context*
Photography: Steve Hall – Hedrich Blessing courtesy of Flad & Associates

ENTRANCE PAVILION AND RECEPTION DESK
TOWER 42, OLD BROAD STREET, LONDON, UK
GMW Partnership

1

2

3

1   Entrance from Old Broad Street
2&5   Details of entrance pavilion
3   Reception desk
4   Detail section through north elevation

Tower 42 (formerly NatWest Tower) sustained considerable damage in the bomb blast of 1993. Subsequently, NatWest Bank decided that they would not reoccupy the building themselves and commissioned GMW Partnership to refurbish it to a quality equal to current new developments.

Discussions with the City of London Planning Department established that they viewed Tower 42 as a well-known landmark in the city that they would not wish to see radically altered. Therefore, while the external envelope of the building has been completely replaced with a modern double-glazing system that responds to the latest safety technology, the appearance of the tower remains familiar on the city skyline.

The most notable result of the refurbishment is the addition of a new three-storey entrance hall in the form of a glazed pavilion beneath an upswept glass roof. This has been designed to provide an enclosure of sufficient presence to relate to the scale and importance of the tower while not being over dominant in the context of Old Broad Street.

The glazed roof slopes upward to the street frontage, where a gently curved glazed skin is suspended below the cantilevered structure, echoing the parapet lines of adjoining buildings. The frontage is intended to create both a welcoming aspect and allow the visible structure to define a 'portal' or grand entry to the building.

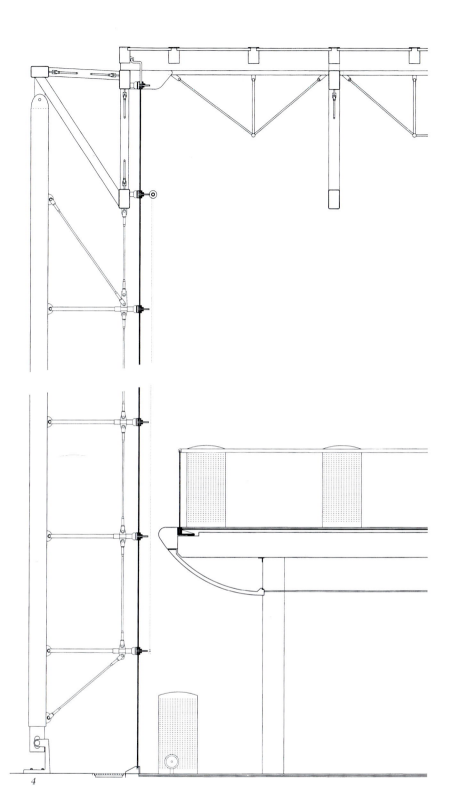

4

5

Its transparency derives from a desire to provide a visual continuity between the street, the external and internal spaces at the entrance and the tower above – in effect to visually 'connect' the street to the tower and provide simplicity and clarity of access.

On entering the building, occupants and visitors ascend via escalators or lifts to the large first-floor reception and waiting area. From here they pass on to either the first floor lift lobby, or via further escalators to a mezzanine lift lobby, which facilitates access to the dual-level lift cars.

The structure of the entrance hall reinforces the theme of transparency, allowing clear views to the tower core as the 'trunk' of its tree-like structure. The enclosure is constructed as a finely engineered lattice with side mullions hung from a roof structure limited to four points of support. A combination of unclad carbon steel for the principal elements and stainless steel for the secondary elements and glazing members, has allowed the most slender structural members. Adjustable solar blinds provide shading when required.

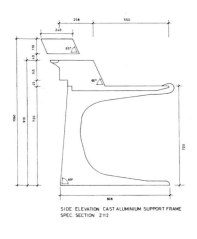

SIDE ELEVATION CAST ALUMINIUM SUPPORT FRAME
SPEC. SECTION Z112

ISOMETRIC PROJECTION

PLAN AT A

PLAN AT B

PLAN AT C

PLAN A

PLAN B

PLAN C

FRONT ELEVATION

END ELEVATION OF DESK

NEST OF DRAWS FRONT ELEVATION
SPEC. SECTION Z10

SECTION A-A   SCALE 1:2

PIGEON HOLES FRONT ELEVATION
SPEC. SECTION Z10

SECTION B-B   SCALE 1:2

BELOW DESK DRAW UNIT
SPEC. SECTION Z10

SECTION C-C   SCALE 1:5

BELOW DESK CUPBOARD UNIT
SPEC. SECTION Z10

SECTION D-D   SCALE 1:5

6

6   Detail of reception desk
*7   South elevation of new entrance pavilion
     showing relationship to base of tower*
8   Reception desk general arrangement
9   Entrance pavilion with tower behind
10 Section through west (street) elevation
*Photography: Anthony Weller (1,2,9), Alan
Williams (3), Peter Cook (5)*

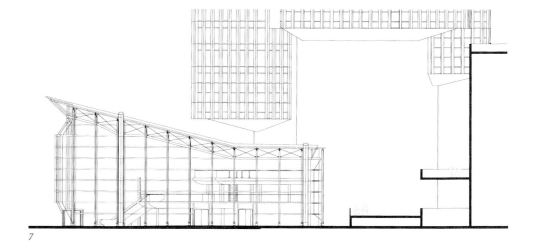

7

Maximum transparency was an overriding objective in the design of the new entrance hall for Tower 42. However, because the building was constructed above three existing basement storeys the weight of the new hall had to be carefully located. None of the weight of the external envelope could be transferred to the existing floor slab, and the entire external walling is suspended from triangulated trusses around the perimeter of the building with loads being transferred to the foundations from only four points of support. Stainless steel glazing trusses carry the weight of the 20 millimetre thick triple-laminate glass and resist all lateral wind loads, yet allow the differential movement between the new building and the existing basement structure with a weather-tight sliding joint at the base of the wall. Main structural elements are in carbon steel.

At 11.5 metres long the reception desk at the entrance hall combines with six glass security pass gates to provide a welcoming focal point for the visitor, and also the first line of separation between the public and private areas of this multi-tenancy building. The desk is constructed using purpose-made cast aluminium frame members, which support a top of African Nero Granite. The glass facing comprises nine handcrafted, slumped-glass panels by artist Graham Jones.

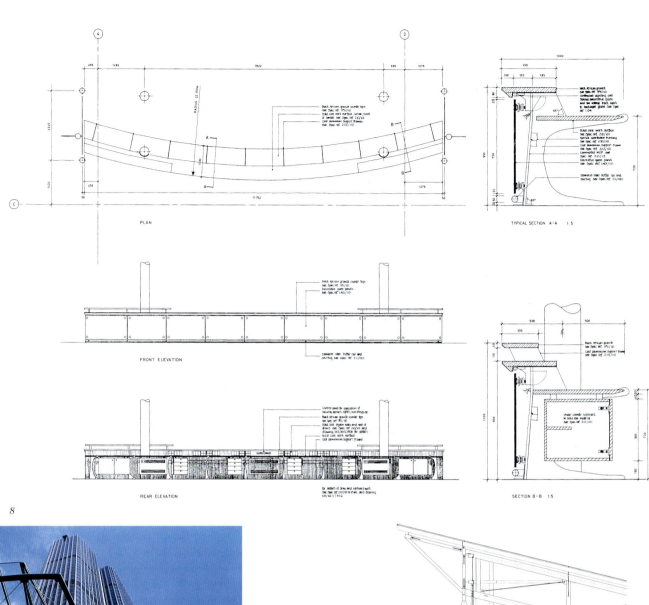

PLAN

TYPICAL SECTION A-A 1:5

FRONT ELEVATION

SECTION B-B 1:5

REAR ELEVATION

8

9

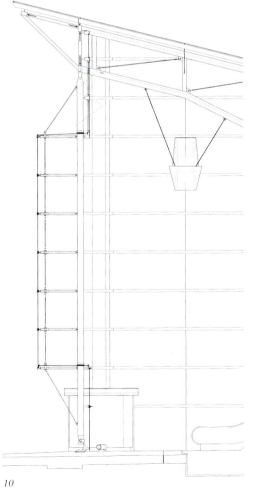

10

TRUSS

PADDINGTON STATION, PADDINGTON, LONDON, UK
Nicholas Grimshaw & Partners

1

1   General view of the Lawn
2   Detail cross section through truss
3   Stainless steel casting used to connect rods
     to outriggers, thus forming the curve of the
     bottom boom of each truss
*Photography: Peter Cook VIEW (1), Peter
Strobel Photodesign/Cologne (Germany) (3),
image 2 reproduced with the kind permission
of The Architects Journal*

Paddington Station is the first mainline terminus to be completely refurbished by Railtrack as part of its station regeneration program. The challenge for Nicholas Grimshaw & Partners has been to prepare this grade-one listed station for its enhanced role as a major transportation hub, since the Heathrow Express service and new private rail initiatives have greatly increased passenger numbers in the station.

The key addition to the fabric of Paddington Station has been the new passenger waiting and check-in facility to the town-end of the Brunel sheds in an area called the Lawn. The best of the 1930s work, including the classical stone façades, has been preserved and complemented with a new,

pre-cast concrete structure. Within this structure, transparent bridges, lift shafts, walkways and partitions are housed under a light-weight steel and glass trussed roof, designed with reference to the 'Paxton' type ridge and furrow original.

The use of castings has ensured that the large quantities of complex elements that make up each truss have been produced economically, without compromising attention to detail. Thus the roof enhances the exuberant Victorian detailing and inventive technical solutions of the adjoining Brunel gables restored by Nicholas Grimshaw & Partners as part of the project.

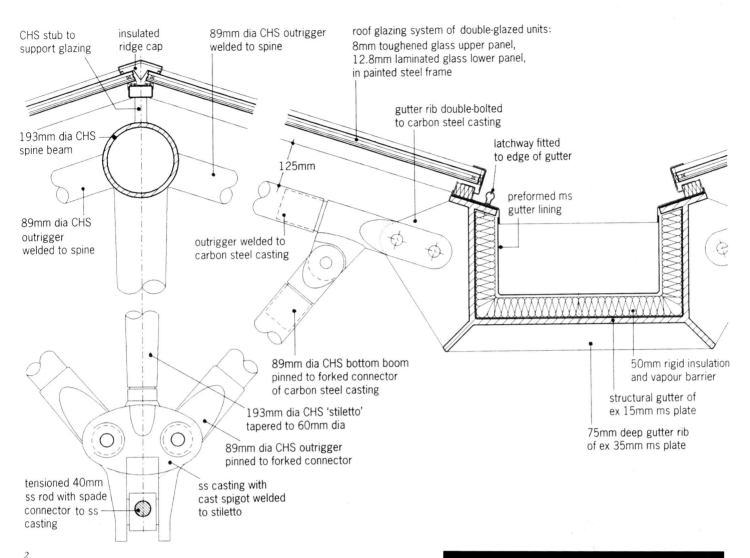

CHS stub to support glazing

insulated ridge cap

89mm dia CHS outrigger welded to spine

roof glazing system of double-glazed units: 8mm toughened glass upper panel, 12.8mm laminated glass lower panel, in painted steel frame

gutter rib double-bolted to carbon steel casting

latchway fitted to edge of gutter

193mm dia CHS spine beam

125mm

preformed ms gutter lining

89mm dia CHS outrigger welded to spine

outrigger welded to carbon steel casting

89mm dia CHS bottom boom pinned to forked connector of carbon steel casting

50mm rigid insulation and vapour barrier

193mm dia CHS 'stiletto' tapered to 60mm dia

structural gutter of ex 15mm ms plate

89mm dia CHS outrigger pinned to forked connector

75mm deep gutter rib of ex 35mm ms plate

tensioned 40mm ss rod with spade connector to ss casting

ss casting with cast spigot welded to stiletto

2

3

GREENHOUSE

BARRETT RESIDENCE, SANTA FE, NEW MEXICO, USA
Jeff Harnar Architects

1

1   *Conceptual model of residence showing
    greenhouse on the left*
2   *Schematic isometric*
3   *Construction details*

The program for this project called for a green-house off the workshop, for passive solar heat gain, light and plants. This structure's sculptural form and the bright yellow colour draws attention to and anchors the end of a curved wall, which leads the arriving visitor to the home's entry. Corner glazing details, without mullions, create a crispness, continuity and indoor/outdoor connection consistent with the theme of the house.

The structure itself is a simple welded steel framework, which receives an electrostatic polyester powder coat finish. Glazing is attached by means of a combination of a mechanical and a structural silicone system using commercially available glazing extrusions, gaskets and caps. Operable metal sash windows are inserted into the framework for ventilation.

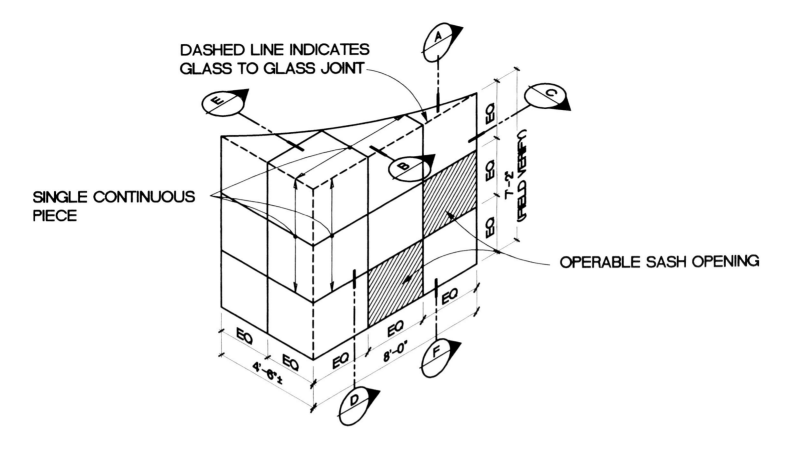

DASHED LINE INDICATES
GLASS TO GLASS JOINT

SINGLE CONTINUOUS
PIECE

OPERABLE SASH OPENING

EO EO EO

4'-6"± 8'-0"

7'-2" (FIELD VERIFY)

GREENHOUSE SCHEMATIC

N.T.S.

2

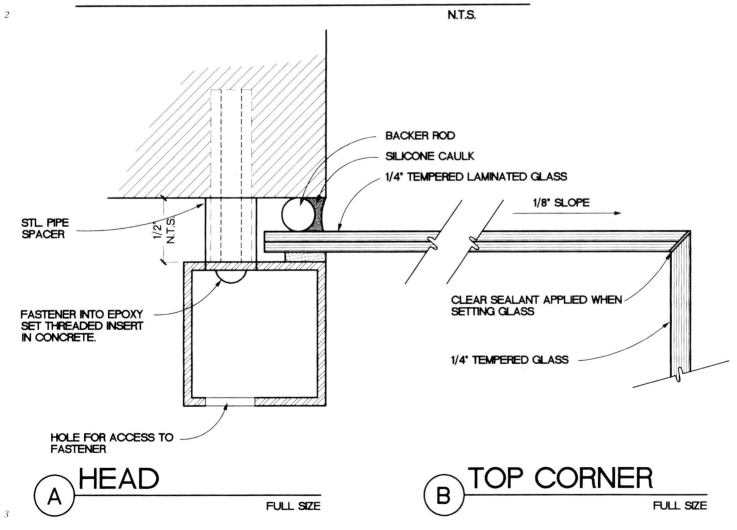

BACKER ROD

SILICONE CAULK

1/4" TEMPERED LAMINATED GLASS

1/8" SLOPE

STL. PIPE
SPACER

1/2" N.T.S.

FASTENER INTO EPOXY
SET THREADED INSERT
IN CONCRETE.

CLEAR SEALANT APPLIED WHEN
SETTING GLASS

1/4" TEMPERED GLASS

HOLE FOR ACCESS TO
FASTENER

A HEAD

FULL SIZE

3

B TOP CORNER

FULL SIZE

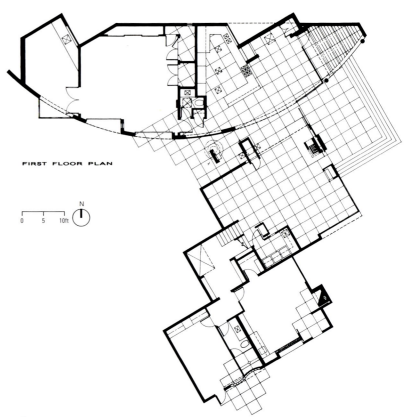

FIRST FLOOR PLAN

0   5   10ft   N

4   Plan of residence with greenhouse at the left
    side of the curved form
5   View of greenhouse, looking toward entry
6   Construction details

4

5

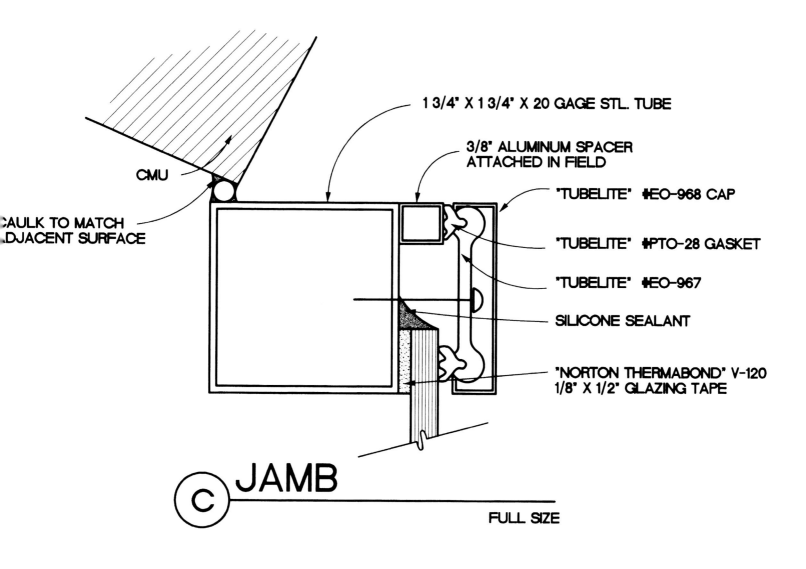

CMU

CAULK TO MATCH
ADJACENT SURFACE

1 3/4" X 1 3/4" X 20 GAGE STL. TUBE

3/8" ALUMINUM SPACER
ATTACHED IN FIELD

"TUBELITE" #EO-968 CAP

"TUBELITE" #PTO-28 GASKET

"TUBELITE" #EO-967

SILICONE SEALANT

"NORTON THERMABOND" V-120
1/8" X 1/2" GLAZING TAPE

C JAMB

FULL SIZE

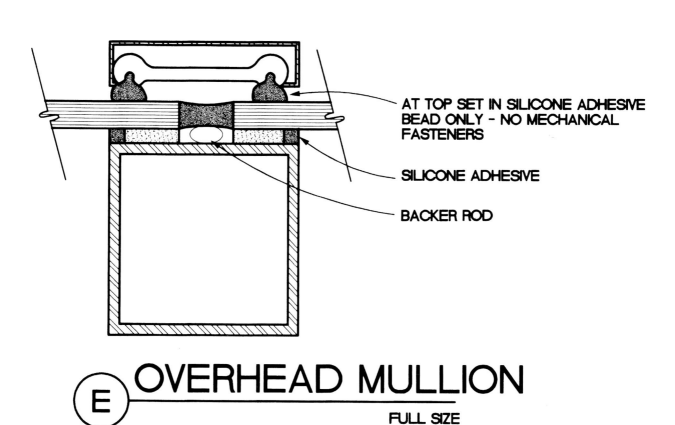

AT TOP SET IN SILICONE ADHESIVE
BEAD ONLY - NO MECHANICAL
FASTENERS

SILICONE ADHESIVE

BACKER ROD

E OVERHEAD MULLION

FULL SIZE

6

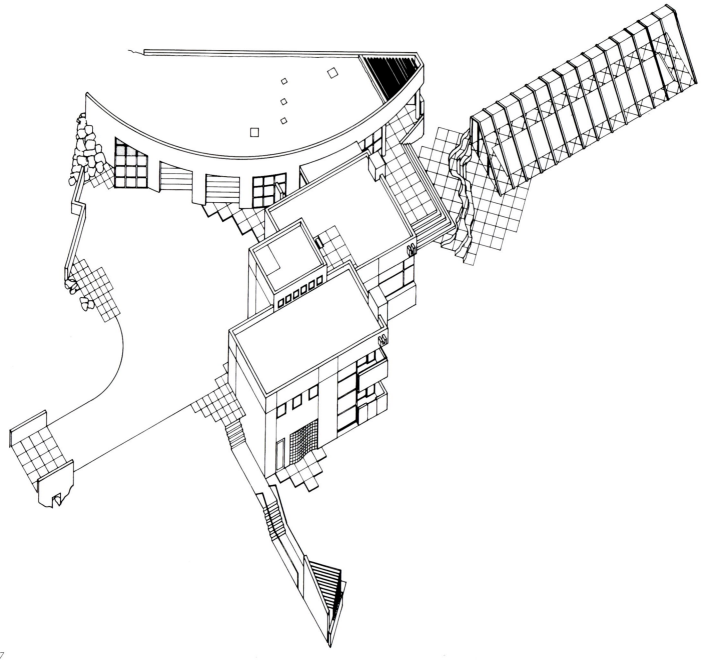

7

8

Photography: Douglas Kahn (5,8), Robert Reck (1)

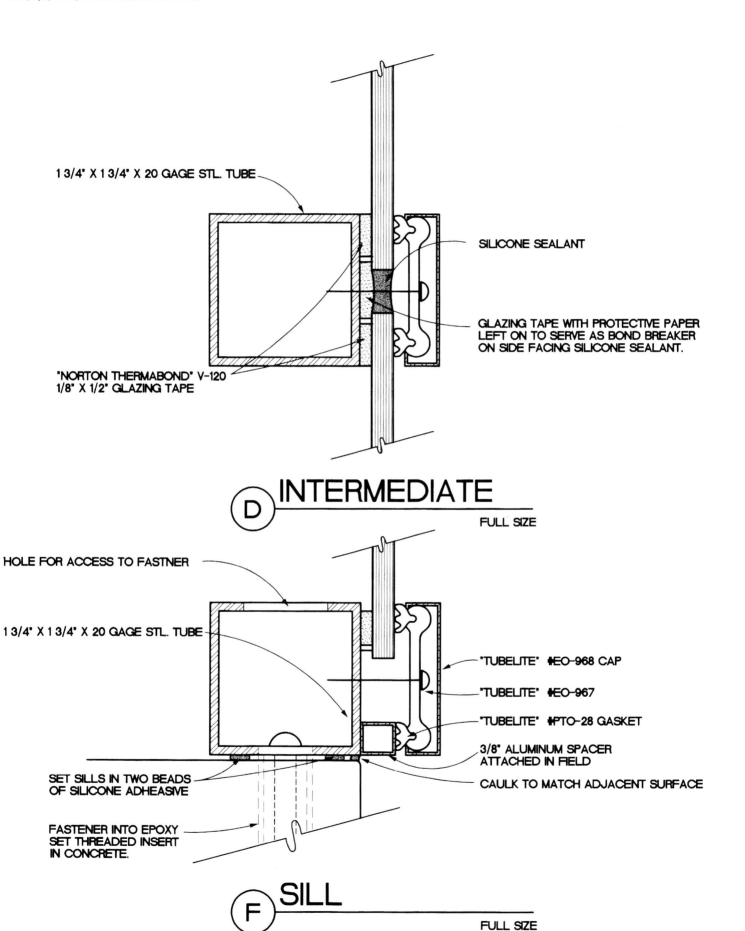

1 3/4" X 1 3/4" X 20 GAGE STL. TUBE

SILICONE SEALANT

GLAZING TAPE WITH PROTECTIVE PAPER
LEFT ON TO SERVE AS BOND BREAKER
ON SIDE FACING SILICONE SEALANT.

"NORTON THERMABOND" V-120
1/8" X 1/2" GLAZING TAPE

D INTERMEDIATE

FULL SIZE

HOLE FOR ACCESS TO FASTNER

1 3/4" X 1 3/4" X 20 GAGE STL. TUBE

"TUBELITE" #EO-968 CAP

"TUBELITE" #EO-967

"TUBELITE" #PTO-28 GASKET

3/8" ALUMINUM SPACER
ATTACHED IN FIELD

SET SILLS IN TWO BEADS
OF SILICONE ADHEASIVE

CAULK TO MATCH ADJACENT SURFACE

FASTENER INTO EPOXY
SET THREADED INSERT
IN CONCRETE.

F SILL

FULL SIZE

9

GLASS BRIDGE

SCHOOL OF ART, ARNHEM, THE NETHERLANDS
Hubert-Jan Henket architecten bna

1

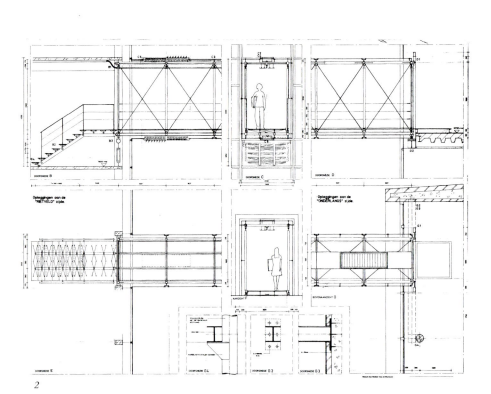

2

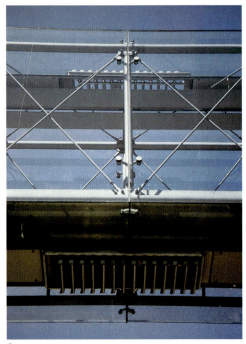

3

1   Glass bridge
2&5   Sections
3   Detail
4   Detail plan
6   Fragment
Photography: H. J. Henket (1,3,6)

Gerrit Rietveld designed the School of Art in Arnhem in 1961 as a transparent solitary element in the park. He chose a small construction grid of 1.8 metres and by so doing, was able to create minimal construction sizes and visually open corners in the building. He also designed a flat glass curtain wall by trying to maximise the technical possibilities available at the time. The result was a beautiful light and transparent building with a simple plan.

During the early 1990s the old PGEM office building, which was extended within 18 metres of Rietveld's north elevation in the late 1960s, was bought by the School of Art and was to become a conservatorium. A bridge was needed to connect the old PGEM building with Rietveld's building. The architectural value of Rietveld's building was respected by using his horizontal and vertical grid in the design. It was also very important to incorporate his transparent themes and open corners and to design a flat glass façade with minimal construction. Due to the fact that the grid and floor levels of Rietveld's building do not correspond with those of the PGEM building, Rietveld's grid was used and the PGEM building was adjusted where necessary.

Industrial ventilation shutters in both the top of the roof and the ceiling were used. These shutters open automatically when it becomes too warm and they close automatically when it rains.

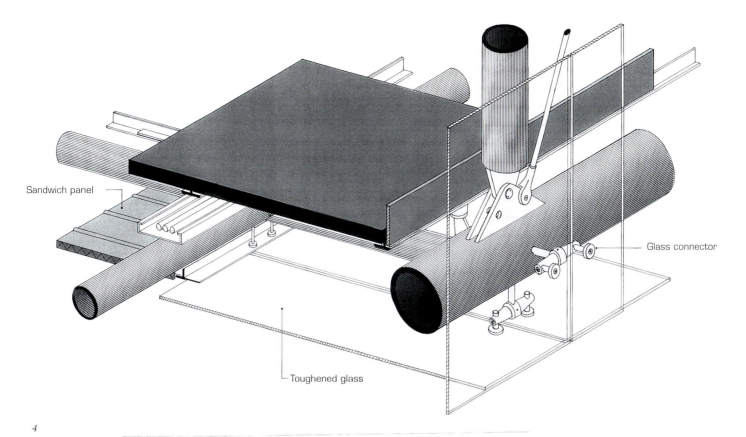

Sandwich panel

Glass connector

Toughened glass

4

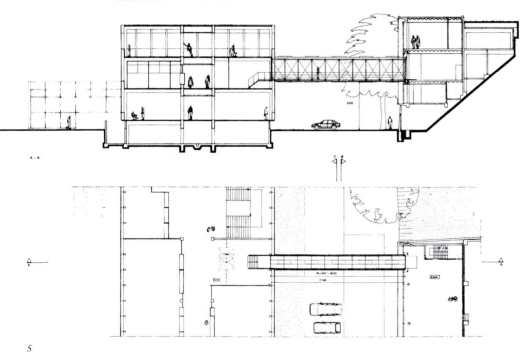

5

6

Radiation panels produce extra comfort during cold periods. Light fittings are incorporated between the radiation panels as well as a large cable gutter, which incorporates all the electrical communication data facilities between the two buildings.

One of the most important design problems of the façade design and development was to prevent the horizontal or vertical distortion as a result of the loads caused by wind, snow and people. The details for the glass connection fittings and the size of the joints between the panes of glass were the result of a careful study of these loads.

MULLIONS
TEYLERS MUSEUM EXTENSION, HAARLEM, THE NETHERLANDS
Hubert-Jan Henket architecten bna

1

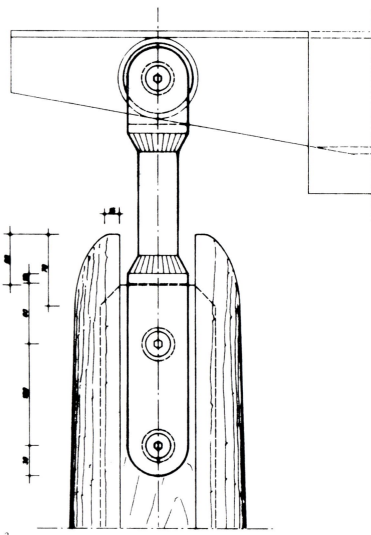

2

1   *Interior of connection*
2   *Top connector*
3   *Bottom connector*
4   *DVW mullions with glass connection*
5   *Connection between old and
    new building*
Photography: Sybolt Voeten

Densified veneer wood (DVW) is a material that has a long tradition in the process industry as a precursor to the use of stainless steel and plastic. The development of those new materials stopped further development and application of DVW until now. New interest for the design of DVW has come up because it can generate production methods that allow size tolerances, freedom of form, better manufacturing and labour circumstances; all not common in the building industry. It also provides the possibility of decreasing dimension and arriving at forms of wood construction never associated with timber before. These are the reasons that DVW was chosen as a material for

mullions in the Teylers Museum extension. DVW is the product of a special technique wherein beech veneer in combination with synthetic resins is glued together under great pressure and temperature. The result is a composit material with greater strength than ordinary types of timber.

According to *Technologie des Holzes und der Holzwerk-stoffen* by Franz Kollman, 1951, all timbers except ring porous non-coniferous species, like oak, and coniferous species with very many resin pockets, are usable to make DVW. This also creates opportunities to use Finnish wood; for example, birch for DVW. As such, experiments are

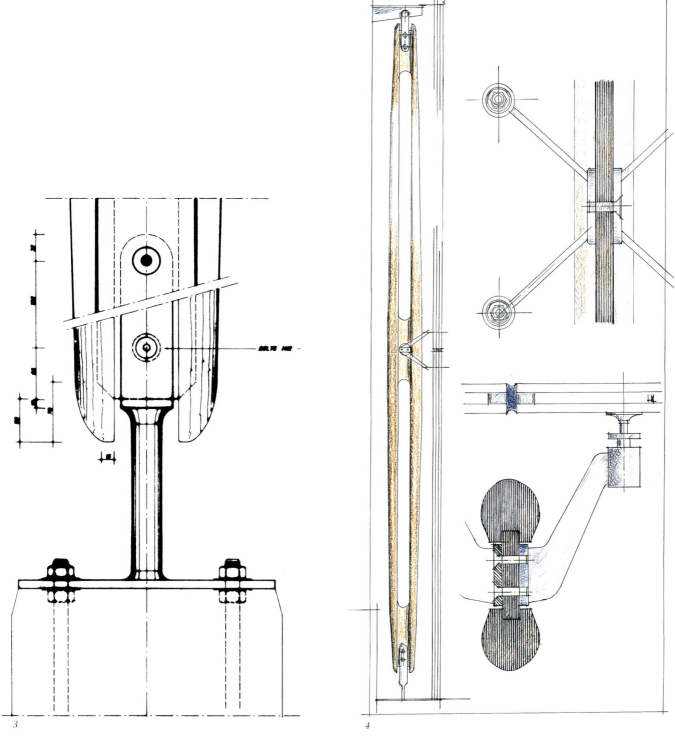

3

4

being done with maritime pine at the Department of Civil Engineering at the University of Technology in Delft, The Netherlands.

Up until this first experiment with DVW it was never used as a building construction material before. The producer of DVW in Holland offered a method by which it is possible to produce parts in greater number and with very low tolerances by means of a computerised three-dimensional milling machine. This machinery is normally used to make hockey sticks, golf club parts, tools, gymnastic appliances, electric insulators for high voltage switches, and so on.

The restriction of a maximum length of 2.4 metres was solved by developing a glue-welded finger joint. The method in which the mullion was developed also creates possiblities for steel or aluminium tube connectors, normally made out of iron or aluminium castings. The cost of developing those castings is almost not feasible due to the relative small numbers normally needed in building construction. Developments to combine DVW and glass in order to create more transparent constructions are on the way. The advantages of DVW architecturally are its beautiful warm and varying colour (due to the pressure technique) and its freedom of form.

5

VENTILATION
STATE OFFICES CERAMIQUE, MAASTRICHT, THE NETHERLANDS
Hubert-Jan Henket architecten bna

1

2

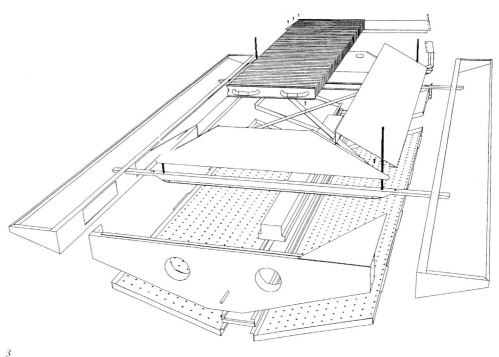

3

To save energy and to create a healthy working environment, natural ventilation was introduced in the working areas on levels 1, 2 and 3 of the State Offices Ceramique. By reducing the energy consumption for cooling and airconditioning to a minimum, the consumption costs for heating would be reduced. The natural airing in the building results from the wind, thermal and sun energy. The ventilation of the ground floor, where a restaurant and other facilities are situated, and of the fourth floor, is mechanically regulated. In those areas where the internal and external heat load will be excessive, mechanical airconditioning systems are installed. The outside air supply for the offices is regulated by self-controlled façade ventilation ducts, one every 180 metres of the building grid. The ventilation ducts can be closed during winter, and opened on summer nights in order to cool the building. Along the façade, radiators are placed below the windows. At ceiling level the incoming fresh air is warmed by the heat exchange with the steel plenum. Redundant air is guided through channels, which end up in the so-called solar chimneys where the air rises through sun thermal energy. The excessive heat, before leaving the chimneys, is used to generate power for cooling purposes. An open glass roof covers the atrium, which is placed on the inside of the

1 Solar chimneys
2 Plenums installed
3 Plenum design
4 View upwards in solar chimney
5 Ventilation scheme solar chimney

4

building. This construction makes an air supply
and a circulation of the air in the atrium possible.
The warm air from the adjacent offices to the
atrium makes a rapid cooling of the inward façade
impossible. The temperature of the rooms is
further regulated by cooling through the radiators,
and during warm periods, extra cooling elements
above the plenums can add to comfort in rooms
with many computers.

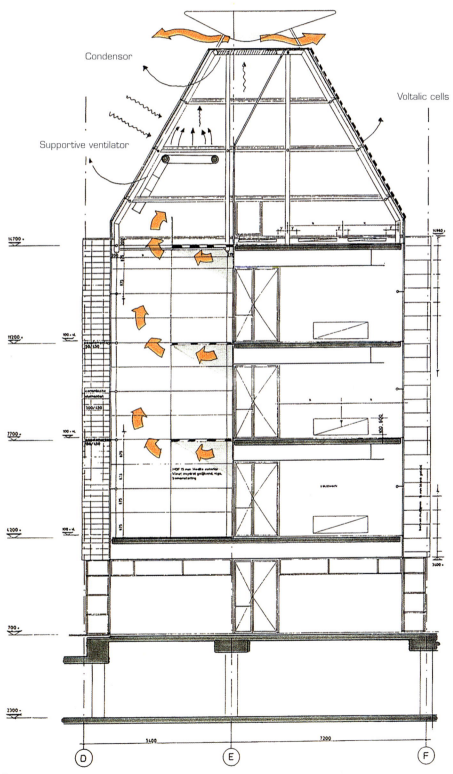

5

Condensor

Voltalic cells

Supportive ventilator

D E F

111

6

7

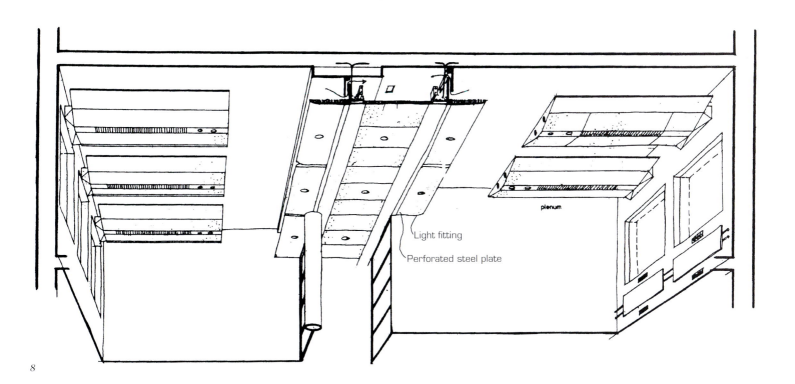

8

Light fitting

Perforated steel plate

plenum

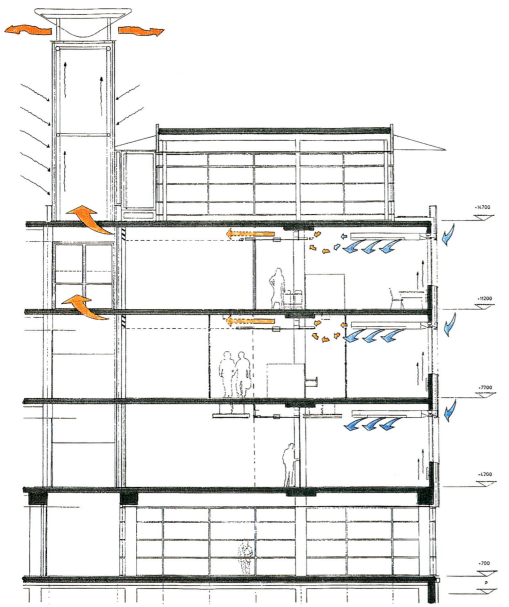

9

+14700

+11200

+7700

+4200

+700

P

6   Front façade
7   Open office concept
8   Isometric of ceiling with plenums and
    lighting
9   Ventilation scheme offices
Photography: Sybolt Voeten

EXHIBITION STANDS

AUDI AG MESSESTAND IAA, FRANKFURT 1999, GERMANY

Ingenhoven Overdiek und Partner

1

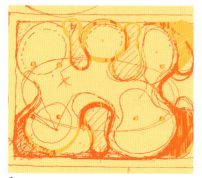

2

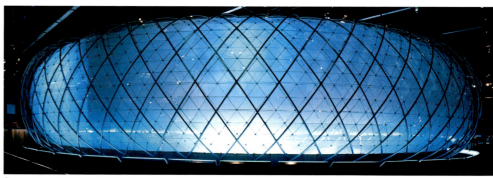

3

1 Model (1:87)
2 First sketch
3 The Loop
4 Isometric projection
5 Meeting room

The exhibition area for the latest Audi exhibition stand is enclosed in a multi-dimensionally curved façade (developed length approximately 320 metres) – known as the loop – made from corundum blasted finish stainless steel tubes, cable nets and glass panels.

The loop features the vehicles and exhibition for the first time in an original environment enclosed in its own specially designed engineering structure. Architecture, engineering, the presentation of the vehicles, light and projection technology, information communication and services define an integrated entry to the exhibition for the visitor.

The floor plan layout and the curved section of the loop form a continuum of through spaces. The directional lighting and image projection technique, with a floor that slopes slightly upwards, amalgamate to create the stand's own special environment. The exhibition space (approximately 4,250 square metres) spreads out like an extensive landscape. Curved opening portals connect all the stand's exhibition and functional areas.

A total of 12,000 triangular glass panes in 3,000 different formats define the loop's surface (approximately 1,800 square metres). Areas of transparent and satinised glazing alternate along

structure

4

the access ways. The transparency of the glass provides a series of changing views of exhibition vehicles, engines and lounges.

Continuously changing pictures are projected onto the loop throughout the day. The software-controlled video projection system is supplemented by lighting, smoothly blending the colour changes cast onto the periphery of the loop.

This form of complex façade design, never designed or built before, defines, and at the same time limits, the space, while acting as the conduit for the communication of information, and providing transparent and translucent projection surfaces. The suitability of the printed, etched and

satinised glass for projection was proved in a series of tests. Finally a degree of satinised finish was found that fulfilled all the technical requirements. All components of the light, picture and film projection display harmonise with one another on the glass surfaces. Powerful hardware and software systems control 25 of the latest generation of video projectors to ensure the best audiovisual performance.

The exhibition stand was used again in slightly different plan arrangements – using the structural components and assembly elements specially developed for the IAA Frankfurt – at Tokyo, Detroit, Geneva and Paris in 2000.

5

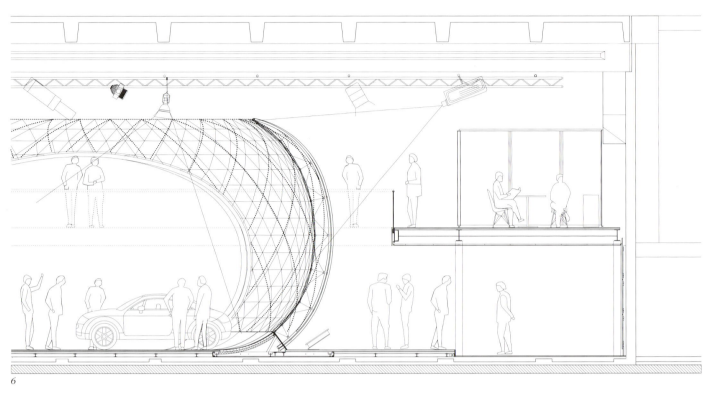

6

7

8

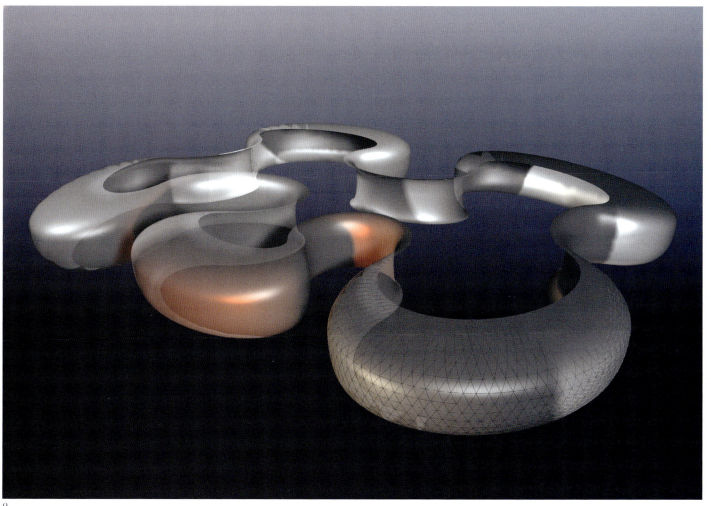

9

10&12   Detail of the loop joint
   11   Detail of the loop surface
   13   Coral
Photography: courtesy Ingenhoven Overdiek
und Partner

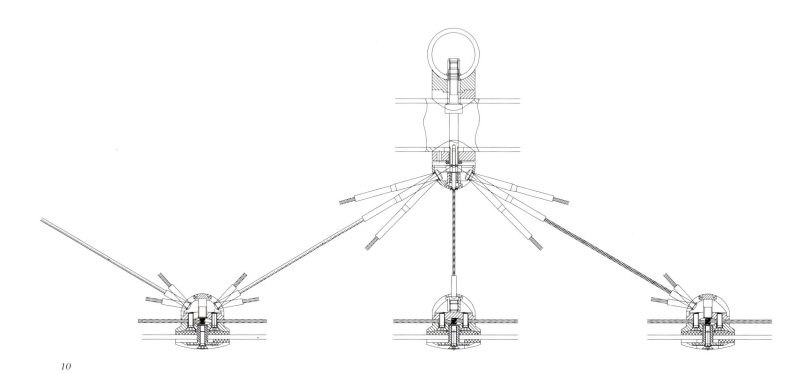

10

11

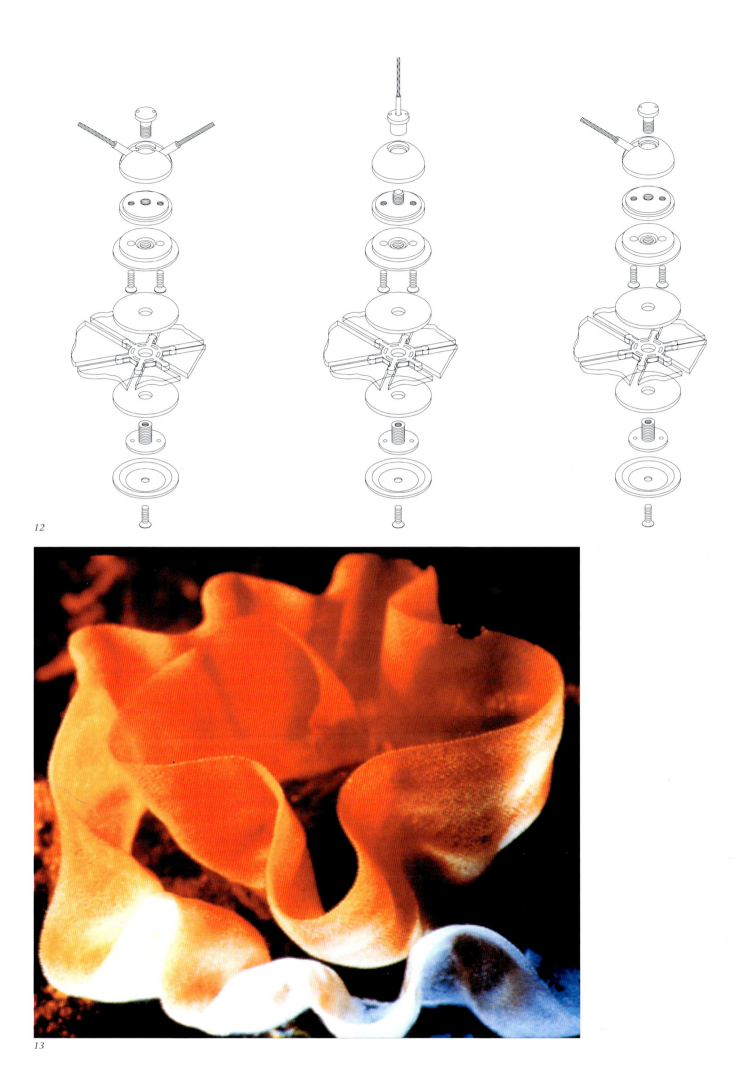

12

13

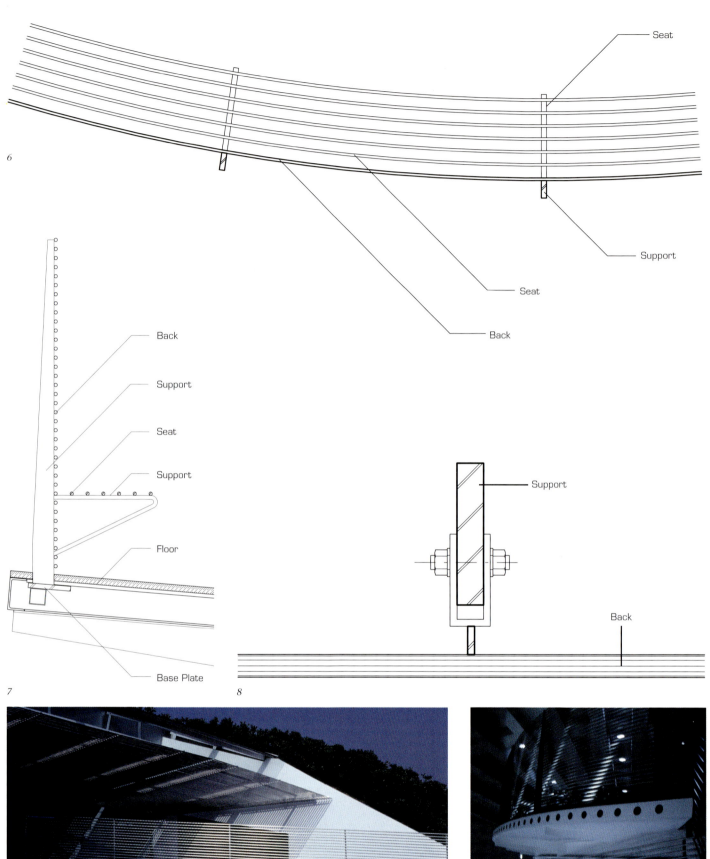

6

Seat

Support

Seat

Back

Back

Support

Support

Seat

Support

Floor

Base Plate

7

8

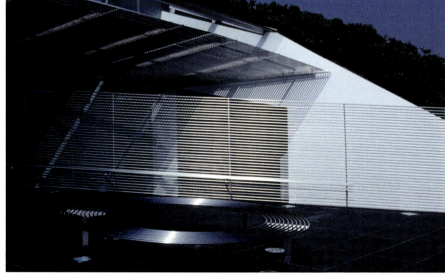

9

10

11

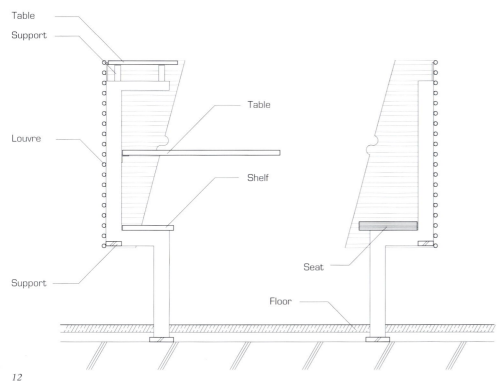

Table

Support

Louvre

Table

Shelf

Support

Seat

Floor

12

13

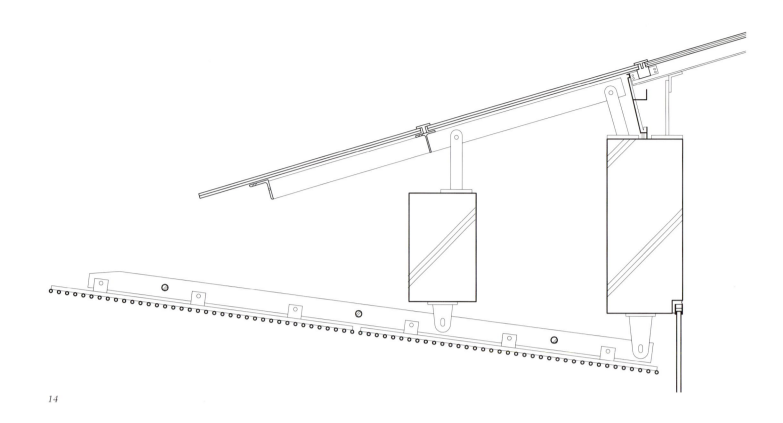

14

15

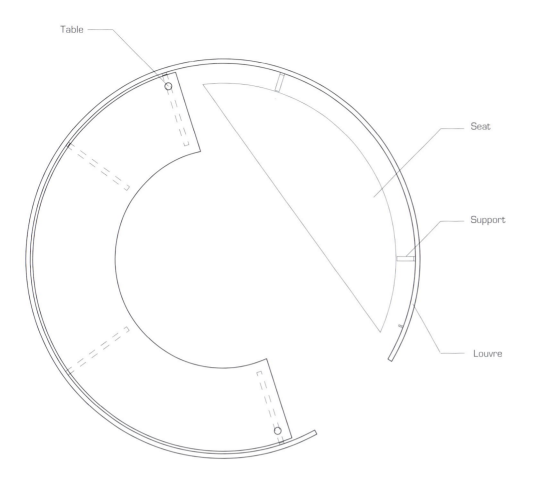

Table

Seat

Support

Louvre

14 Hisashi section
15 Hisashi detail
16 Counter plan
17 View to the Kitakami River
Photography: Fujitsuka Mitsumasa

16

17

CEILING

SHIGA KOGEN ROMAN ART MUSEUM, YAMANOUCHI, JAPAN
Kisho Kurokawa Architect & Associates

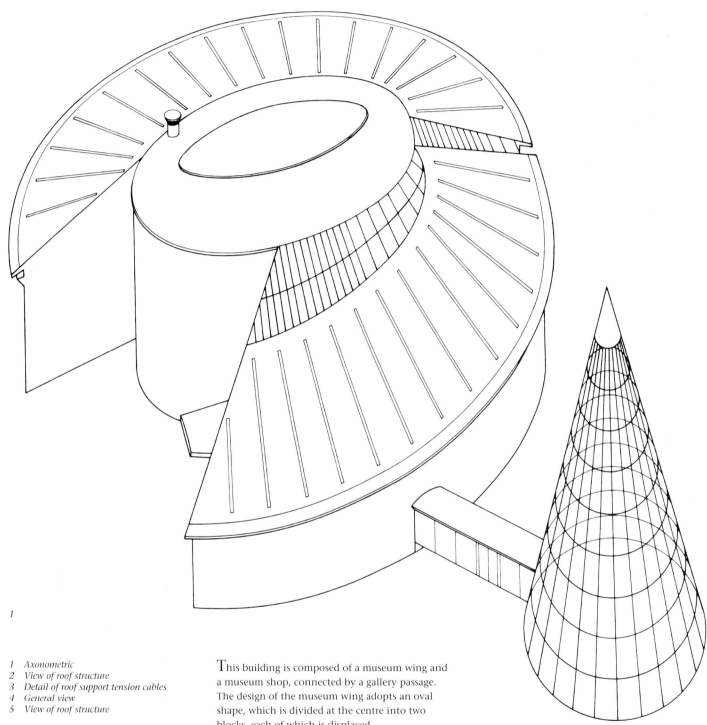

1

1 Axonometric
2 View of roof structure
3 Detail of roof support tension cables
4 General view
5 View of roof structure

This building is composed of a museum wing and a museum shop, connected by a gallery passage. The design of the museum wing adopts an oval shape, which is divided at the centre into two blocks, each of which is displaced.

The exhibition hall has a two-storied atrium with ceilings that adopt the shape of the base of a ship, and the exhibition rooms are placed around this hall.

The roof consists of glue-laminated timbers and roof truss tension cables, creating a rhythm in the spiraling roof.

2

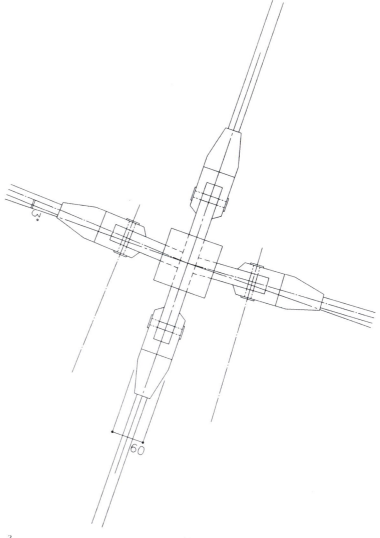

3

4

5

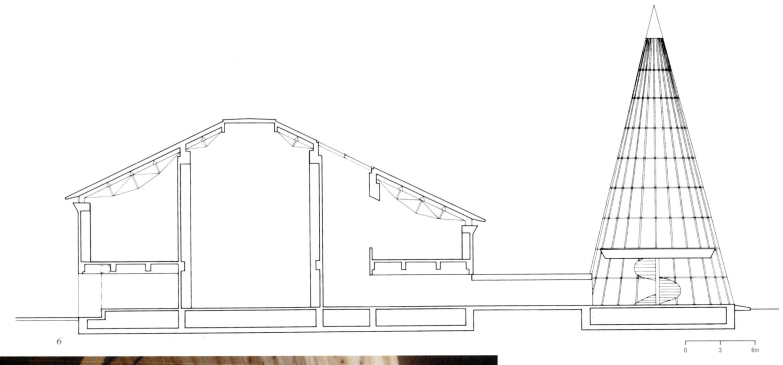

6

6   Section
7   Staircase and EV shaft in second floor
    exhibition room
8   Roof support detail
9   Entrance hall
10 Looking up roof light of the entrance hall
Photography: Tomio Ohashi

7

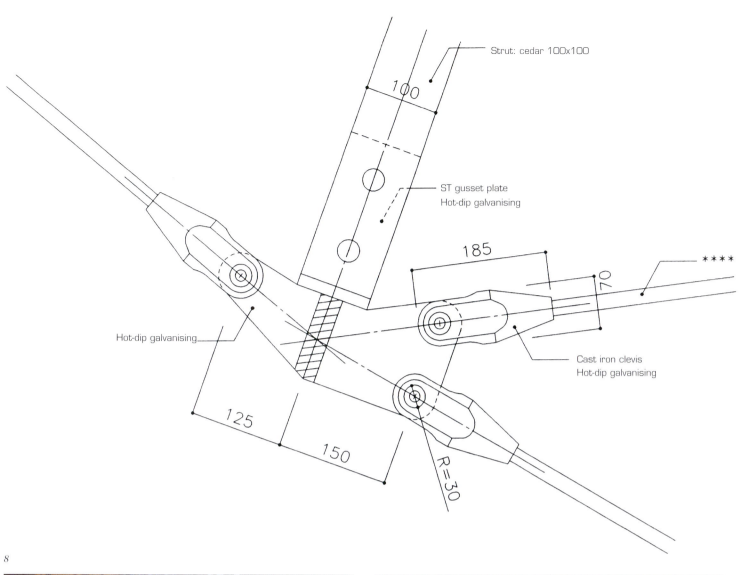

Strut: cedar 100x100

100

ST gusset plate
Hot-dip galvanising

185

70

****

Hot-dip galvanising

Cast iron clevis
Hot-dip galvanising

125

150

R=30

8

9

10

EXTERIOR SKYLIGHT
THE NEW WING OF THE VAN GOGH MUSEUM, AMSTERDAM, THE NETHERLANDS
Kisho Kurokawa Architect & Associates

1

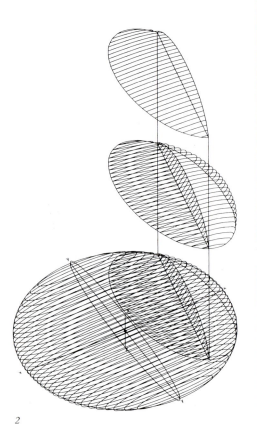

2

3

4

1   *View from east*
2   *Roof curve simulation*
3   *Detail view from south*
4   *Staircase view from second floor*
5   *Detail of skylight*
6   *View from south-east*
Photography: Sels-Clerbourt

The new wing of the Van Gogh Museum is constructed on the Museumplein that is called 'the most important heart of the city' of Amsterdam, The Netherlands.

The shape of the roof is a cut part of a revolving ellipsoid, and the whole surface is finished with titanium sheets.

The curved surface of the exterior wall of the building that faces the museum is covered with 90 centimetre square granite panels.

The in-between space, from the top part of this exterior wall to the underside of the roof, is filled with a high-side skylight – the exhibition rooms receive natural light from these. Roll-blind shades have been installed in the skylight to control the amount of natural light.

The new wing adopts abstract forms and careful placement of space – off-centered, twisted and asymmetrical – in order to express Japanese aesthetics and the concept of order in the age of modernism – this is called a *non-Bourbakian* system.

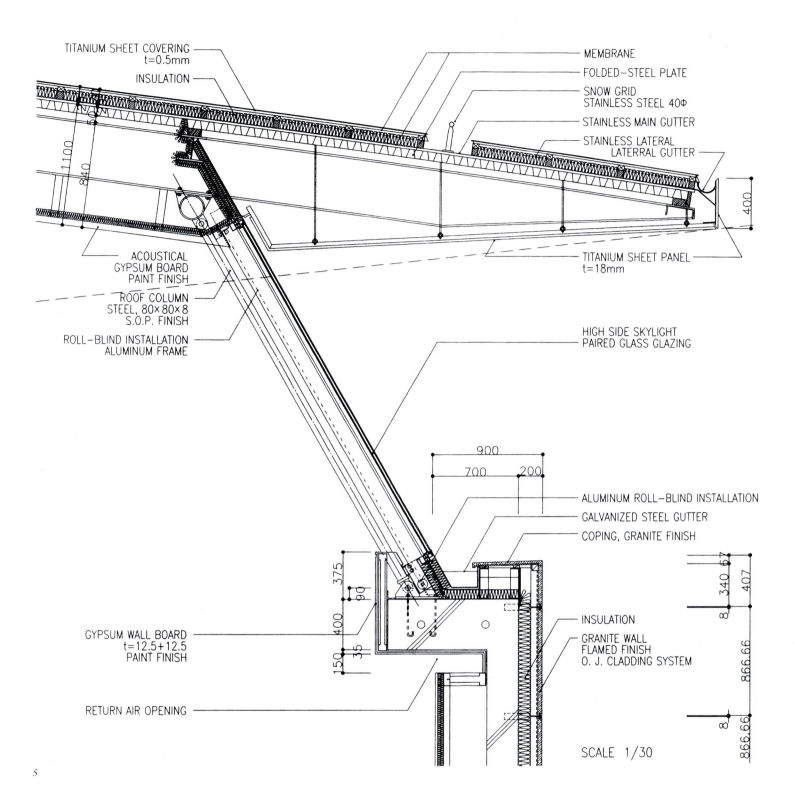

TITANIUM SHEET COVERING
t=0.5mm

INSULATION

MEMBRANE

FOLDED-STEEL PLATE

SNOW GRID
STAINLESS STEEL 40Φ

STAINLESS MAIN GUTTER

STAINLESS LATERAL
LATERRAL GUTTER

1100

840

400

ACOUSTICAL
GYPSUM BOARD
PAINT FINISH

ROOF COLUMN
STEEL, 80×80×8
S.O.P. FINISH

ROLL-BLIND INSTALLATION
ALUMINUM FRAME

TITANIUM SHEET PANEL
t=18mm

HIGH SIDE SKYLIGHT
PAIRED GLASS GLAZING

900

700

200

ALUMINUM ROLL-BLIND INSTALLATION

GALVANIZED STEEL GUTTER

COPING, GRANITE FINISH

375

90

400

150

35

340

67

407

8

INSULATION

GRANITE WALL
FLAMED FINISH
O. J. CLADDING SYSTEM

866.66

GYPSUM WALL BOARD
t=12.5+12.5
PAINT FINISH

RETURN AIR OPENING

SCALE 1/30

866.66

8

5

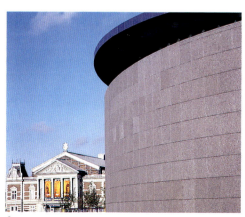

6

131

HANDRAIL
EHIME PREFECTURAL MUSEUM OF GENERAL SCIENCE, NIIHAMA CITY, SHIKOKU ISLAND, JAPAN
Kisho Kurokawa Architect & Associates

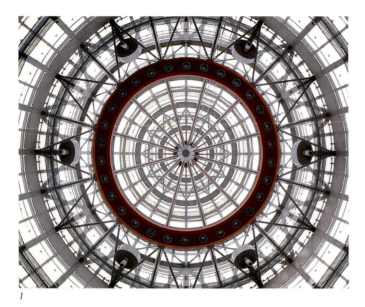

1

2

3

1 Entrance hall atrium
2 View of planetarium (left), exhibition hall (right) and entrance hall (centre) over pond
3 Entrance hall with descending ramp and handrail
4 Section of handrail
5 View of glass cone atrium
6 Section and details of handrail
Photography: Tomio Ohashi

This site is located in the suburb of Niihama City of Shikoku Island, where a future highway interchange is planned adjacent to the base of the mountains. In order to create a relationship with the surrounding area, the buildings are individually articulated into four fragments. Each fragment has its own function, including an administrative facility and a planetarium.

Simple geometric forms were adopted: a crescent, a cube, a square, a cone and a triangle. The layout and design of each fragment is based on the image of the Japanese garden as a free arrangement of stepping stones; this is another way of expressing the asymmetry of Japanese traditions.

The entrance hall is a glass cone atrium 38 metres high. There is a spiral ramp ascending from the first floor to the fourth floor, connecting the exhibition rooms adjacent to the cone atrium. People can come down the spiral ramp into the glass cone atrium.

The balustrade of the ramp is composed of curved tempered glass. The handrail is composed of aluminium casting, and the design is truss shaped. The tempered glass is attached to the handrail by bolts. There are two handrails: the upper handrail, for adults, composed of a stainless flat bar, and the lower handrail for children and the elderly, composed of a stainless pipe.

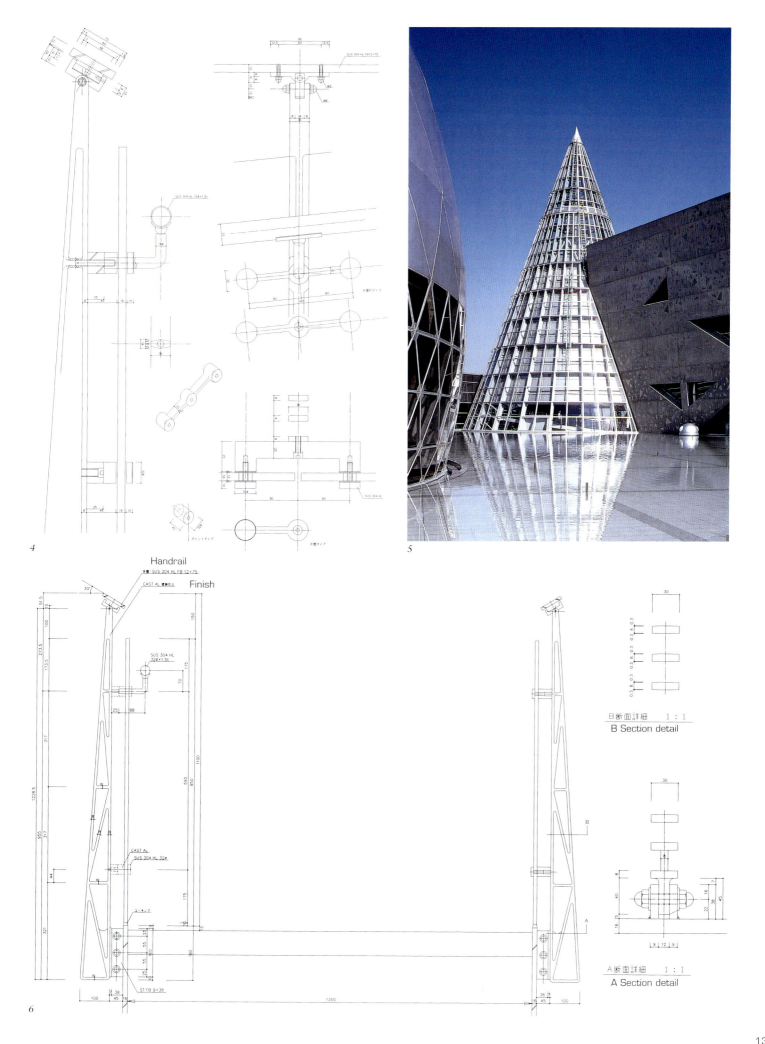

4

5

Handrail
手摺 : SUS 304 HL FB 12×75
CAST AL 塗装仕上
Finish

SUS 304 HL
32ø×1.5t

CAST AL
SUS 304 HL 32ø

ST FB 9×38

6

30
B断面詳細　1 : 1
B Section detail

30
A断面詳細　1 : 1
A Section detail

ROOF

GIFU RESEARCH LABORATORIES, AMANO PHARMACEUTICAL CO. LTD., JAPAN
Kisho Kurokawa Architect & Associates

1

2

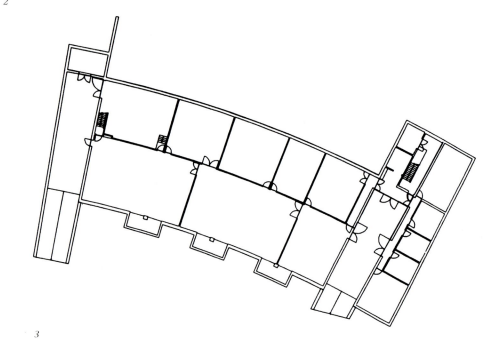

3

1 *Aluminium louvre roof eaves*
2 *Night view of entrance*
3 *Floor plan*
4 *Section*
5 *Roof detail*
6 *View of entrance glass roof*
Photography: Koji Kobayashi

Amano Pharmaceutical Co. Ltd. is a leading company in the world in the field of enzyme research. The theme of this new laboratory is 'interactive communication among researchers in different fields in an open space'. The design requirement was to create a flexible space structure for the various types of research and experiments. For this reason, the large laboratory has no columns in between the mechanical room and the study room.

To create a clean environment for research and experiments, the building consists of plain ceiling surfaces, ceilings without ducts, and plumbing under the first floor and the mezzanine floor, with outlets placed at the floors and walls. For the same reason, the beams and the columns are placed as frames outside the building envelope, supporting the roof of the large laboratory on triangle box trusses that produce segmented arches.

Aluminum louvers have been installed on the eaves on the upper part of the south elevation for shade and protection from rainwater.

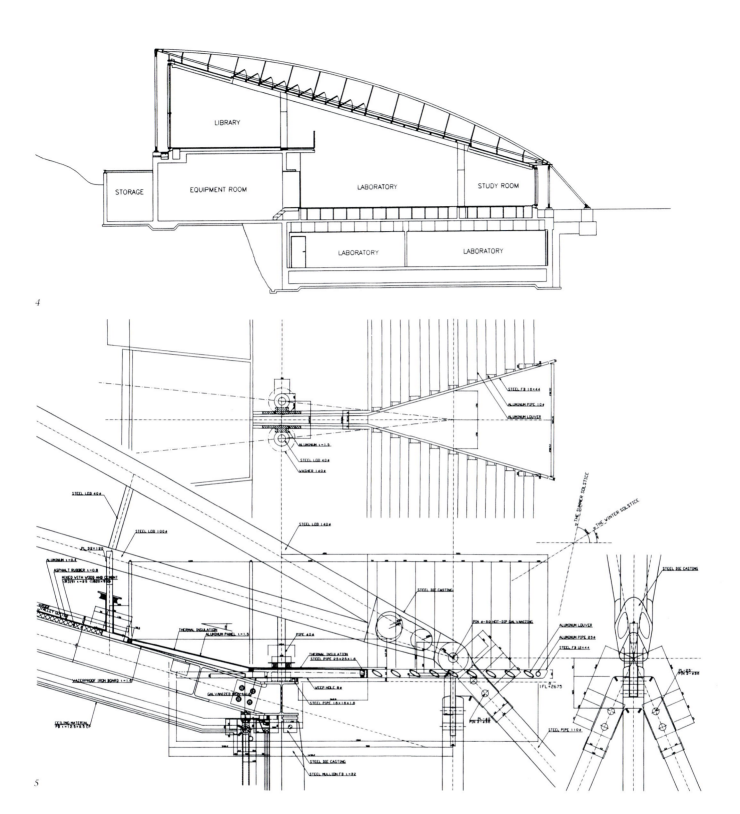

4

STORAGE

EQUIPMENT ROOM

LIBRARY

LABORATORY

STUDY ROOM

LABORATORY

LABORATORY

5

STEEL FB 10×44
ALUMINUM PIPE 10φ
ALUMINUM LOUVER

ALUMINUM t=1.5
STEEL LOD 40φ
WASHER 140φ

THE SUMMER SOLSTICE
THE WINTER SOLSTICE

STEEL LOD 40φ

STEEL LOD 100φ

STEEL LOD 140φ

PL 32×120

ALUMINUM t=0.7
ASPHALT RUBBER t=0.8
MIXED WITH VOID AND CEMENT

STEEL DIE CASTING

STEEL DIE CASTING

THERMAL INSULATION
ALUMINUM PANEL t=1.5

PIPE 60φ

THERMAL INSULATION
STEEL PIPE 25×25×1.6

PIN 4-SQ HOT-DIP GALVANIZING
ALUMINUM LOUVER
ALUMINUM PIPE 20φ
STEEL FB 12×44

WATERPROOF IRON BOARD t=1.6

WEEP HOLE 8φ

STEEL PIPE 18×18×1.6

1FL +2675

PIN 2-φ88

CEILING MATERIAL
PB t=12.5×6519

PIN 2-φ88

STEEL PIPE 110φ

STEEL DIE CASTING

STEEL MULLION FB t=32

GALVANIZED IRON WIRE

6

ROOF AND COLUMN STRUCTURE
KUALA LUMPUR INTERNATIONAL AIRPORT TERMINAL COMPLEX, KUALA LUMPUR, MALAYSIA
Kisho Kurokawa Architect & Associates

1

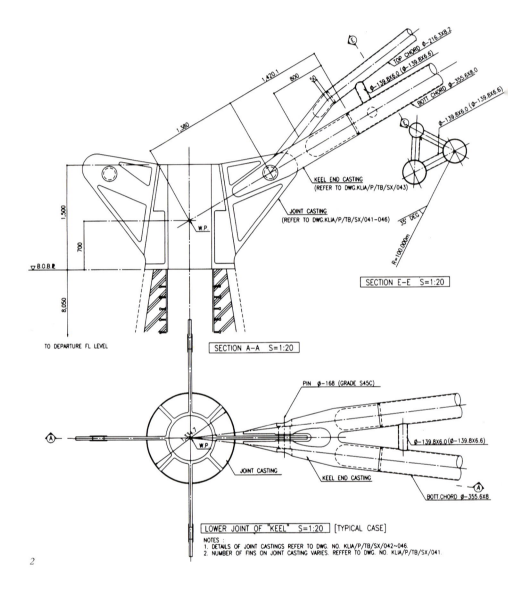

2

1   View of curbside and west elevation from
    short-term parking building
2   Detail of roof support MTB-roof
3   Detail of MTB skylight truss
4   Curbside view of column structure
5   Detail of MTB skylight joint
6   Curbside view from Flight Crew
    Briefing Centre
Photography: Tomio Ohashi

The detail that has generated the most interest in this project is the complex structural connection of the main terminal shell roof elements and the supporting column structure. Coincidentally, this is also the lowest part of the roof system and therefore the drainage point. The column detail was developed into an elegant, hollow conical concrete structure. It incorporates, in addition to the rainwater drainage, a plenum for chilled air supply, discharged through jet nozzle diffusers located half-way up the column.

The joint node evolved into an elaborate column capital detail, designed as conical steel casting with four-gusset plate fins, each to receive the triangu-

lated skylight truss. In perimeter conditions, additional, smaller gusset fin plates were introduced to accommodate the specific structural requirements of the arched canopies and gutter pan details. The joint node was fabricated as a single, 6 tonne steel casting component, with a height of 1.6 metres and a width of 3.2 metres. Additional castings were made for the pin joint components for the lower end of the skylight truss, and for the smaller scale gusset plates and pin joint components.

During the construction stage, the joint node developed beyond its original structural form. The inclusion of granite cladding and the limiting

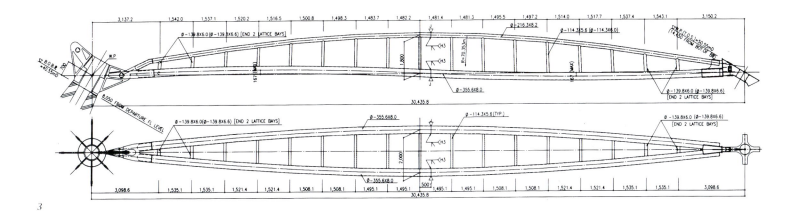

3

4

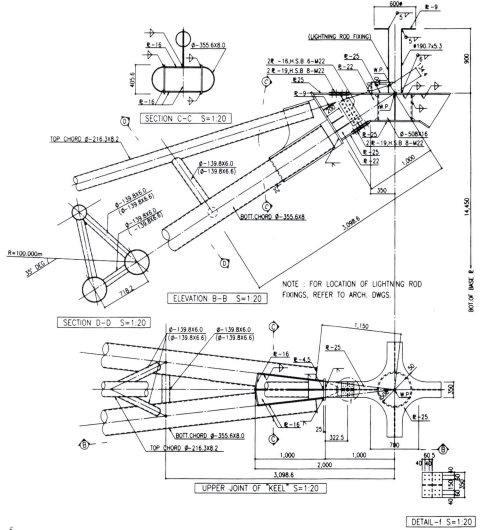

5

dimensions of the concrete column meant that, due to the structural reasons, the original method of using cast-in holding down bolts was no longer feasible. The bolts were omitted in favour of a studded cylindrical component, welded to the base of the joint casting, this was then cast-in-situ within the upper portion of the conical concrete column.

6

ENTRANCE PAVILION

LONG ISLAND RAIL ROAD, PENNSYLVANIA STATION, NEW YORK, NEW YORK, USA
R.M.Kliment & Frances Halsband Architects

1

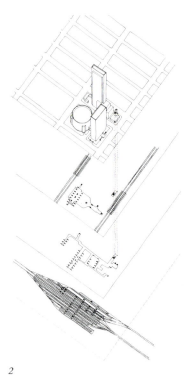

2

3

The entrance pavilion to the Long Island Rail Road (LIRR) at Pennsylvania Station serves 90,000 commuters each day. The entrance pavilion is the only component of the LIRR station visible above ground, and is located in a block of single-storey commercial buildings surrounded by office buildings, hotels, Madison Square Garden and Macy's Department Store.

The pavilion shelters pedestrian access to the station, and accommodates climate control equipment for the entire LIRR concourse below. It is comprised of four elements: the masonry

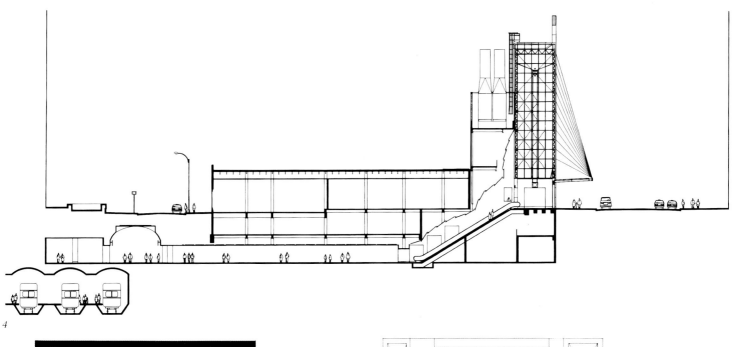

4

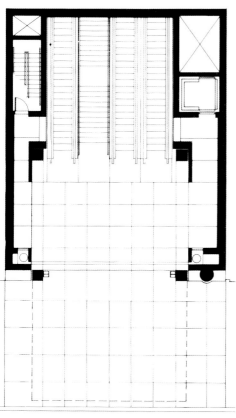

5

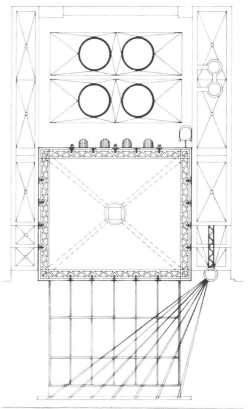

6

outer shell, the steel and glass tower, the marquee suspended by stainless steel rods from a stainless steel mast, and the escalator/stair hall.

The masonry outer shell, framed in steel, supports the cooling tower and other components of the mechanical system. The structure of the tower is similar to those of early train sheds, bridges and the glazed concourse of the old Penn Station itself. The glass of the walls is clear and supported by a mullionless stainless steel flush-bolt system. A clock, salvaged from the old Penn Station, is suspended in the tower. The tower is illuminated by a pendant fixture and by uplights set in the four corner columns.

The marquee, supported by a stainless steel mast and rods, is made of glass and painted steel, with a stainless steel counterweight. The top section of the mast is an illuminated beacon.

The escalator/stair hall connects the street with the concourse. The ceiling is formed by suspended folded metal panels with integral lighting.

1 Night view from 34th Street looking east
2 Site stacking diagram
3 Tower detail
4 Section through concourse
5 Plan at street level
6 Plan through tower

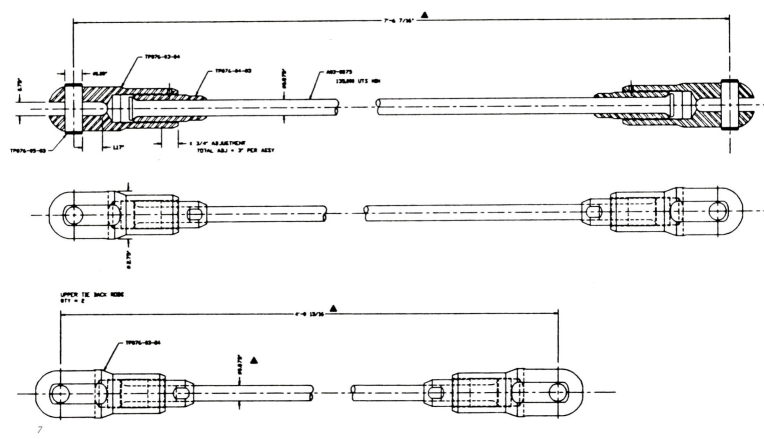

7

8

Thank you for riding the Long Island Rail Road

9

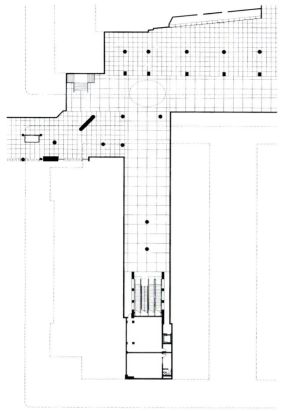

10

11

7 Mast tie back rods
8 Detail of canopy support
9 View into tower from escalator, with clock from
original Pennsylvania Station
10 Plan at concourse level
11 Corner of Seventh Avenue and 34th Street
12 Typical canopy tie up rod
Photography: Cervin Robinson

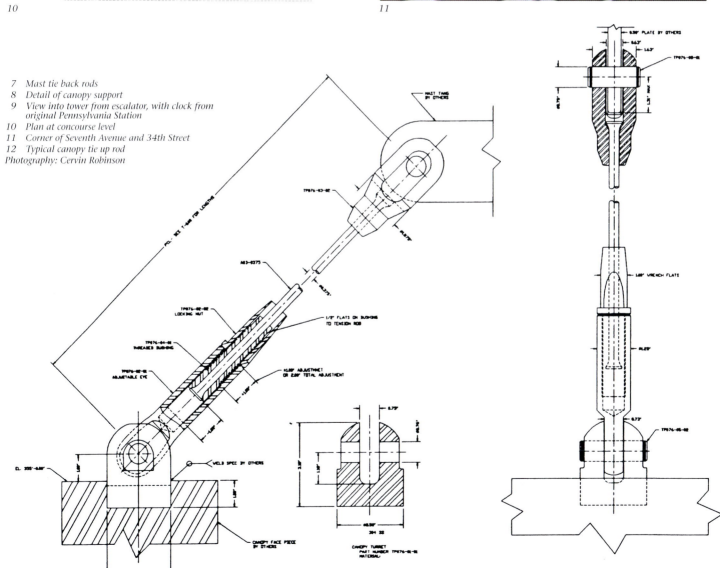

12

POND AND WATERFALL

KOREA LIFE INSURANCE SUJI TRAINING CENTER, YONG-IN CITY, KOREA

Kunchook-Moonhwa Architects & Engineers

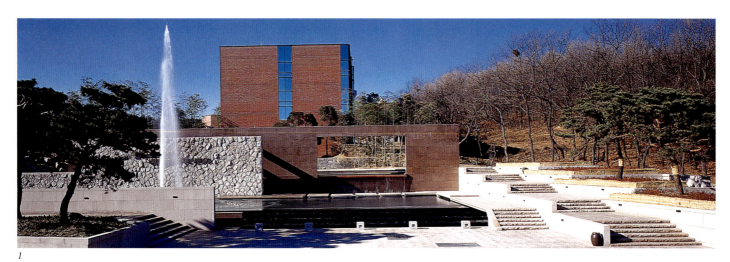
1

2

1   Front view
2   West side view of pond
3   Pond site plan
4   Waterfall cross section and perspective

The water flows out of the stone chasms and then through large wall planes and a bamboo bush to form a big stream. The stream then flows into a large pond of some 600 square metres with black cobbles spread at its base. Finally, the water drops down the staircase and passes the promenade only to disappear into the lowest drainage area.

The water in this lake-side space makes the sounds of 'hush', 'screaming', 'boiling', and other various sounds as it flows down. In spring, a cool water nozzle rises 20 metres from the centre of the pond.

This jet fountain skyrockets powerfully to respond to the resurrection sound generated in spring by the grass seeds and shrubs on the sunny parts of the artificial hill.

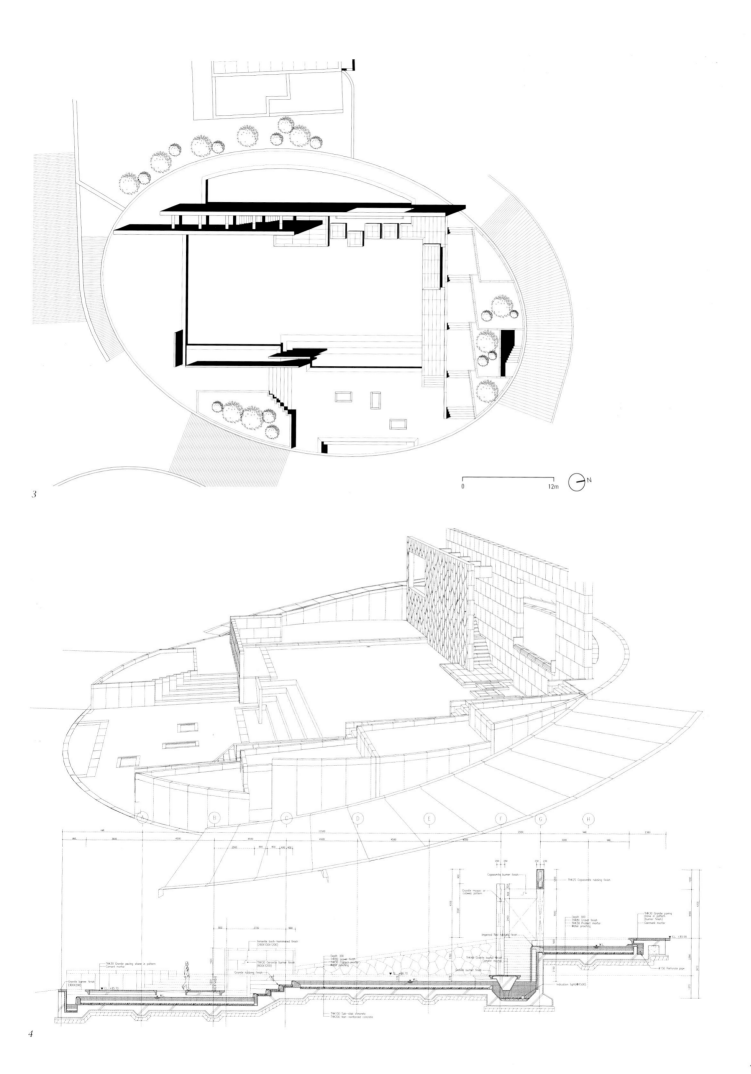

3

0   12m   N

4

5   *Detail section and perspective*
6   *Detail view of stone step*
*Photography: Jae-Kyeong Kim and
Young-sub Kim*

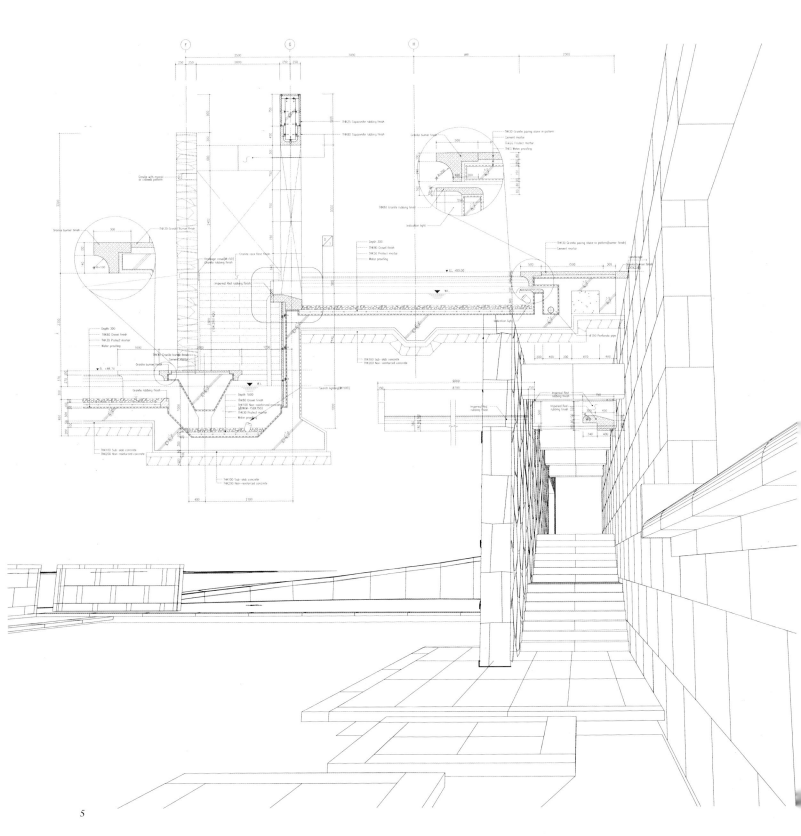

5

CANOPY, COAT RACKS AND RECEPTION COUNTER

NOKIA NETWORKS, HELSINKI, FINLAND
KVA Architects Ltd

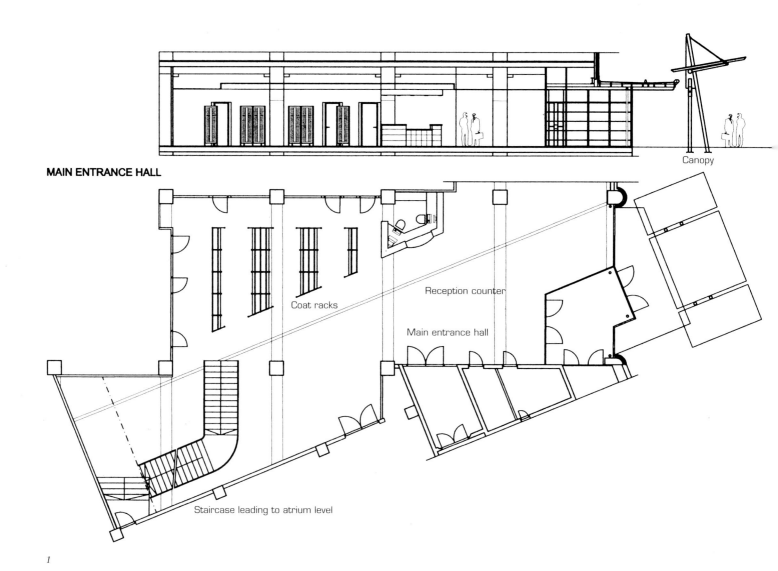

MAIN ENTRANCE HALL

Canopy

Reception counter

Coat racks

Main entrance hall

Staircase leading to atrium level

1

1 Section and plan
2&3 Canopy

A former industrial building was entirely reno-vated for Nokia Networks. The triangular courtyard was converted into an atrium, and the surrounding offices, and the research and development spaces were joined by corridors suspended from the skylight. The redesigned main entrance, entrance hall, conference rooms and auditorium are now joined by an open staircase leading up to the atrium level, which also contains a 200-seat staff restaurant. The entire complex is 29,054 square metres.

The layout and design of the main entrance, reception counter and freestanding coat racks all direct the way to the atrium level. The granite used in the entrance hall floor and reception counter are from Finnish quarries. The granite floor tiles were installed during the first building phase but withstood the wear throughout the entire renovation process, during which the building was in use. The surface area of the entrance hall was tripled and the massive columns of the old repair shop were coated with a soft grey glaze, creating a refined finish.

The entrance hall ceiling is made of acoustically perforated wood gypsum board panels, while the wind box ceiling in perforated anodised aluminium continues on to the canopy outside.

146

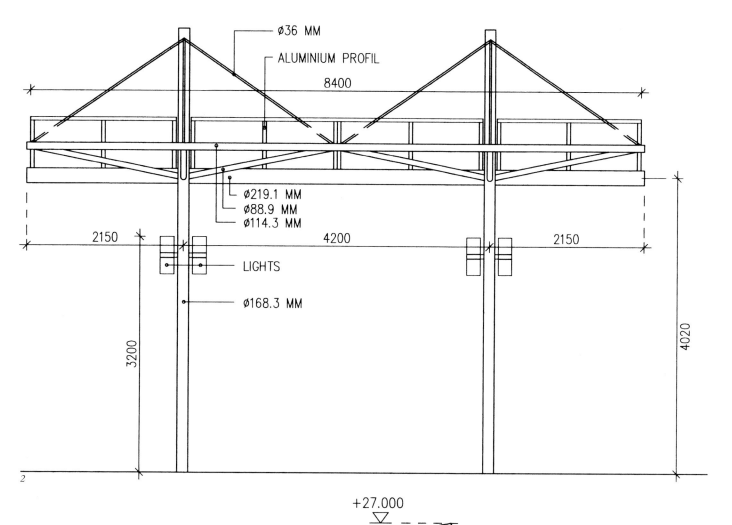

Ø36 MM

ALUMINIUM PROFIL

8400

Ø219.1 MM
Ø88.9 MM
Ø114.3 MM

2150   4200   2150

LIGHTS

Ø168.3 MM

3200

4020

2

The open staircase leading up to the atrium level offers an uninterrupted view through glass balustrades.

The staff restaurant, conference rooms, dining/ conference rooms and auditorium are also accessible to Nokia staff from outside. It was desirable to create a more easily approachable and discernible, as well as quickly mountable, canopy over the main entrance. The materials are stainless steel and toughened glass. The canopy was delivered pre-assembled, while the glazing was installed on-site.

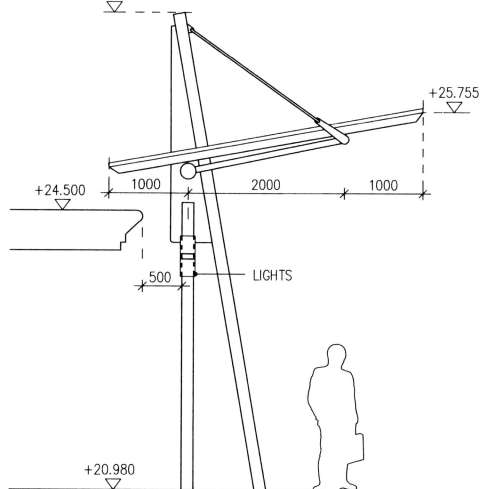

+27.000

+25.755

+24.500

1000   2000   1000

500   LIGHTS

+20.980

3

MATERIALS

**5 PERFORATED MDF-BOARD
STAINED**
6 MIRROR WITH BEVELLED EDGES
7 STEEL FRAME, STOVE ENAMELLED

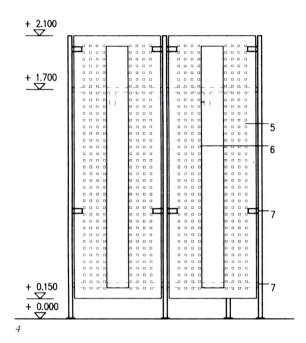

+ 2.100

+ 1.700

5

6

7

+ 0.150
+ 0.000

7

4

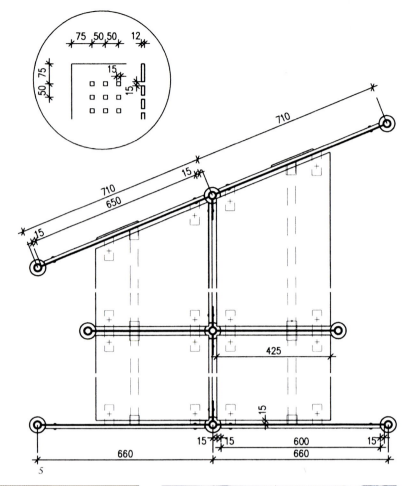

75 50 50 12

50 75

15

15

710

710
650

15

15

425

15

15 15 600 15

660

660

5

6

7

8

MATERIALS

1 BRUSHED STAINLESS STEEL
2 "MOSS" GRANITE 298 x 298 x 10
   POLISHED
3 "MOSS" GRANITE POLISHED
4 STAINED BEECH

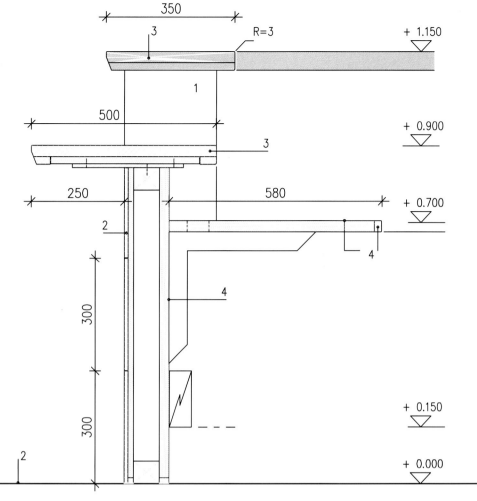

9

MATERIALS:

1 BRUSHED STAINLESS STEEL
2 "MOSS" GRANITE 298 x 298 x 10
   (FINLAND) POLISHED
3 "MOSS" GRANITE POLISHED

4   Entrance hall coat racks
5   Coat rack, horizontal section
6   Main entrance hall
7   Canopy
8   Staircase leading to atrium level
9   Reception counter, section
10 Reception counter
Photography: Jussi Tiainen and
KVA Architects Ltd

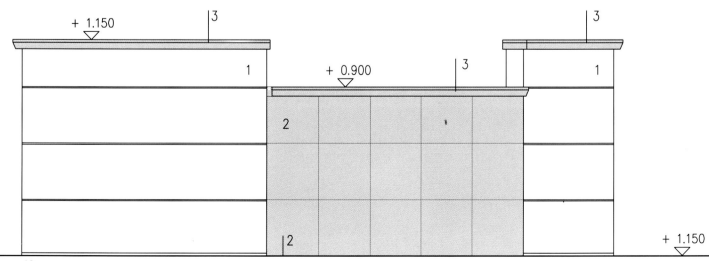

10

GALLERY

ARTS OF KOREA GALLERY, METROPOLITAN MUSEUM OF ART, NEW YORK, NEW YORK, USA
Kyu Sung Woo Architect, Inc.

1

2

3

1   Section
2&3 Gallery views
4   Section detail

Within the context of a large museum, the gallery is designed to provide an emotive space of calmness and light that conveys the spirit of Korea. A diffused, natural light washes the white surfaces of the gallery to create an openness and light quality germane to Korean Architecture.

The gallery is a square room defined by perimeter glass display cases that provide for the flexible display of ceramics, painting and sculpture. A removable, central partition allows for a variety of exhibit configurations, including the display of larger scroll paintings. The extension of the traditional wood flooring into the display case

blurs the separation between object and viewer, and further contributes to a sense of spaciousness within the room.

The restrained yet deliberate use of architectural elements within the gallery communicates Korean sensibilities without the application of traditional materiality. The limited use of architectural elements and ephemeral play of light in the space heightens the experience of art and provides an innovative display environment. The white oak flooring is articulated in an abstract, grey finish. A screen of mylar within the display case, which recalls the light quality of rice paper, allows for a

150

more intimate view of smaller objects. Door frames crafted in blackened steel plate mark the two openings into the gallery. The overall intent of the design is to create a gallery Korean in nature that is quietly restrained and foremost an outstanding space for the display of art.

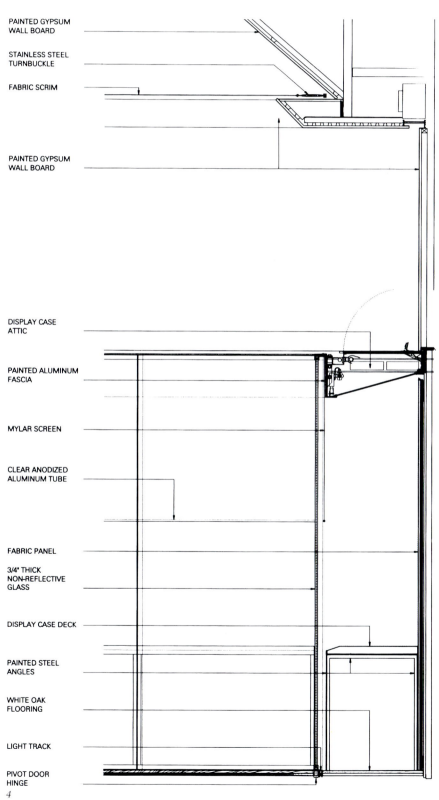

PAINTED GYPSUM WALL BOARD

STAINLESS STEEL TURNBUCKLE

FABRIC SCRIM

PAINTED GYPSUM WALL BOARD

DISPLAY CASE ATTIC

PAINTED ALUMINUM FASCIA

MYLAR SCREEN

CLEAR ANODIZED ALUMINUM TUBE

FABRIC PANEL

3/4" THICK NON-REFLECTIVE GLASS

DISPLAY CASE DECK

PAINTED STEEL ANGLES

WHITE OAK FLOORING

LIGHT TRACK

PIVOT DOOR HINGE

4

5

6

5&6   Gallery views
  7   Plan
Photography: Chuck Choi

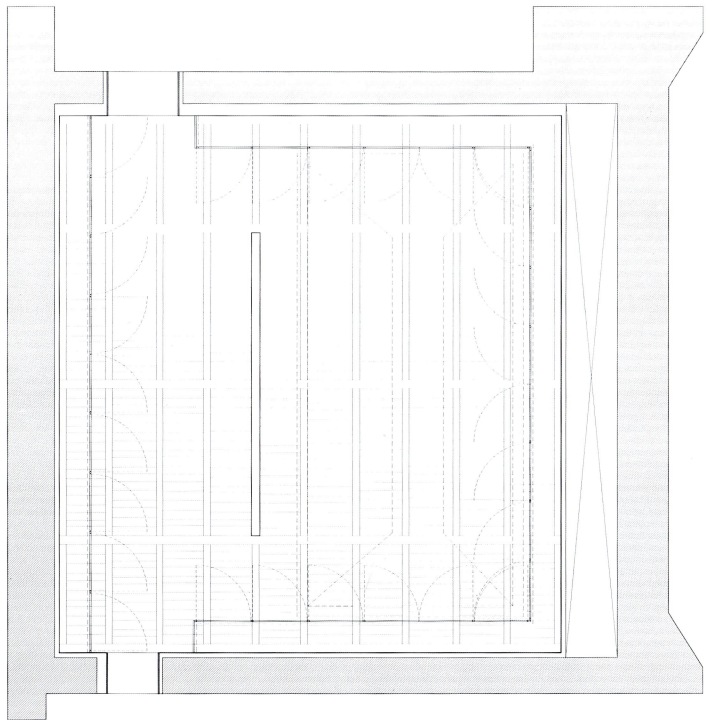

7

WALKWAY, CANOPY AND RECEPTION

BLUE CROSS BLUE SHIELD OF ILLINOIS HEADQUARTERS, CHICAGO, ILLINOIS, USA
Lohan Associates

1

1   Interior, security desk at reception
2   Reception desk and canopy detail

With the construction of its new building at 300 East Randolph, Blue Cross Blue Shield sought to achieve three primary objectives: to improve the efficiency of the organisation; to enhance the quality of the working environment; and to provide flexibility to accommodate the need for change and growth.

The base building configuration of each floor plate is exactly the same and is designed for the efficient layout of the non-hierarchical team/group open office working environment, and to accommodate the need for constantly changing operational needs.

Perhaps the most unique aspect of the building is that it is designed to be expanded vertically adding 22 floors without disrupting the operation of the building. An unprecedented 30-storey atrium incorporates exciting features such as exposed elevators, open interconnecting stairs and dedicated team areas. Breathtaking in its openness, the atrium benefits BC/BS in a very tangible way: it facilitates the interaction essential for today's less-hierarchical, more consensus-oriented corporate culture while at the same time heightening the awareness of the organisation as a whole.

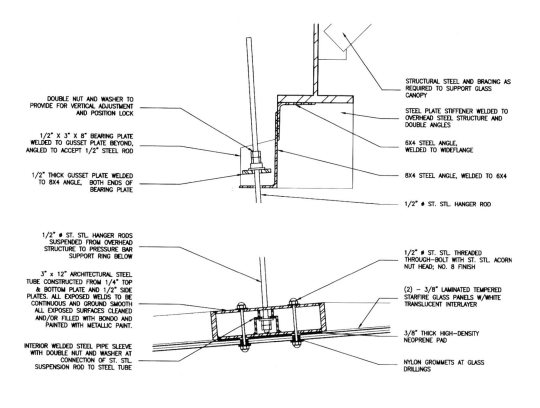

DOUBLE NUT AND WASHER TO PROVIDE FOR VERTICAL ADJUSTMENT AND POSITION LOCK

1/2" X 3" X 8" BEARING PLATE WELDED TO GUSSET PLATE BEYOND, ANGLED TO ACCEPT 1/2" STEEL ROD

1/2" THICK GUSSET PLATE WELDED TO 8X4 ANGLE, BOTH ENDS OF BEARING PLATE

STRUCTURAL STEEL AND BRACING AS REQUIRED TO SUPPORT GLASS CANOPY

STEEL PLATE STIFFENER WELDED TO OVERHEAD STEEL STRUCTURE AND DOUBLE ANGLES

6X4 STEEL ANGLE, WELDED TO WIDEFLANGE

8X4 STEEL ANGLE, WELDED TO 6X4

1/2" ⌀ ST. STL. HANGER ROD

1/2" ⌀ ST. STL. HANGER RODS SUSPENDED FROM OVERHEAD STRUCTURE TO PRESSURE BAR SUPPORT RING BELOW

3" x 12" ARCHITECTURAL STEEL TUBE CONSTRUCTED FROM 1/4" TOP & BOTTOM PLATE AND 1/2" SIDE PLATES. ALL EXPOSED WELDS TO BE CONTINUOUS AND GROUND SMOOTH ALL EXPOSED SURFACES CLEANED AND/OR FILLED WITH BONDO AND PAINTED WITH METALLIC PAINT.

INTERIOR WELDED STEEL PIPE SLEEVE WITH DOUBLE NUT AND WASHER AT CONNECTION OF ST. STL. SUSPENSION ROD TO STEEL TUBE

1/2" ⌀ ST. STL. THREADED THROUGH-BOLT WITH ST. STL. ACORN NUT HEAD; NO. 8 FINISH

(2) - 3/8" LAMINATED TEMPERED STARFIRE GLASS PANELS W/WHITE TRANSLUCENT INTERLAYER

3/8" THICK HIGH-DENSITY NEOPRENE PAD

NYLON GROMMETS AT GLASS DRILLINGS

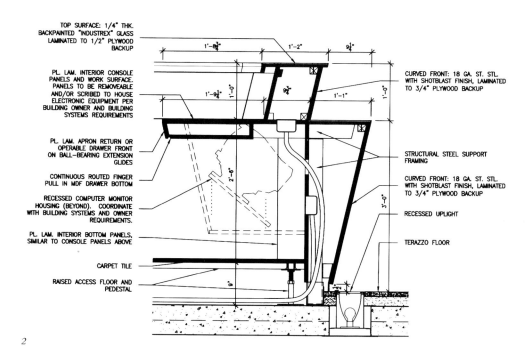

TOP SURFACE: 1/4" THK. BACKPAINTED "INDUSTREX" GLASS LAMINATED TO 1/2" PLYWOOD BACKUP

PL. LAM. INTERIOR CONSOLE PANELS AND WORK SURFACE. PANELS TO BE REMOVEABLE AND/OR SCRIBED TO HOUSE ELECTRONIC EQUIPMENT PER BUILDING OWNER AND BUILDING SYSTEMS REQUIREMENTS

PL. LAM. APRON RETURN OR OPERABLE DRAWER FRONT ON BALL-BEARING EXTENSION GLIDES

CONTINUOUS ROUTED FINGER PULL IN MDF DRAWER BOTTOM

RECESSED COMPUTER MONITOR HOUSING (BEYOND). COORDINATE WITH BUILDING SYSTEMS AND OWNER REQUIREMENTS.

PL. LAM. INTERIOR BOTTOM PANELS, SIMILAR TO CONSOLE PANELS ABOVE

CARPET TILE

RAISED ACCESS FLOOR AND PEDESTAL

CURVED FRONT: 18 GA. ST. STL. WITH SHOTBLAST FINISH, LAMINATED TO 3/4" PLYWOOD BACKUP

STRUCTURAL STEEL SUPPORT FRAMING

CURVED FRONT: 18 GA. ST. STL. WITH SHOTBLAST FINISH, LAMINATED TO 3/4" PLYWOOD BACKUP

RECESSED UPLIGHT

TERAZZO FLOOR

2

A 275 foot long section of the Chicago Loop pedway system connects the new corporate headquarters facility at 300 East Randolph Street with the Monroe Street Parking Garage. The structure is suspended between the upper and intermediate levels of a three-level roadway system that connects Lake Shore Drive and Michigan Avenue.

The problem was to create an economical, lightweight structure and enclosure system that could be constructed quickly (to minimise disruption to traffic below), be easily maintained and provide a sense of security. The solution was an assembly of prefabricated components, carefully selected based on the programmatic requirements mentioned above, their individual intrinsic visual qualities as well as their visual compatibility as an assembly. These components include a structural steel truss, painted yellow with circular holes; a vertical enclosure system – laminated glass on an aluminum frame, with two different frit patterns; a precast concrete roof deck and floor – spanning between the trusses; and a lighting system that unifies the assembly and highlights the individual components.

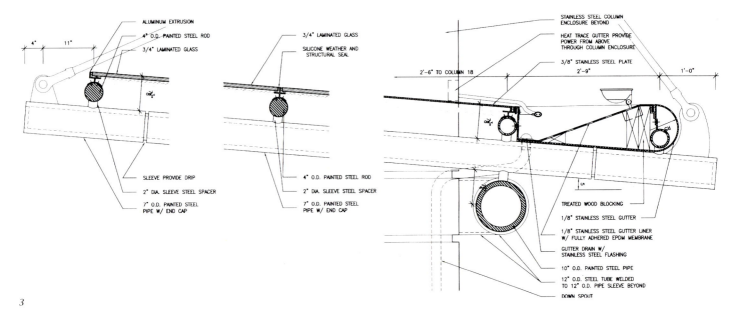

ALUMINUM EXTRUSION
4" O.D. PAINTED STEEL ROD
3/4" LAMINATED GLASS

4"   11"

SLEEVE PROVIDE DRIP
2" DIA. SLEEVE STEEL SPACER
7" O.D. PAINTED STEEL PIPE W/ END CAP

3/4" LAMINATED GLASS
SILICONE WEATHER AND STRUCTURAL SEAL

4" O.D. PAINTED STEEL ROD
2" DIA. SLEEVE STEEL SPACER
7" O.D. PAINTED STEEL PIPE W/ END CAP

STAINLESS STEEL COLUMN ENCLOSURE BEYOND
HEAT TRACE GUTTER PROVIDE POWER FROM ABOVE THROUGH COLUMN ENCLOSURE
3/8" STAINLESS STEEL PLATE

2'-6" TO COLUMN 18   2'-9"   1'-0"

TREATED WOOD BLOCKING
1/8" STAINLESS STEEL GUTTER
1/8" STAINLESS STEEL GUTTER LINER W/ FULLY ADHERED EPDM MEMBRANE
GUTTER DRAIN W/ STAINLESS STEEL FLASHING
10" O.D. PAINTED STEEL PIPE
12" O.D. STEEL TUBE WELDED TO 12" O.D. PIPE SLEEVE BEYOND
DOWN SPOUT

3

3 Entrance canopy section detail
4 View from canopy
5 Entrance canopy plan and section
6 Pedway section detail
7 Walking through pedway
Photography: Hedrich Blessing (1,7),
Steinkamp/Ballogg (4)

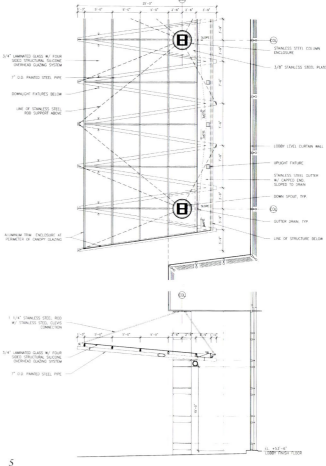

3/4" LAMINATED GLASS W/ FOUR SIDED STRUCTURAL SILICONE OVERHEAD GLAZING SYSTEM
7" O.D. PAINTED STEEL PIPE
DOWNLIGHT FIXTURES BELOW
LINE OF STAINLESS STEEL ROD SUPPORT ABOVE

STAINLESS STEEL COLUMN ENCLOSURE
3/8" STAINLESS STEEL PLATE

LOBBY LEVEL CURTAIN WALL
UPLIGHT FIXTURE
STAINLESS STEEL GUTTER W/ CAPPED END, SLOPED TO DRAIN
DOWN SPOUT, TYP.
GUTTER DRAIN, TYP.
LINE OF STRUCTURE BELOW

ALUMINUM TRIM ENCLOSURE AT PERIMETER OF CANOPY GLAZING

1 1/4" STAINLESS STEEL ROD W/ STAINLESS STEEL CLEVIS CONNECTION
3/4" LAMINATED GLASS W/ FOUR SIDED STRUCTURAL SILICONE OVERHEAD GLAZING SYSTEM
7" O.D. PAINTED STEEL PIPE

LOBBY FINISH FLOOR

4   5

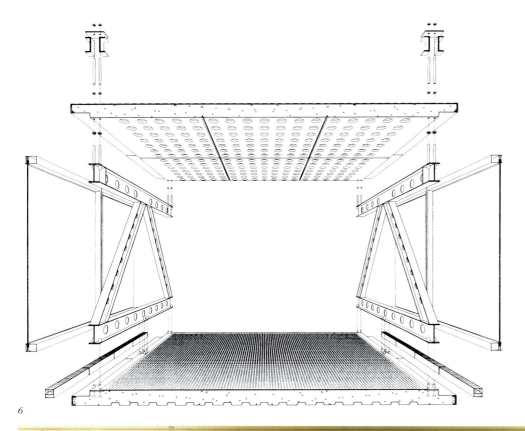

6

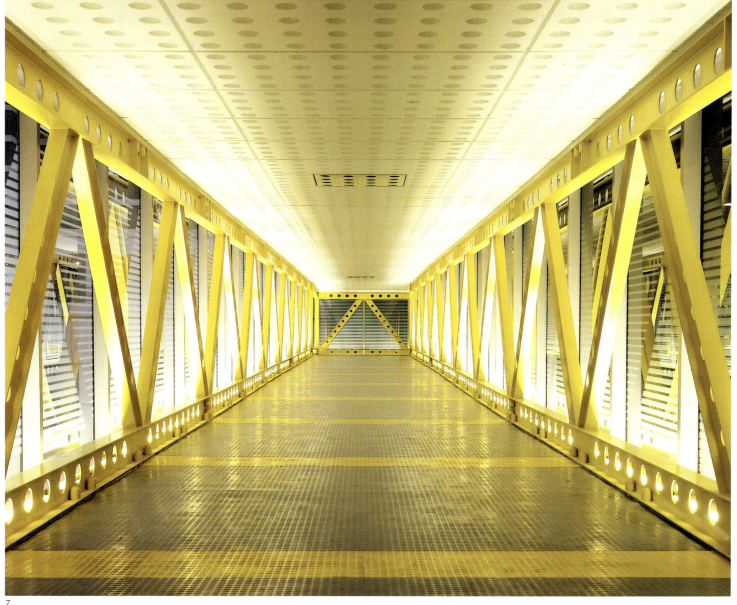

7

ENTRANCE CANOPY

WHITNEY APPLIED TECHNOLOGY CENTER, ONONDAGA COMMUNITY COLLEGE, SYRACUSE, NEW YORK, USA
Mitchell/Giurgola Architects

1

2

1 Detail view, south elevation
2 South elevation
3 Section
4 Elevation
Photography: Jeff Goldberg/Esto

The Whitney Applied Technology Center, the first project built at Onondaga Community College in over thirty years, presented the college with the opportunity to create a new front door to the campus. The entrance canopy for the Center provides protection from the elements and conveys the high technological nature of the building's program.

The entrance is defined by a tensile suspension structure intended to give the entry a dynamic presence. Its taut, floating quality acts as a counterpoint to the 190,000 square foot, Roman brick building element beyond. The structural

articulation of the canopy is an extension of the open expression of the structural and mechanical systems in the lobby.

The building design creates a new quad by enclosing the area on campus flanked by the gymnasium and the student centre. The campus context is referenced through the use of light beige masonry that acts as a visual counterpoint to the existing buildings. The building establishes a sheltered connection with the Gorge Bridge. Lounge spaces and glazed stairways at the western end of the building overlook the gorge and take advantage of its dramatic site.

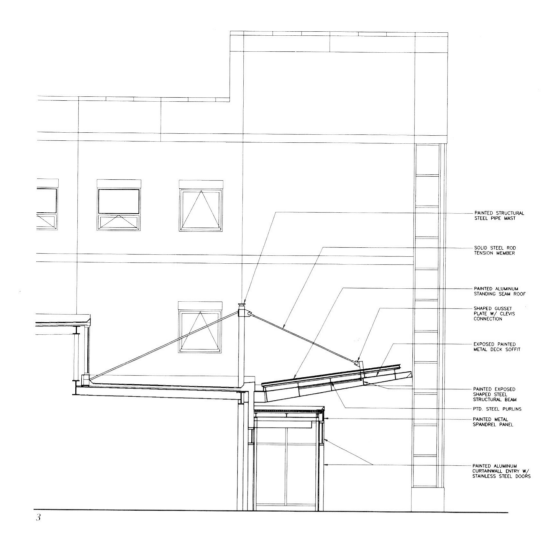

3

PAINTED STRUCTURAL
STEEL PIPE MAST

SOLID STEEL ROD
TENSION MEMBER

PAINTED ALUMINUM
STANDING SEAM ROOF

SHAPED GUSSET
PLATE W/ CLEVIS
CONNECTION

EXPOSED PAINTED
METAL DECK SOFFIT

PAINTED EXPOSED
SHAPED STEEL
STRUCTURAL BEAM

PTD. STEEL PURLINS

PAINTED METAL
SPANDREL PANEL

PAINTED ALUMINUM
CURTAINWALL ENTRY W/
STAINLESS STEEL DOORS

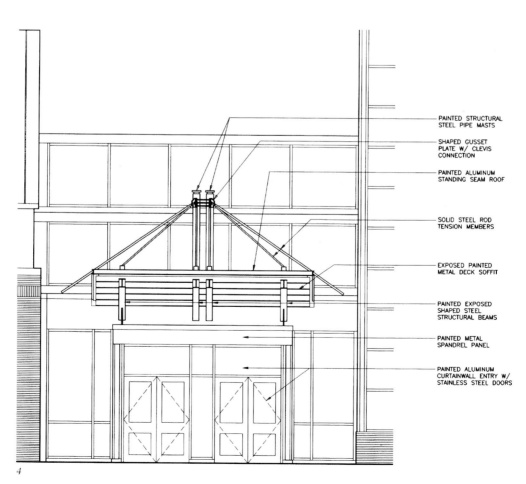

4

PAINTED STRUCTURAL
STEEL PIPE MASTS

SHAPED GUSSET
PLATE W/ CLEVIS
CONNECTION

PAINTED ALUMINUM
STANDING SEAM ROOF

SOLID STEEL ROD
TENSION MEMBERS

EXPOSED PAINTED
METAL DECK SOFFIT

PAINTED EXPOSED
SHAPED STEEL
STRUCTURAL BEAMS

PAINTED METAL
SPANDREL PANEL

PAINTED ALUMINUM
CURTAINWALL ENTRY W/
STAINLESS STEEL DOORS

ROOF TRELLIS

CHANCELLORS HALL, SOUTHAMPTON COLLEGE, LONG ISLAND UNIVERSITY, SOUTHAMPTON, NEW YORK, USA
Mitchell/Giurgola Architects

1

1 Classroom wing with trellis in foreground
2 Trellis section
Photography: Jeff Goldberg/Esto

Chancellors Hall, a 38,000 square foot classroom building, was the first constructed on Long Island University's Southampton Campus in over thirty years. Although the building is modest in its dimension, it is prominent on the campus. Its site creates the edge to a newly formed quadrangle. The primary building circulation runs along the edge of the building and engages Chancellors Hall and the quadrangle. The long sloping roof projects over the lawn with supporting struts to mediate between the building and the landscape.

A roof trellis gives intimate scale and provides shade to the building. The trellis also provides seating on a low roof terrace. Like the roof overhang, the trellis extends out over the edge of the building connecting building and landscape. The trellis is formed out of southern red cedar detailed with simple overlapping boards, consistent with a typical garden trellis. With time vines will grow over the trellis casting shadows on the wall and blurring the distinction between the building and landscape.

Detailing of the trellis is geared to the need for an economical solution and to satisfy the demands of durability and longevity for an institutional building. Galvanized steel anchors the trellis to the masonry wall. The cedar boards are detached from the wall and secured with bolted connections.

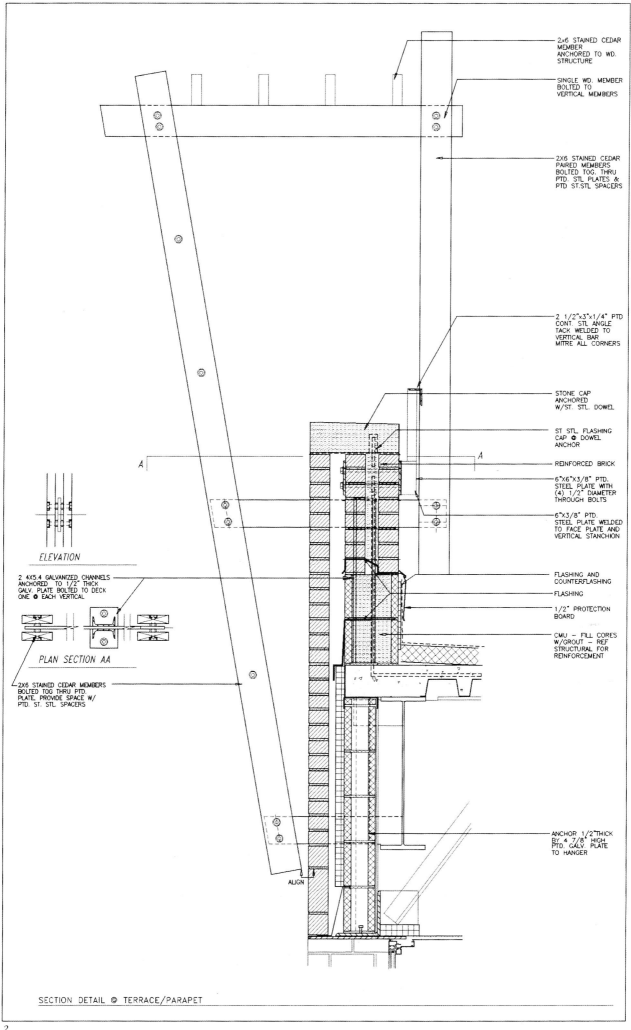

2x6 STAINED CEDAR
MEMBER
ANCHORED TO WD.
STRUCTURE

SINGLE WD. MEMBER
BOLTED TO
VERTICAL MEMBERS

2X6 STAINED CEDAR
PAIRED MEMBERS
BOLTED TOG. THRU
PTD. STL PLATES &
PTD ST.STL SPACERS

2 1/2"x3"x1/4" PTD
CONT. STL ANGLE
TACK WELDED TO
VERTICAL BAR
MITRE ALL CORNERS

STONE CAP
ANCHORED
W/ST. STL. DOWEL

ST STL FLASHING
CAP @ DOWEL
ANCHOR

REINFORCED BRICK

6"X6"X3/8" PTD.
STEEL PLATE WITH
(4) 1/2" DIAMETER
THROUGH BOLTS

6"X3/8" PTD.
STEEL PLATE WELDED
TO FACE PLATE AND
VERTICAL STANCHION

FLASHING AND
COUNTERFLASHING

FLASHING

1/2" PROTECTION
BOARD

CMU — FILL CORES
W/GROUT — REF
STRUCTURAL FOR
REINFORCEMENT

ANCHOR 1/2"THICK
BY 4 7/8" HIGH
PTD. GALV. PLATE
TO HANGER

A

A

ELEVATION

2 4X5.4 GALVANIZED CHANNELS
ANCHORED TO 1/2" THICK
GALV. PLATE BOLTED TO DECK
ONE @ EACH VERTICAL

PLAN SECTION AA

2X6 STAINED CEDAR MEMBERS
BOLTED TOG THRU PTD.
PLATE. PROVIDE SPACE W/
PTD. ST. STL SPACERS

ALIGN

SECTION DETAIL @ TERRACE/PARAPET

2

161

GUARDRAIL

MOODY GARDENS AQUARIUM, GALVESTON ISLAND, TEXAS, USA
Morris Architects

2

1

1   Entrance to the South Atlantic exhibit
2–5   Guardrail aluminium panels
6   Atrium and skylight above
7   1 million gallon Caribbean exhibit
     featuring a 60 foot long acrylic tunnel
     and viewing dome
Photography: Aker/Zvonkovic Photography

Housing creatures of the seas, the 2 million gallon Moody Gardens Aquarium Pyramid transports the visitor into the depths of the oceans from the four corners of the world and offers an opportunity to observe and interact with some of the world's most intriguing marine life.

The aquarium building is a composition of geometric forms with honest expressions of circulation, direction and exhibition. The exterior of the aquarium is composed of blue glass to reinforce its nautical theme and differentiate it from the existing pyramids of Moody Gardens. A sculptural wave wall invites visitors to the aquarium entrance.

The interior public spaces, exhibit viewing areas and habitats are fully integrated through design of materials, textures, colour and lighting to provide an aesthetic transferral to the marine world. Building systems and operations are concealed allowing reflections of colour-washed shadows to provide an illusion of submergence into the alien and beautiful ocean realm.

Directly beneath the aquarium's pyramid apex is an oculus in the second floor slab that allows the natural light to illuminate the otherwise dim first level. The guardrail that protects visitors from this opening therefore becomes a focal point. A simple

3

4

5

6

7

radiused guardrail was used, broken into 16 equal arcs with a continuous 2¹/₂ inch (63.5 millimetres) diameter, clear anodised aluminium rail welded atop ¹/₄ inch (6 millimetre) x 2 inch (51 millimetre) support bars. In the centre of each arc, four of the marine animals species found in the aquarium are emphasised. Cut by lasers, the ¹/₄ inch (6 millimetre) thick aluminium panels feature playful seals, handsome penguins, graceful angel fish and majestic sharks on a background of waves, which is another theme carried throughout the building in ceiling and wall details. The plates are tack welded to a radiused bar that interrupts the regular ³/₄ inch (19 millimetre) diameter balusters.

With the exception of the aluminium top rail and marine image panels, the rail assembly is painted by alkyd rust-inhibitive primer and alkyd enamel finish coat to withstand the inherently salt-laden Galveston atmosphere. The entire assembly is mounted to the concrete slab opening by anchoring embeds. Clip angles welded to the embeds allow for a 4¹/₄ inch (11 centimetre) thick gypsum board furring construction around the oculus opening. That furring accommodates two radiused neon light features on the first level ceiling. The use of neon is another universal theme used most often in conjunction with the waved ceilings.

Exhibit architecture seems to constantly struggle with the idea that either the building design or the exhibits must somehow have prominence over the other. The Aquarium at Moody Gardens was approached with the intent to create a showcase of a building and infuse exhibits that had the visual impact to stand on their own. To unify the many elements of the aquarium, a marine theme was carried throughout the buildings from the 110-foot (33-meter) high atrium awash in natural light filtered through blue glazing to the interlocking wave patterns used as signage background.

MESH FAÇADE

FKB PARKHAUS, COLONGE/BONN AIRPORT, GERMANY
Murphy/Jahn Inc. Architects

1

1   Transparent screenwall at night
2   Section
3   Elevation
4   Solid screenwall in daytime
5   Detail connection
Photography: courtesy Murphy/Jahn Inc.
Architects

The Parkhaus was kept as low as possible in order to preserve the views across the airport landscape to the existing Terminal 1 and future Terminal 2. The structure is composed of four 65 metre wide units separated by a 10 metre wide light court. Highly detailed steel structures clad the basic rough steel construction. They include the shimmering stainless steel mesh façade cladding, the vine walls in the light courts, and railings of stainless steel cables. The elevator/stair towers are also steel structures with cantilevering platforms of stainless steel planks in front of the point-fixed glazing of the elevator towers. The glass elevator cabs ride in open-air shafts and are designed to function in extreme weather conditions.

The Parkhaus 2 is the first building component in the expansion of the Colonge/Bonn Airport and lies on a trapezoidal site bounded by the existing elevated roadway, the new Terminal 2 future train station and a new road network. There are six levels with 5,850 parking spaces, which are linked by two cylindrical ramp structures. The structure has vehicular access at its east and west ends at level with the main exit feeding directly into the existing terminal road network. The upper level has an additional entrance/exit directly to the future elevated departures roadway in front of Terminal 2 and is intended for short-term parking.

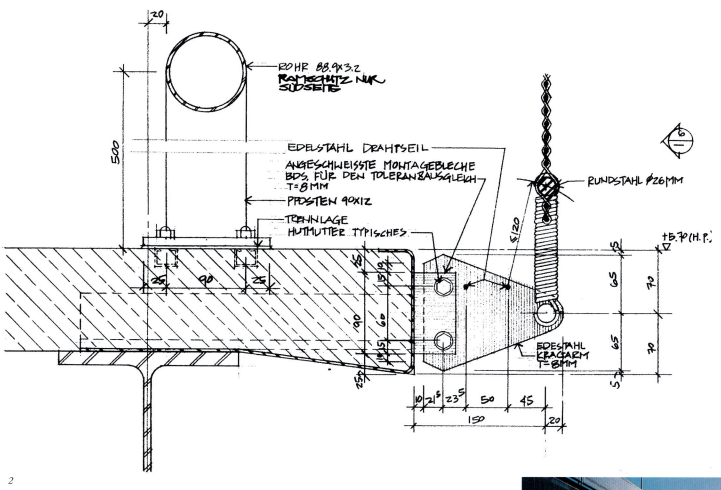

ROHR 88.9x3.2
RAMMSCHUTZ NUR
SÜDSEITE

EDELSTAHL DRAHTSEIL

ANGESCHWEISSTE MONTAGEBLECHE
BDS. FÜR DEN TOLERANZAUSGLEICH
T=8MM

PFOSTEN 90x12

TRENNLAGE

HUTMUTTER TYPISCHES

RUNDSTAHL Ø26MM

+5.70 (H.P.)

EDELSTAHL
KRAGARM T=8MM

20

500

45

90

60

25

250

150

25   90   25

10 21⁵ 23⁵   50   45

150   20

15   65   65   70   70   57

2

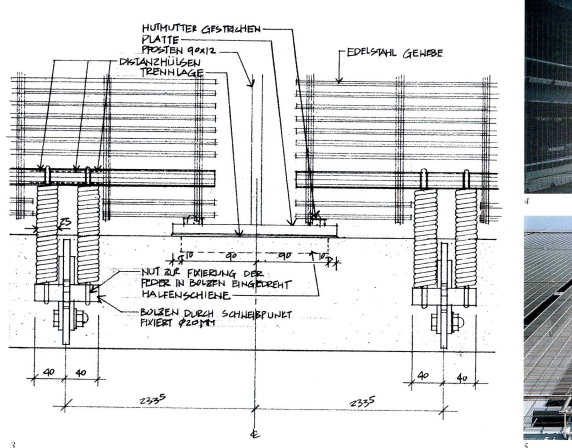

HUTMUTTER GESTRICHEN
PLATTE
PFOSTEN 90x12
DISTANZHÜLSEN
TRENNLAGE

EDELSTAHL GEWEBE

NUT ZUR FIXIERUNG DER
FEDER IN BOLZEN EINGEDREHT
HALFENSCHIENE

BOLZEN DURCH SCHWEISSPUNKT
FIXIERT Ø20MM

25

10   90   90   10

40   40

233⁵

40   40

233⁵

3

4

5

ROOF

MUNICH AIRPORT CENTER WEST, GERMANY
Murphy/Jahn Inc. Architects

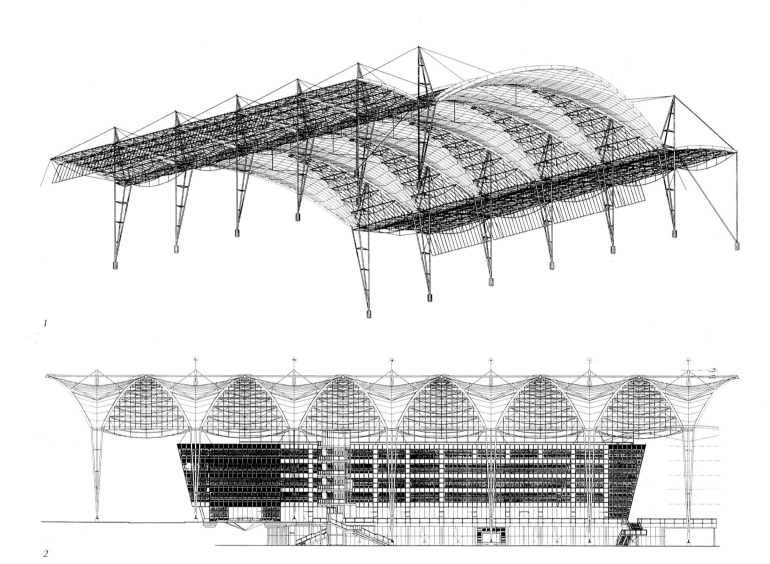

1

2

1 *Axonometric – ground view of forum roof/
   structure*
2 *Section longitudinal through forum*
3 *Forum – pavilion roof*
4 *Aerial – looking towards future terminal*

The Munich Airport Center West (MAC) is situated on the main east/west crossing between the existing Terminal 1 and the planned Terminal 2, and as such it forms a spatial connecting element between these structures. It is the centrepoint of the total urban concept, which extends the functional area of the airport to the commercial functions, as well as providing possibilities for expanding the airport and rail facilities.

Seen from the entry road to the airport, behind and above the Terminal 1 building, the form of the MAC forum roof will become a visible symbol for

the airport. It creates a significant spatial and orientation axis for the passenger terminal area and gives the airport identity and order.

The forum roof is not only an important element for the urban identity of the airport, but also an integral engineering element of the MAC: the exterior sunshading, which is normally necessary on building façades, can be eliminated in the forum due to the sunshading effect of the roof.

Between the masts, the main steel beams run diagonally. The resulting diamond-shaped areas are covered with a saddle-shaped membrane. Parallel to the arch, cables are integrated to receive

3

the resulting tension forces. The membrane consists of Teflon-coated glass fibre and is fireproof. The colour of the membrane is white and allows 10–15 per cent daylight transmission (ultraviolet light is almost totally blocked).

The remaining roof area is glazed using a clear laminated glass with a substructure and framing consisting of steel pipe, bow trusses and tension rod crosses for bracing. The roof skin is light and transparent/translucent. The roof protects the forum from hot direct sunlight. The forum receives, however, changing natural sunlight to create a lively urban space. At night, the roof is uplit with artificial lighting, which transforms the roof into a large visible lighted signal.

4

5   Mast detail
6   East elevation
7   Looking into forum
8   Perspective forum structure
9   Forum plan
*Photography: courtesy Murphy/Jahn Inc.
Architects*

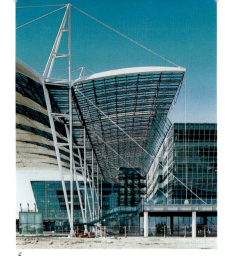

5

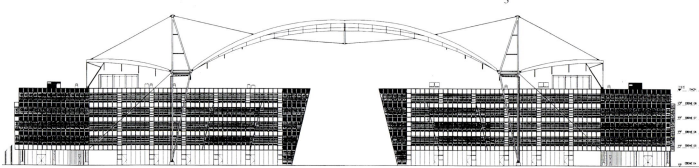

6

7

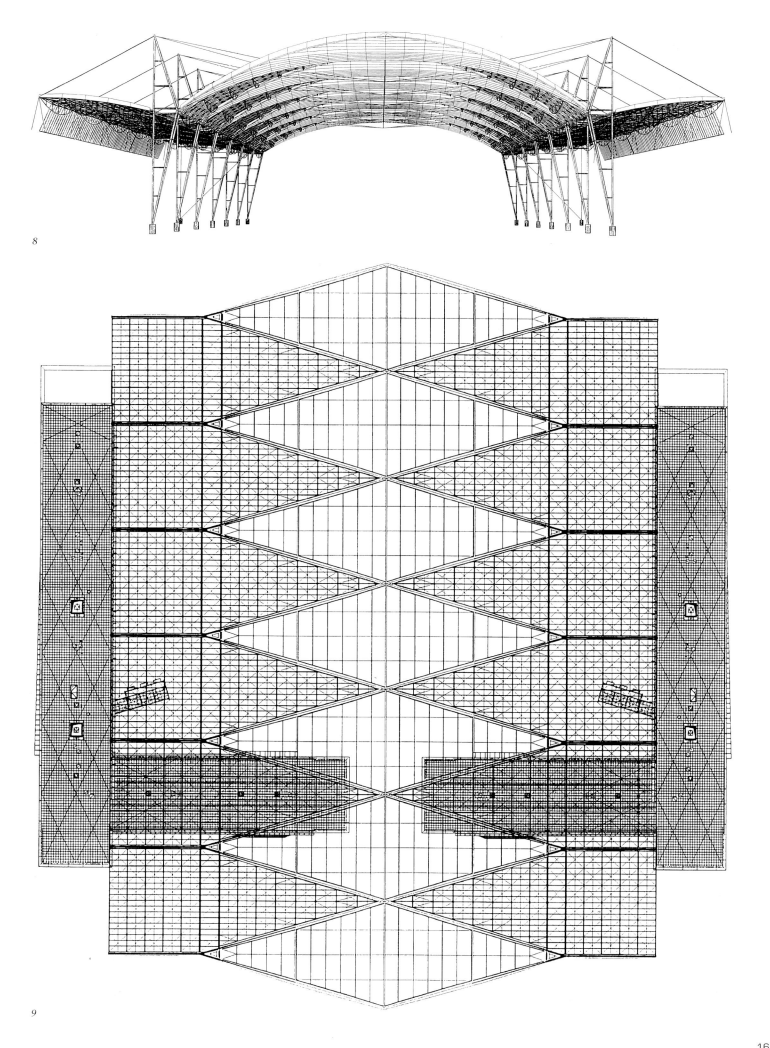

8

9

GLASS WALL

BRITISH AIRWAYS HEADQUARTERS 'WATERSIDE', HEATHROW, LONDON, UK
Niels Torp AS Arkitekter MNAL

1

2

3

4

1   *The light-filled street forms a dignified and welcoming circulation and social axis*
2   *Executive dining room (showing glass wall)*
3   *Main entrance through a sloping glass wall at the south-west end of the spinal street*
4   *Courtyard*
5   *Typical elevation and typical side elevation (section side street bridge) of glass bracket*
6&7 *Details of glass wall*
Photography: Peter Cook, London

To ensure a more rational operation of the company, British Airways secured a large site immediately outside the airport for a headquarters for its 2,800 staff.

The Heathrow area is totally devoid of urban structure. This large number of people will have to rely on themselves and the interior and exterior environment of the office building.

How does one provide a stimulating environment for 2,800 people in the middle of a field, with one of the largest airports in the world as its neighbour? The office building is envisaged as a *place,* and the large number of users as a *community*.

The 55,000 square metre offices have been split into six U-shaped buildings. The pavilions are individually expressed and contain various functions, such as schools, sports facilities, restaurants, computer centre, and so on. Between the pavilion and the office building, a small 'formal garden' was developed as an environmental centre or hub for each of the six office complexes. Around each of these complexes, a landscape is modelled with distinctly shaped landscape forms, emanating from the building body behind. These elements are grouped and related to one another, so that a network of streets – main streets and side streets – stretch out into

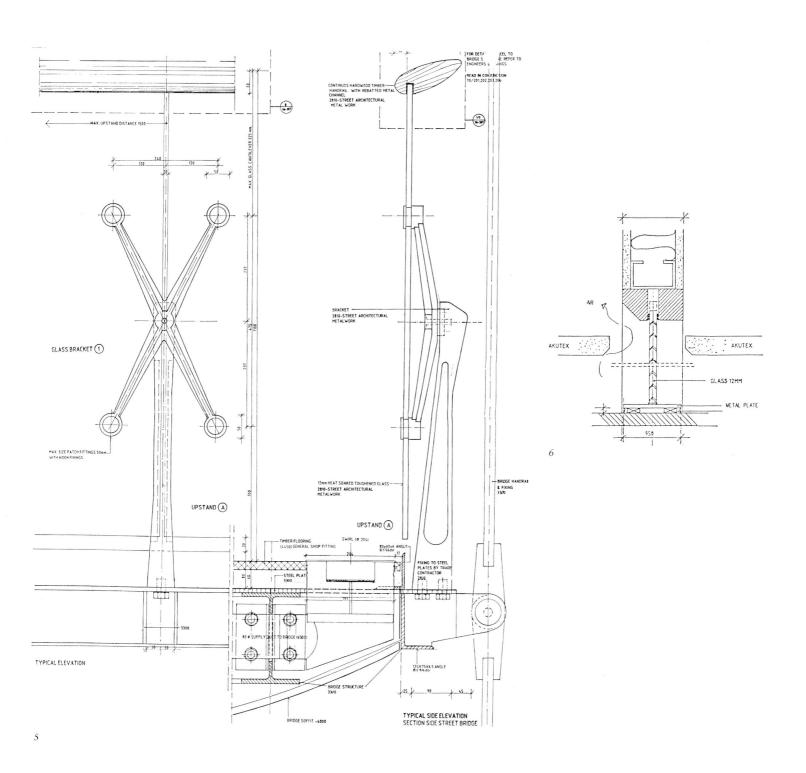

MAX. UPSTAND DISTANCE 1500

MAX GLASS CANTILEVER 325 mm

240
120 120
20 50

237
1100
475
237
50

GLASS BRACKET ①

MAX SIZE PATCH FITTINGS 50mm
WITH HIDEN FIXINGS.

UPSTAND Ⓐ

300

TYPICAL ELEVATION

TIMBER FLOORING
(4450) GENERAL SHOP FITTING

SWIRL (@ 204)

30

80x60x6 ANGLE
BY 6500

STEEL PLAT
3300

80 Ø SUPPLY DUCT TO BRIDGE (6500)

BRIDGE STRUCTURE
3300

BRIDGE SOFFIT -4000

5

CONTINUOS HARDWOOD TIMBER
HANDRAIL WITH REBATTED METAL
CHANNEL
2810-STREET ARCHITECTURAL
METAL WORK

FOR DETA   EEL TO
BRIDGE S   E REFER TO
ENGINEERS   NGS
READ IN CONJUNCTION
70/201,202,203,204

BRACKET
2810-STREET ARCHITECTURAL
METALWORK

12mm HEAT SOAKED TOUGHENED GLASS
2810-STREET ARCHITECTURAL
METALWORK

UPSTAND Ⓐ

FIXING TO STEEL
PLATES BY TRADE
CONTRACTOR
2400

BRIDGE HANDRAI
& FIXING
3300

125X75X6 S ANGLE
BY 6600

25 90 65

TYPICAL SIDE ELEVATION
SECTION SIDE STREET BRIDGE

AIR

AKUTEX   AKUTEX

GLASS 12MM

METAL PLATE

950

6

---

the flat landscape. The main street is orientated with the church and barn as a backdrop, and at the opposite end a large lake is formed. From the surrounding park, the buildings are seen with their slim gables between the heavily planted hillocks; these gables are a light, warm-grey stone.

Along the street the more 'traffic'-generating activities are found and where larger numbers of people gather. The main social element is a terraced square in the middle of the extent of the street, with a capacity to accommodate most of the users at a single occasion.

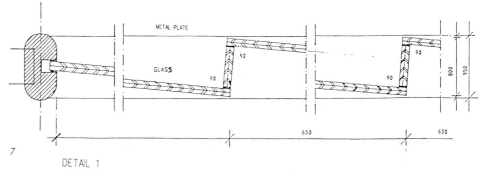

METAL PLATE

GLASS

90
90
90
90

800
950

600   600

7

DETAIL 1

ELEVATOR

AXA CENTRE, SYDNEY, NEW SOUTH WALES, AUSTRALIA
Rihs Architects Pty Ltd

1

2

3

4

1   View of cast aluminium ceiling light and
    panel detailing
2   Typical lobby
3   Cast aluminium ceiling lighting frame and
    ceiling panels
4   Detail showing call button stand
5   Sections
6   Preliminary sketches: rear and side
    elevation
Photography: courtesy Rihs Architects Pty Ltd

Toughness, lightness, flexibility and good design were the owner's requirements for the refurbishment of 13 elevator cars in the AXA Centre in Sydney.

It was natural to turn to the aviation industry for technical inspiration. A system of sandwich panels comprising strong resin facings, honeycomb base and laminate backing was designed and tested successfully for resistance to damage and for easy removal if required. The panels are fixed within strong stainless steel vertical ribs to further absorb a range of possible impacts.

Previous experience with aluminium casting led to the further development of cast lighting troffers, which brace as well as provide a visual relief to the otherwise stark geometry of the wall paneling. The successful combination of old and new technology, with a consistency and imagination of design, has achieved the desired outcomes of performance and visual tension in an otherwise passive environment.

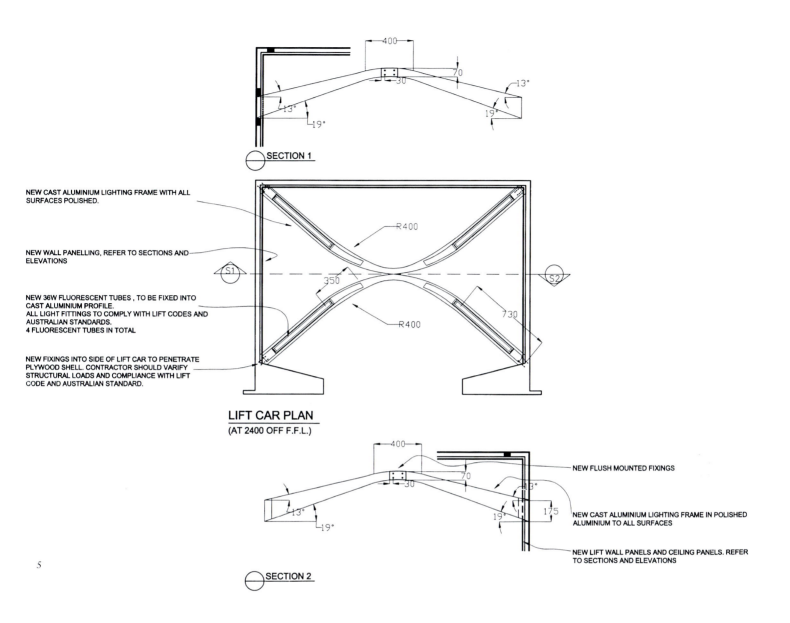

Ⓢ **SECTION 1**

NEW CAST ALUMINIUM LIGHTING FRAME WITH ALL SURFACES POLISHED.

NEW WALL PANELLING, REFER TO SECTIONS AND ELEVATIONS

NEW 36W FLUORESCENT TUBES , TO BE FIXED INTO CAST ALUMINIUM PROFILE.
ALL LIGHT FITTINGS TO COMPLY WITH LIFT CODES AND AUSTRALIAN STANDARDS.
4 FLUORESCENT TUBES IN TOTAL

NEW FIXINGS INTO SIDE OF LIFT CAR TO PENETRATE PLYWOOD SHELL. CONTRACTOR SHOULD VARIFY STRUCTURAL LOADS AND COMPLIANCE WITH LIFT CODE AND AUSTRALIAN STANDARD.

400

R400

350

R400

730

LIFT CAR PLAN
(AT 2400 OFF F.F.L.)

5

400
70
30
175
13°
19°
13°
19°

NEW FLUSH MOUNTED FIXINGS

NEW CAST ALUMINIUM LIGHTING FRAME IN POLISHED ALUMINIUM TO ALL SURFACES

NEW LIFT WALL PANELS AND CEILING PANELS. REFER TO SECTIONS AND ELEVATIONS

Ⓢ **SECTION 2**

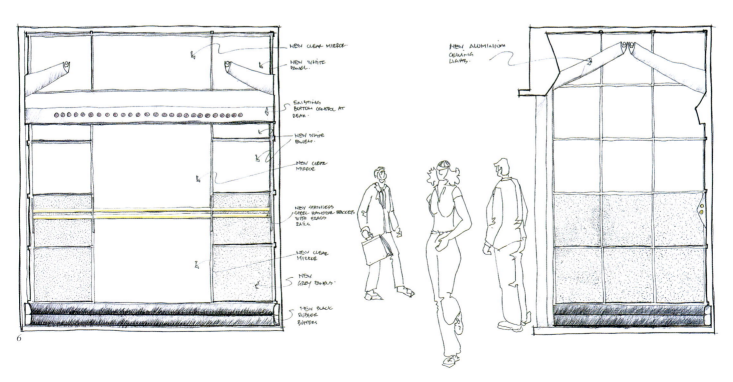

6

LIGHT MASTS

AXA CENTRE, SYDNEY, NEW SOUTH WALES, AUSTRALIA
Rihs Architects Pty Ltd

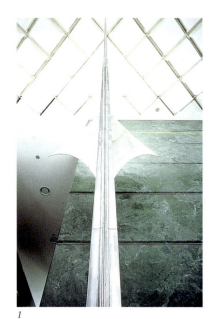

1

2

3

4

5

1   *Top of light mast*
2   *Base detail*
3   *Main foyer looking north*
4   *Foyer with one main lift lobby*
5   *Main foyer looking south*
6   *Elevation*
*Photography: Patrick Crowe International (3)
and Rihs Architects Pty Ltd*

The enduring success of the original building completed in 1976 led the owner of the AXA Centre (originally National Mutual Centre) to upgrade the building in line with current technology, and to redesign the forecourt and main entrance lobby to project a light and fresh image.

Essential to the design was the concept of the complete replacement of downlighting with new uplighting sources, which takes advantage of other architectural features and provides a distinctive and exciting addition to the main foyer.

Rihs Architects designed the dramatic light masts, which have exceeded expectations in performance and have dramatic if not poetic results.

Special skills were required to produce the highly polished cast aluminium. Possibly the most rewarding part of the project was the fact that small factories had to be expanded and special tradespeople found.

Each section of the mast was cast in sandbeds, ground and eventually polished to the standards expected. Close tolerances were required for each section to fit around the steel structural section of the mast.

Prototypes were built to test all aspects of the mast, including advanced electronic components for the three lamps and spread of light on the coffered ceiling.

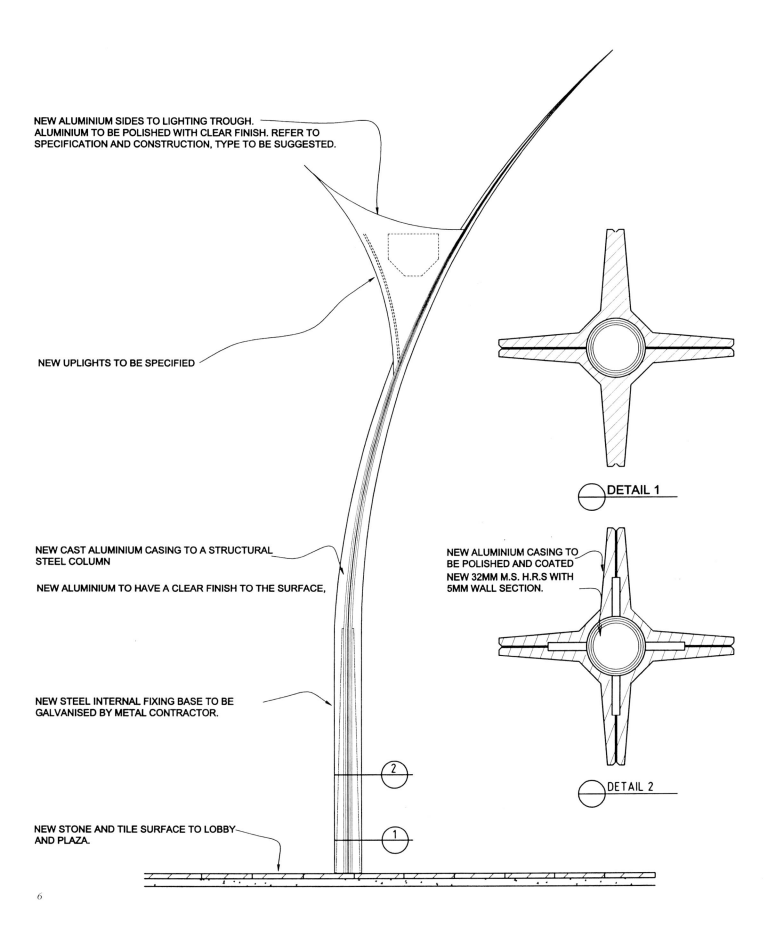

NEW ALUMINIUM SIDES TO LIGHTING TROUGH.
ALUMINIUM TO BE POLISHED WITH CLEAR FINISH. REFER TO
SPECIFICATION AND CONSTRUCTION, TYPE TO BE SUGGESTED.

NEW UPLIGHTS TO BE SPECIFIED

NEW CAST ALUMINIUM CASING TO A STRUCTURAL
STEEL COLUMN

NEW ALUMINIUM TO HAVE A CLEAR FINISH TO THE SURFACE,

NEW STEEL INTERNAL FIXING BASE TO BE
GALVANISED BY METAL CONTRACTOR.

NEW STONE AND TILE SURFACE TO LOBBY
AND PLAZA.

DETAIL 1

NEW ALUMINIUM CASING TO
BE POLISHED AND COATED
NEW 32MM M.S. H.R.S WITH
5MM WALL SECTION.

DETAIL 2

6

HEATING/COOLING SYSTEM
SAITAMA PREFECTURAL UNIVERSITY, KOSHIGAYA, SAITAMA, JAPAN
Riken Yamamoto & Field Shop

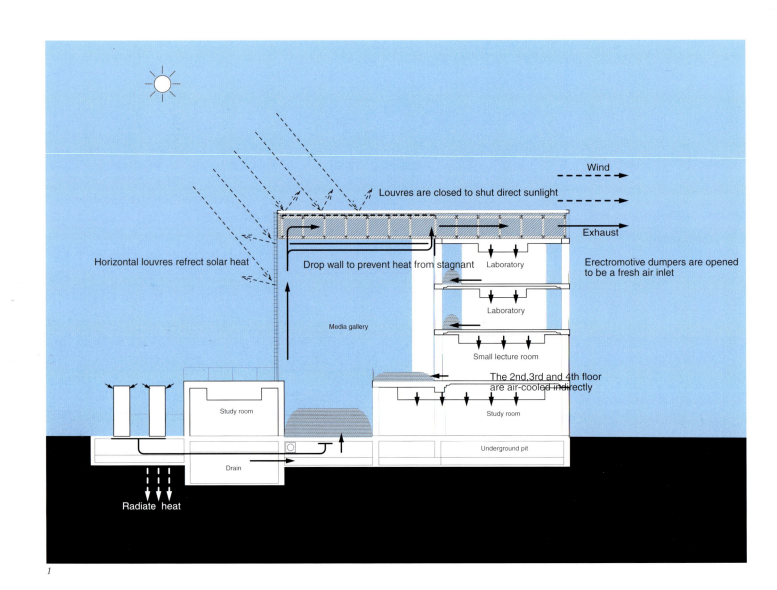

Louvres are closed to shut direct sunlight

Wind

Exhaust

Horizontal louvres refrect solar heat

Drop wall to prevent heat from stagnant

Laboratory

Erectromotive dumpers are opened
to be a fresh air inlet

Media gallery

Laboratory

Small lecture room

The 2nd,3rd and 4th floor
are air-cooled indirectly

Study room

Study room

Underground pit

Drain

Radiate heat

1

1   *Environmental device ('passive solar system') in Summer*
2   *Media Gallery of the University*
3   *View of roof decks from Media Gallery*
4   *South-north section*
5   *Bird's eye view of Saitama Prefectural University*
Photography: courtesy Tomio Ohashi (2,3), courtesy Gantan Beauty Industry Co., Ltd. (5)

The university complex consists of two parallel building tracts containing The Media Gallery, laboratories and seminar rooms, with a platform area between them. The Media Gallery is a four-storey glazed atrium (length: 200 metres, height: 16 meters); various scenes can be viewed here, including lectures in progress and people relaxing.

For high visibility, the Media Gallery is structured using extremely thin horizontal and vertical stays, rather than a diagonal rod. There is no obstruction of the view from the roof decks to the inside of the Media Gallery due to uncomplicated support hardware for the louvres and glass.

Summers are very hot in Koshigaya, and because the Media Gallery faces the south side, it is equipped with outer horizontal louvres for screening direct sunlight in summer. The airconditioning devices used in this big transparent 'box' are designed not to waste artificial energy. The Media Gallery serves as an environmental device in itself in terms of being a 'passive solar system'.

The Vierendeel steel truss is placed between roof panels and ceiling panels and are used for airconditioning. In the winter, the pockets

2

3

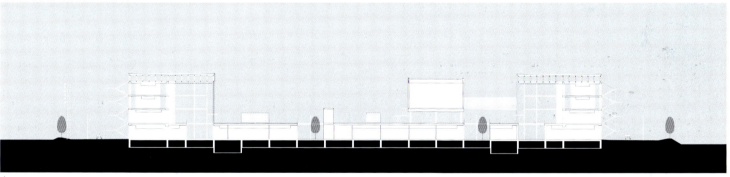

4

function as a regenerator by taking sunlight inside. The electromotive blinds installed to the base of top-lights shut out direct sunlight in summer. Hot air on the surface of the glass is evacuated to the top-lights through the slits on the ceiling panels; the air is then ventilated through the grilles.

5

CURTAIN WALL
DEPOT AND OFFICE, KWUN TONG, HONG KONG
RMJM

1

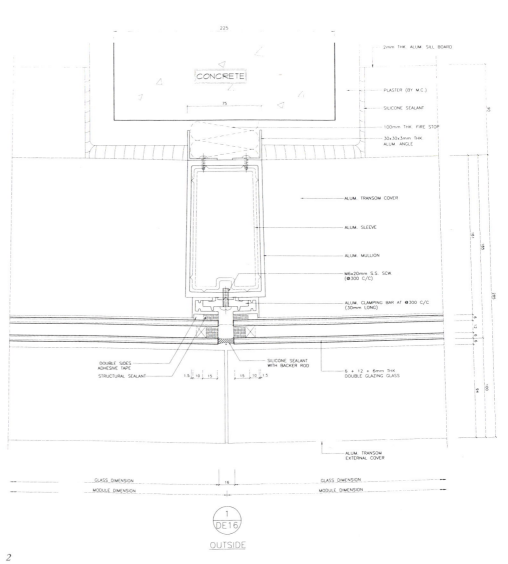

2

The proposed Southeast Regional Depot provides a permanent and combined depot for the Water Supplies Department (WSD) at the junction of Kai Fuk Road and Wai Yip Street of Kwun Tung.

The project comprises of storage areas, workshops, administration offices, canteen and other ancillary areas. The project consists of 11 stories including the ground floor loading and unloading bays; four floors of naturally ventilated ramp-side parking areas accommodating 127 spaces for service vehicles, visitors and essential users; and six floors of offices and ancillary spaces.

Architecturally, the building form follows the round profile of the allocated site with a setback of 5.7 metres from the property line to allow emergency vehicle access all round the building. The ground floor and lift core are enhanced by tile cladding and projecting horizontal fins. The free-standing architrave is clad with metal and the suspended metal canopy serves as a focal point of interest to the main entrance along the elevated road. This interest is enhanced by the vertical metal fins above. The glass curtain wall on the curved façade maximises views from the office floors. The double-glazed curtain wall was proposed in consideration of the solar and noise pollution. The ring beam on the parking/roof deck level and vertical fins accentuate the continuity and verticality of the building.

1 External view from the north
2 Curtain wall plan detail
3 Curtain wall section detail
4 External view from the south
Photography: Kerum Ip

4

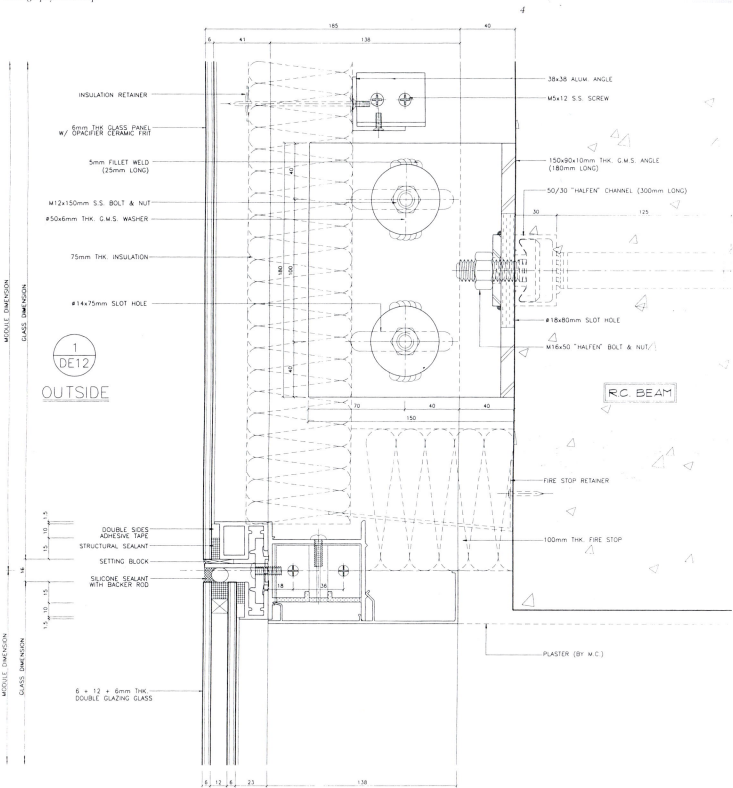

INSULATION RETAINER

6mm THK GLASS PANEL
W/ OPACIFIER CERAMIC FRIT

5mm FILLET WELD
(25mm LONG)

M12x150mm S.S. BOLT & NUT

Ø50x6mm THK. G.M.S. WASHER

75mm THK. INSULATION

Ø14x75mm SLOT HOLE

1
DE12

OUTSIDE

DOUBLE SIDES
ADHESIVE TAPE

STRUCTURAL SEALANT

SETTING BLOCK

SILICONE SEALANT
WITH BACKER ROD

6 + 12 + 6mm THK.
DOUBLE GLAZING GLASS

38x38 ALUM. ANGLE

M5x12 S.S. SCREW

150x90x10mm THK. G.M.S. ANGLE
(180mm LONG)

50/30 "HALFEN" CHANNEL (300mm LONG)

Ø18x80mm SLOT HOLE

M16x50 "HALFEN" BOLT & NUT

R.C. BEAM

FIRE STOP RETAINER

100mm THK. FIRE STOP

PLASTER (BY M.C.)

MODULE DIMENSION
GLASS DIMENSION

MODULE DIMENSION
GLASS DIMENSION

3

PORTE-COCHERE

THE MILL, ROCESTER, STAFFORDSHIRE, UK
Robert Adam Architects

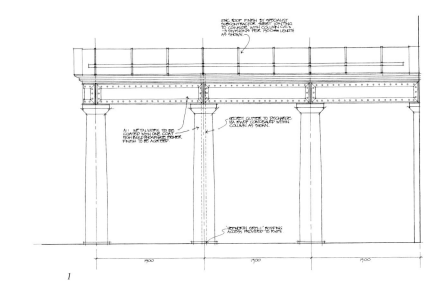

1

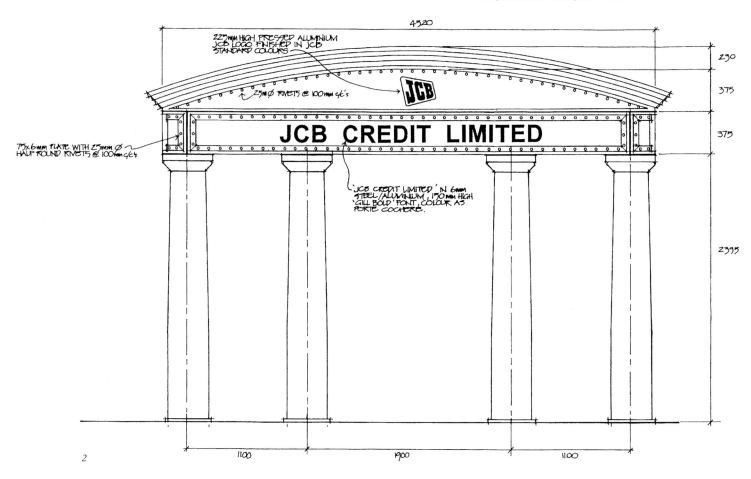

2

1   Side elevation
2   Front elevation
3   Section
4   Front view
Photography: Jonathan Moore

The mill occupies the adjacent site to JCB's principal factory in the village of Rocester in Staffordshire. Part refurbishment of a grade II listed mill and part new-build, the mill provides additional office accommodation for JCB. To complement the existing stone building, the extension is designed with a nineteenth century industrial influence. New work is in red brick laid in Flemish bond, with Staffordshire blue hand-made roof tiles. The classical *porte-cochere*, which covers the main entrance, is constructed in cast iron and steel continuing the industrial theme.

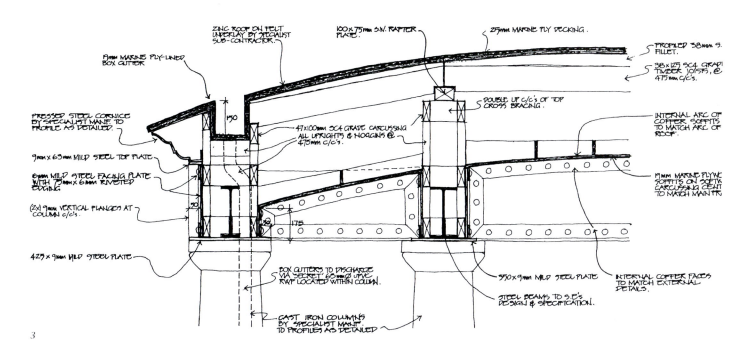

ZINC ROOF ON FELT UNDERLAY BY SPECIALIST SUB-CONTRACTOR.

100 x 75mm S.W. RAFTER PLATE.

25mm MARINE PLY DECKING.

PROFILED 38mm S. FILLET.

6mm MARINE PLY-LINED BOX GUTTER

38 x 125 SC4 GRADE TIMBER JOISTS, @ 475mm c/c's.

PRESSED STEEL CORNICE BY SPECIALIST MANF. TO PROFILE AS DETAILED.

47 x 100mm SC4 GRADE CARCASSING ALL UPRIGHTS & NOGGINS @ 475mm c/c's.

DOUBLE UP c/c's OF TOP CROSS BRACING.

INTERNAL ARC OF COFFER SOFFITS TO MATCH ARC OF ROOF.

9mm x 69mm MILD STEEL TOP PLATE

6mm MILD STEEL FACING PLATE WITH 75mm x 6mm RIVETED EDGING

19mm MARINE PLYWD SOFFITS ON SC4TW CARCASSING CENT TO MATCH MAIN FR

(2 x) 9mm VERTICAL FLANGES AT COLUMN c/c's.

425 x 9mm MILD STEEL PLATE

BOX GUTTERS TO DISCHARGE VIA 'SECRET' 68mm Ø UPVC RWP LOCATED WITHIN COLUMN.

550 x 9mm MILD STEEL PLATE

STEEL BEAMS TO S.E's DESIGN & SPECIFICATION.

INTERNAL COFFER FACES TO MATCH EXTERNAL DETAILS.

CAST IRON COLUMNS BY SPECIALIST MANF. TO PROFILES AS DETAILED

3

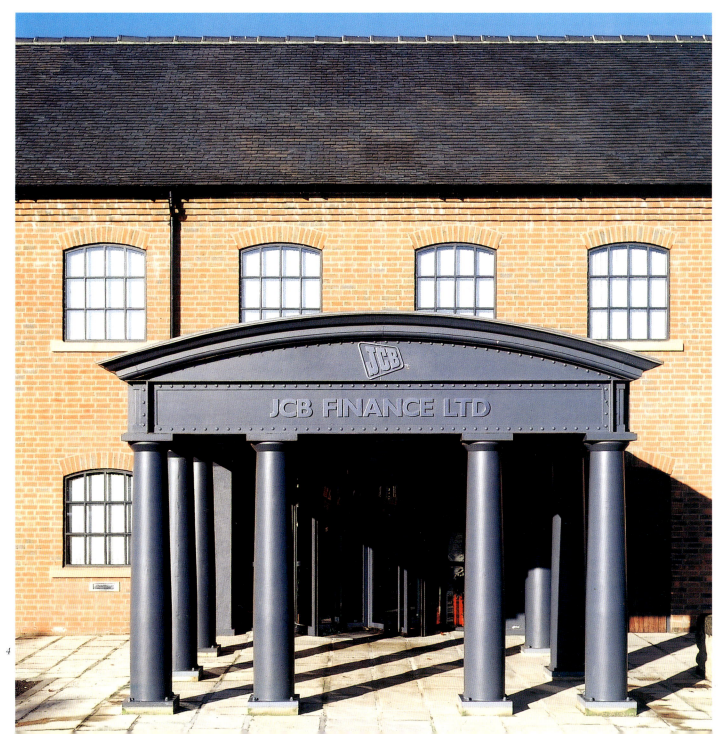

4

183

ARCS
WALLOON BRANCH OF REPRODUCTION FORESTRY MATERIAL, MARCHE-EN-FAMENNE, BELGIUM
Samyn and Partners

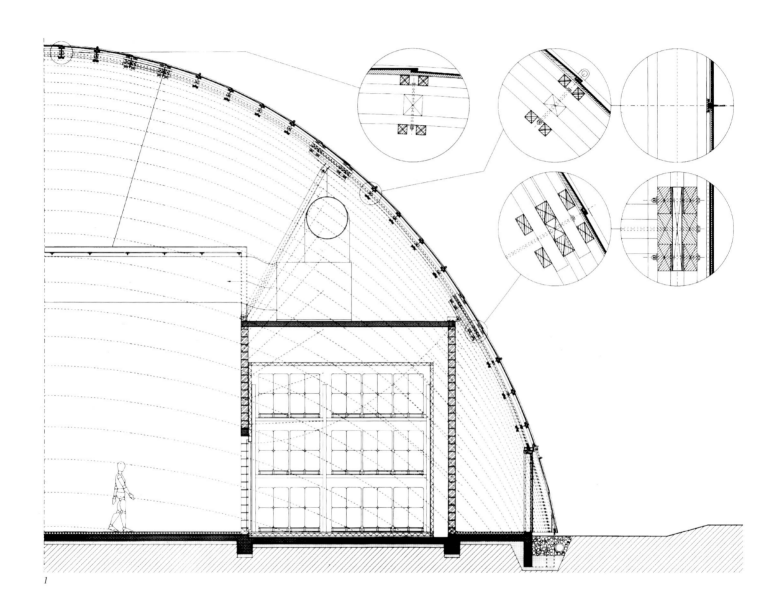

1

1 Cross section that shows one of two
  secondary buildings along longitudinal
  sides of shell
2 Front view
3 Side view; emergency doors were cut out
  after last arches were put into place
4 Final studs that support at joint of
  structure and start on top of secondary
  concrete buildings
5 View of passageway between shell and
  secondary buildings with entrances to
  offices and laboratories; clear view on
  composition of double-layered arch
6 Complete view of all elements shown in
  images 4 and 5

The Forestry Branch, situated at Marche-en-Famenne in the heart of the Ardennes Forest, houses the treatment process of sylviculture grains coming from the domains of the Walloon region. It is essentially made up of a workshop, cold storage areas and a few offices and laboratories.

The actual workshop is composed of a pre-drying zone, storage and an area for treating grain. The irregular polygon shape of the site, timbered with beautiful 200-year-old oaks, made the ovoid form an appropriate choice.

A framework of composed arcs, clamped at the edges in an apron of reinforced concrete, constitutes the structure that covers the whole building. Two secondary buildings are placed in the inside of this shell along its longitudinal sides. They house the cold storage, the administrative rooms and small laboratories; they also help in supporting the arcs of the external structure. The central nave is reserved for large machines that treat and pre-dry grain. The building is covered with 1,691 large tiles of laminated reflecting glass.

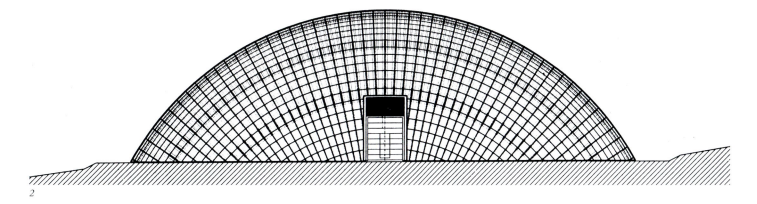

2

3

4

5

6

The initial idea was to use fresh wood because of its capacity to relieve pre-bending stresses from constant curvature. The basic element of the structure is a double-layered arc composed of various rectangular pieces of wood, all being between 6.14 and 6.21 metres long. The arc thus formed of circular segments approximates a funicular curve; the axes of which are all implanted in radian plans forming a torus section. This is an economic design because it requires a limited number of different wood sections.

The idea of using pre-bent perches to create a building is a concept as old as time, used by the Mongolian Yurt to the Zulu Cabin. A revival of interest in this type of construction has taken place recently due to the work of C. Mutschler with F. Otto in Mannheim (1975) and of Kikutake at Nara (1987), and to the experimental buildings in Dorset UK by architects Ahrends Burton and Koralec and engineer Edmund Happopld (1982).

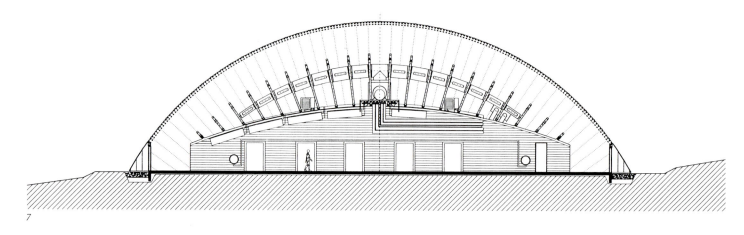

7

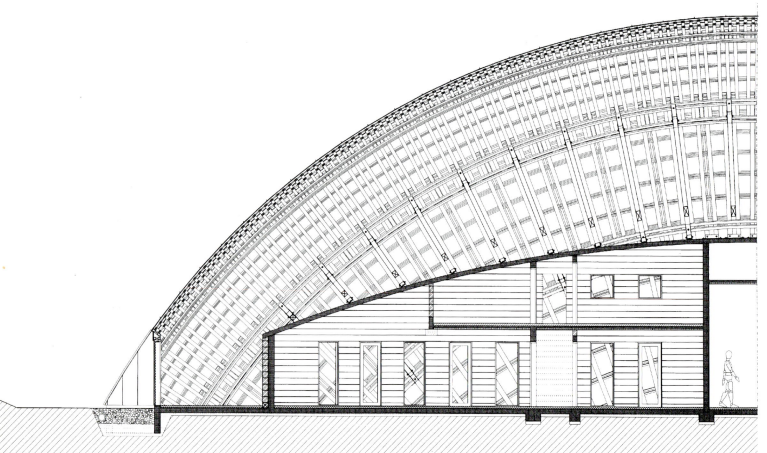

8

7   North longitudinal section that shows
    heating and ventilation systems and doors
    of cold storage rooms
8   Detailed longitudinal section
9   Rear exterior view of shell
10 North longitudinal section showing wood
11 View of passageway between shell and
    secondary buildings with entrances to
    offices and laboratories; clear view of the
    composition of double-layered arch
12 Night view
13 Longitudinal view between two secondary
    buildings; heating and ventilation systems
    still to be put in place
14 Side view showing chimneys that simply
    replace two glass tiles

*Photography: Ch. Bastin, J. Evrard sprl and
Daylight Liége sprl.*

9

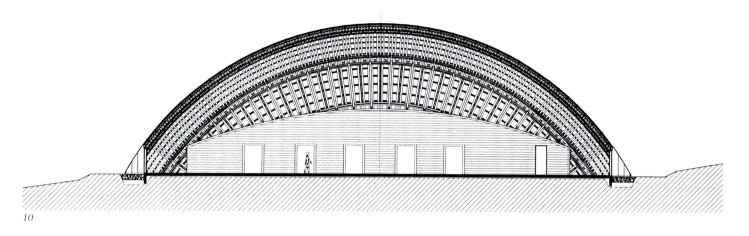

10

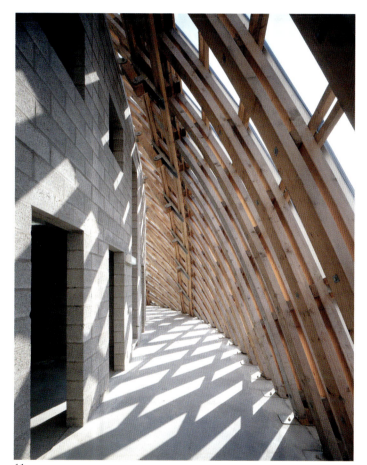

11

12

13

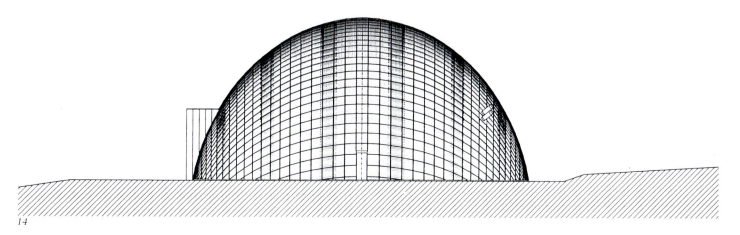

14

HOUSE SECTION

NANON HOUSE, LANAKEN, BELGIUM
Sottsass Associati – Ettore Sottsass, Johanna Grawunder

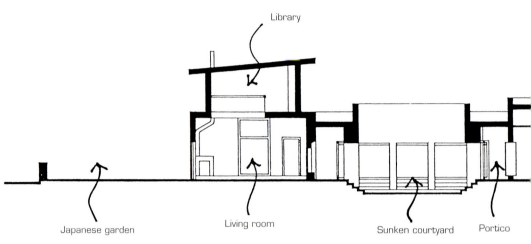

Library

Japanese garden   Living room   Sunken courtyard   Portico

2

1

4

5

3

1   *Rear view of house*
2   *Longitudinal section*
3   *Model*
4&5   *Ground floor plan*
6   *Hall, kitchen and dining room construction details*

This project, located on a large and flat piece of land (800 square metres) surrounded by tall trees, is divided into a family home and garden. The home contains three bedrooms, kitchen, dining area, living room, study and large central courtyard. It also has horse stables, indoor pool, sauna/ steam bath and exercise rooms.

The project develops around different spaces, including gardens, which are voids as well as volumes. The exterior materials follow the movement of the building rather than being simply used for volumetric definition. An internal

project of natural and artificial lighting is used to define the interior spaces through light, colour and texture.

Together the volumes and voids form an architecture that is more like a village than a single building.

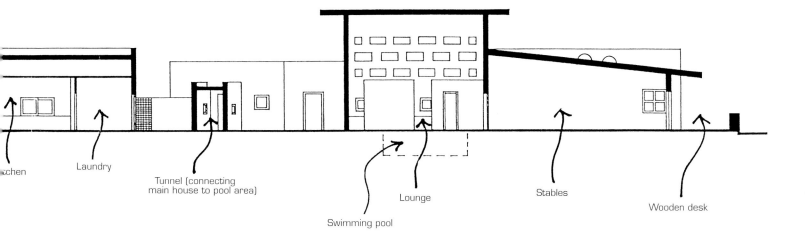

...chen

Laundry

Tunnel (connecting
main house to pool area)

Swimming pool

Lounge

Stables

Wooden desk

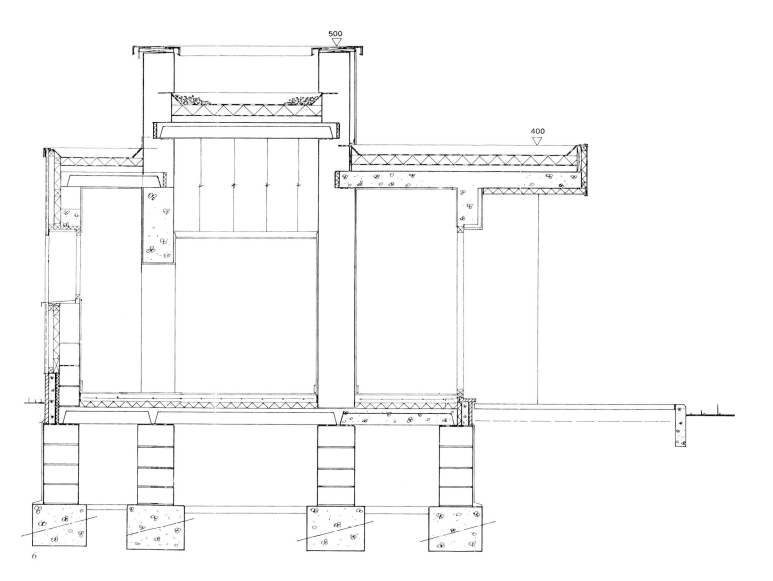

▽ 500

▽ 400

6

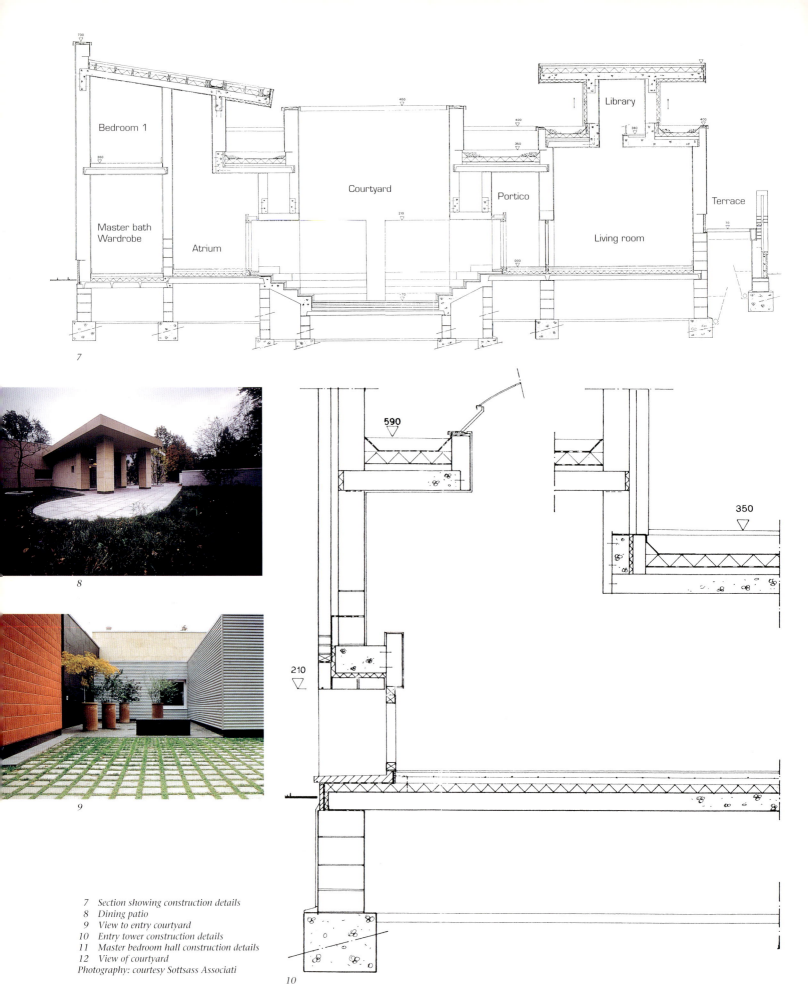

7

8

9

7   Section showing construction details
8   Dining patio
9   View to entry courtyard
10 Entry tower construction details
11 Master bedroom hall construction details
12 View of courtyard
Photography: courtesy Sottsass Associati

10

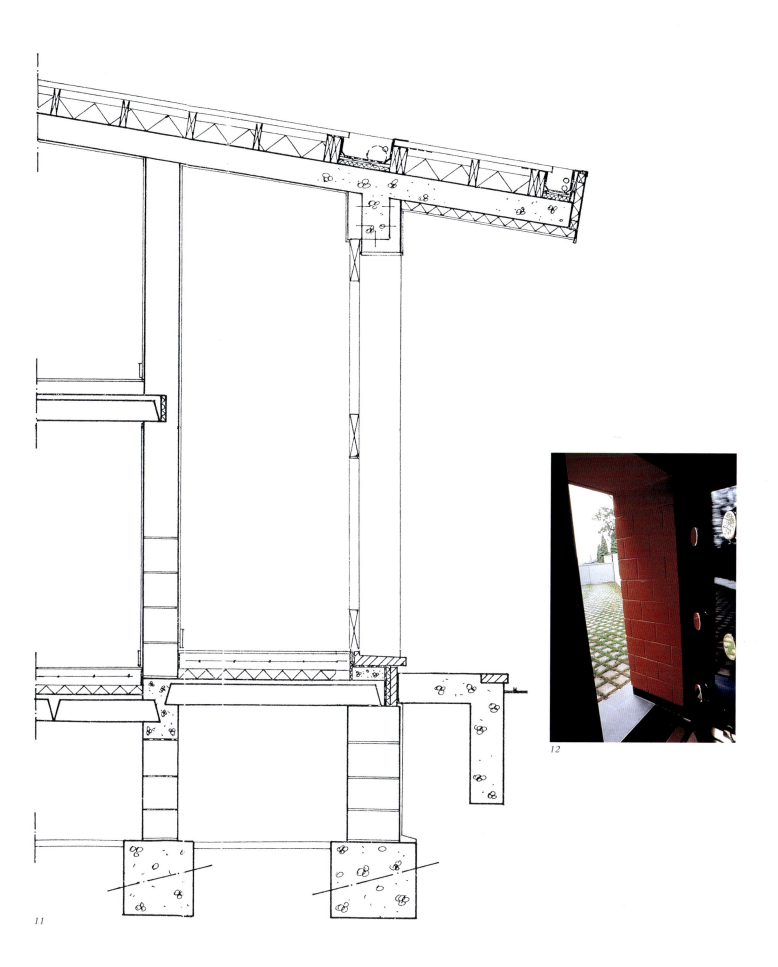

11

12

GLAZED ROOF

THE IMAGE BANK, FITZROY SQUARE, LONDON, UK
Studio*downie*

1

2

1 *View into central courtyard*
2 *Garden wall*
3 *Detail at G*
4 *Detailed courtyard section*

To accommodate their growing collection of films, *StudioDownie* were asked to design a new centre for storage and client viewing for The Image Bank. This involved a new office space plan and creating a hospitality area within an existing courtyard. The main feature is a tall, steel structure placed within this space creating two new floor areas and access to a small, cantilevered garden. The structure extends up to a series of inclined helicopter-type arms upon which a large glass element is placed creating a sunny light wall to the existing building.

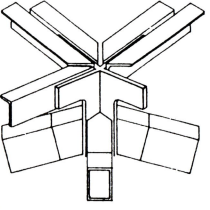

3

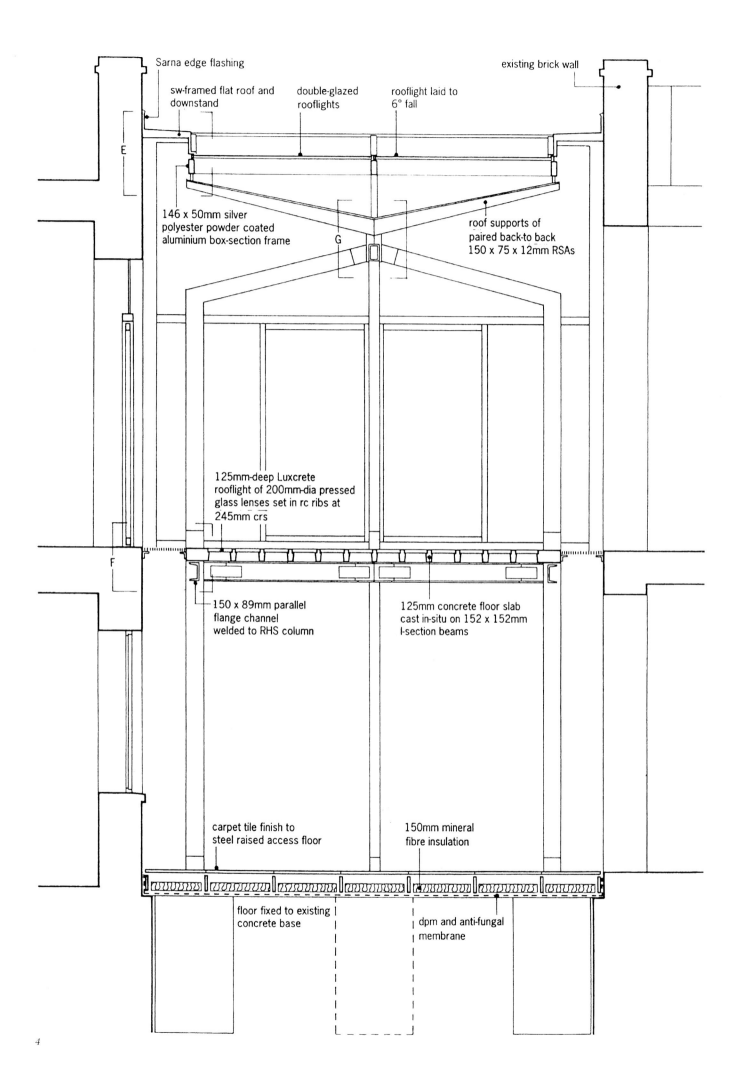

Sarna edge flashing

sw-framed flat roof and downstand

double-glazed rooflights

rooflight laid to 6° fall

existing brick wall

E

146 x 50mm silver polyester powder coated aluminium box-section frame

G

roof supports of paired back-to back 150 x 75 x 12mm RSAs

125mm-deep Luxcrete rooflight of 200mm-dia pressed glass lenses set in rc ribs at 245mm crs

F

150 x 89mm parallel flange channel welded to RHS column

125mm concrete floor slab cast in-situ on 152 x 152mm I-section beams

carpet tile finish to steel raised access floor

150mm mineral fibre insulation

floor fixed to existing concrete base

dpm and anti-fungal membrane

4

ENTRANCE CANOPY

EQUIPMENT FOR TECHNOLOGY AND SCIENCE (ETS), SAN JOSE, CALIFORNIA, USA
STUDIOS Architecture

2

3

1   At night, the building's glowing interior is
    welcome relief on an otherwise barren
    street
2   The steel and glass entry boldly contrasts
    with a natural stone wall
3   The front entrance features detailed
    sunshade system and reflection pond
4   Detail of entrance canopy structure
Photography: Michael O'Callahan

Equipment for Technology and Science (ETS) requested a facility specifically designed as a venue for exhibiting and celebrating their unique business, which specialises in the revitalisation of semiconductor fabrication, precision optical and computer development equipment.

Located in what was previously an agricultural area remote from major transportation corridors, a new highway has made access to San Francisco and the rest of Silicon Valley convenient, opening the area up to new development. The ETS project is the first of a series of 1.1 acre lots intended for small business/entrepreneurial use.

Fundamental needs of the business included a warehouse with truck and trailer docking capability; forklift-accessible service bays; a front showroom; a conference room for visiting vendors; a large conference room for clients; and staff offices with break and recreational spaces. The potential for adaptive reuse of the structure was also a consideration.

The primary structural system is a steel-braced frame and supporting metal deck. The building skin is comprised largely of metal profile panels, with curtain wall and natural stone. The front entrance features a detailed sunshade system and a reflection pond. At night, the building's glowing interior is a welcome relief on an otherwise barren street.

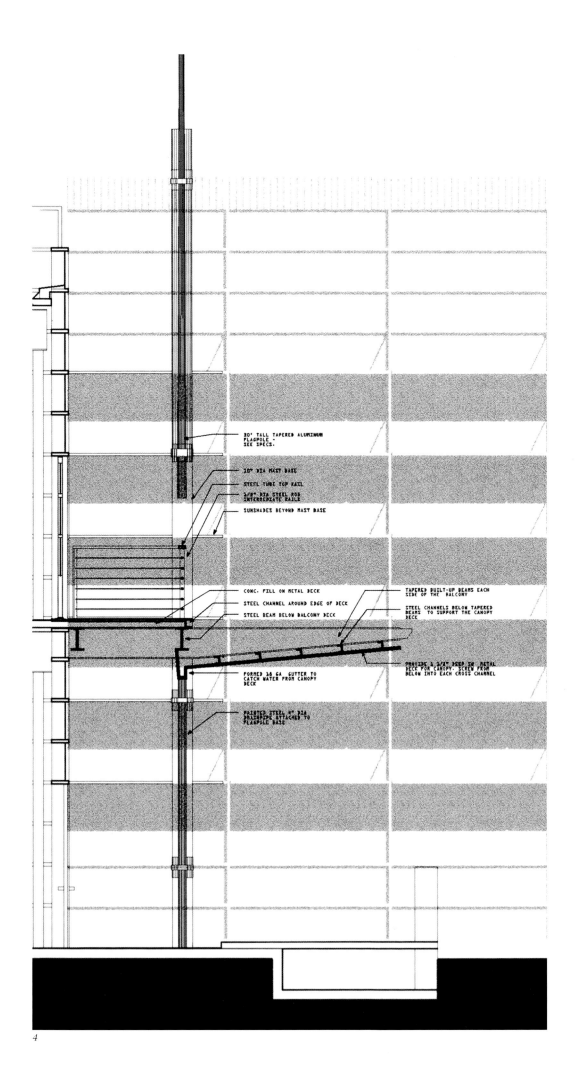

30' TALL TAPERED ALUMINUM
FLAGPOLE -
SEE SPECS.

10" DIA MAST BASE

STEEL TUBE TOP RAIL

1/2" DIA STEEL ROD
INTERMEDIATE RAILS

SUNSHADES BEYOND MAST BASE

CONC. FILL ON METAL DECK

STEEL CHANNEL AROUND EDGE OF DECK

STEEL BEAM BELOW BALCONY DECK

TAPERED BUILT-UP BEAMS EACH
SIDE OF THE BALCONY

STEEL CHANNELS BELOW TAPERED
BEAMS TO SUPPORT THE CANOPY
DECK

PROVIDE 1 1/2" DEEP 20 METAL
DECK FOR CANOPY. SCREW FROM
BELOW INTO EACH CROSS CHANNEL

FORMED 16 GA GUTTER TO
CATCH WATER FROM CANOPY
DECK

PAINTED STEEL 4" DIA
DRAINPIPE ATTACHED TO
FLAGPOLE BASE

4

STEEL SCREENS, ELEVATOR SHAFT AND STAIR
MARCONI COMMUNICATIONS, WARRENDALE, PENNSYLVANIA, USA
STUDIOS Architecture

1

2

3

One of the fastest growing upstart computer companies in the United States had been labouring in relative obscurity in three nondescript buildings miles apart from each other in the north hills of Pittsburgh, Pennsylvania. The brief called for consolidating up to 1,100 employees in manufacturing, administration, and research and development into a single 300,000 square foot complex while maintaining the distinctiveness of each group. The new headquarters would promote corporate identity, inspire employee creativity, and help attract the highest quality of recruitment.

STUDIOS was asked to capture the innovative, yet relaxed, culture that had sustained the young company during its meteoric growth. The architecture challenges preconceptions that perpetuate the monotonous proliferation of the anonymous office building, offering an alternative model that supports the unique creative work processes and almost constant change inherent in the high-tech industry.

The campus is master planned for five two-storey structures along the ridge of a wooded 65 acre hilltop, doubling the area of the first phase. The buildings are connected – and penetrated – by an all-weather pedestrian link that will ultimately extend almost a quarter mile in length. The diverse forms and cladding materials of the individual

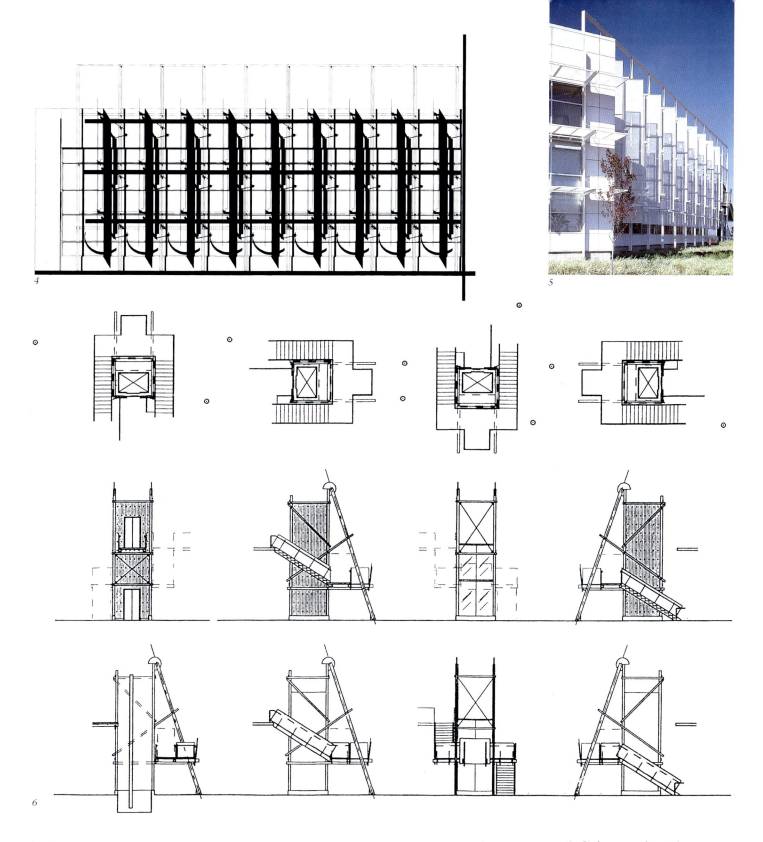

4

5

6

buildings give each their own unique personality, while all the interiors are knit together with strong architectural continuity.

Located at the heart of each building and directly along the circulation spine is an expressive steel structure supporting an open elevator shaft and monumental connecting stair. Inspired by the hauntingly beautiful coal mineheads, or 'tipples' found in the wooded Appalachian foothills, the towers act as orientation landmarks deep within the large floorplates as well as intermittent milestones when navigating prolonged segments of the pedestrian links.

1   Steel screens and protective canopy mark employee entrance
2,3&6 Steel structure supporting open elevator shaft and connecting stair
4&5   Custom fabricated steel screens are oriented to provide protection from sun

Photography: Lockwood Hoehl (3), Richard Barnes (1,2,5)

CANOPY
GUTHRIE PAVILLION, MALAYSIA
T. R. Hamzah & Yeang Sdn. Bhd.

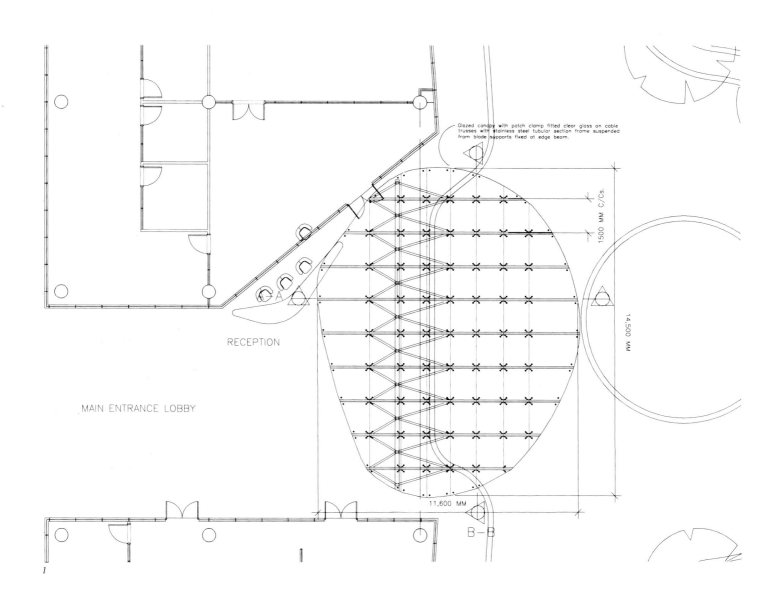

Glazed canopy with patch clamp fitted clear glass on cable trusses with stainless steel tubular section frame suspended from blade supports fixed at edge beam.

1500 MM C/Cs.

14,500 MM

11,600 MM

B — B

RECEPTION

MAIN ENTRANCE LOBBY

1

1   *Arrangement plan*
2   *Long section*
3   *Fixing detail*
4   *Entrance showing canopy*
Photography: T. R. Hamzah & Yeang Sdn. Bhd.

The function of the canopy is two-fold: firstly to announce the entrance of the building, and secondly to provide rain protection at the drop-off point.

The design explores the possibilities of lightweight structure and the expression of the structural systems employed.

The structural system is essentially an array of laminated glass panels supported by stainless steel bowstring trusses to form a single structural member.

The whole canopy is supported by steel brackets fixed back to the RC superstructure of the building (additional stainless steel cables resist wind-loading deflections).

In order to reduce the weight of the structural tubes (100 millimetres diameter), a double bowstring truss was developed to resist positive and negative loading.

Secondary struts actually pass through the glass plane via holes formed at the junctions of the glazed panels to facilitate the differential movement across the plane of the glazed system.

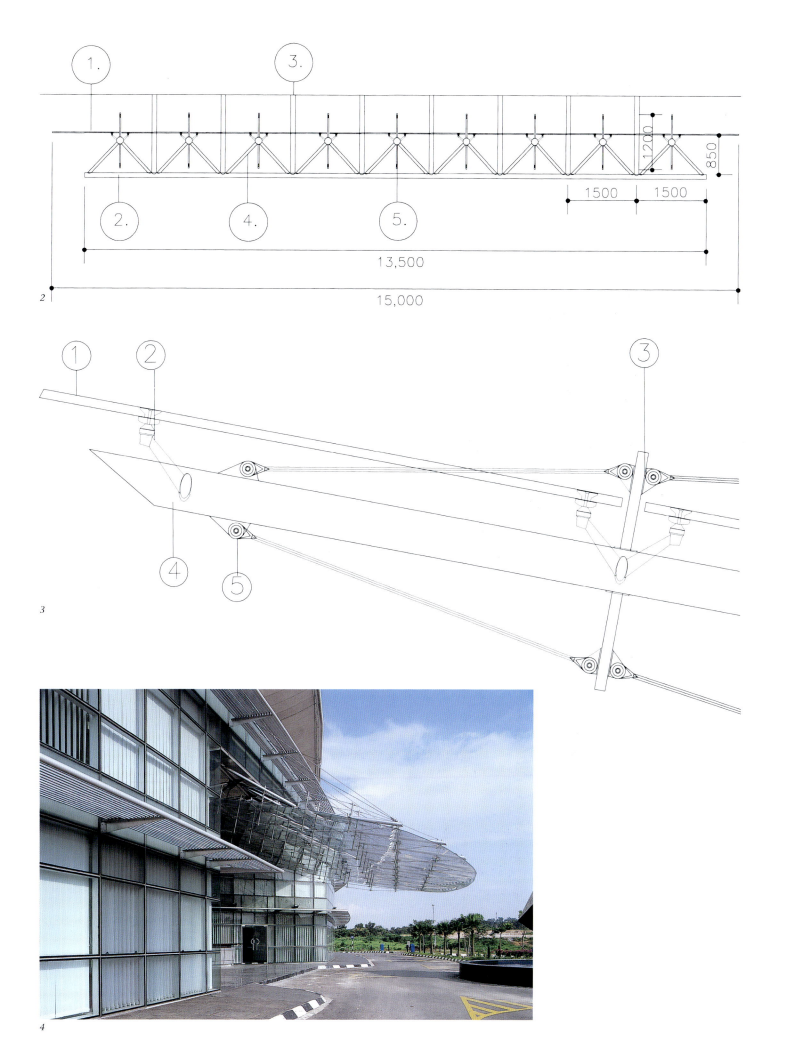

2

1.

3.

1200

850

2.

4.

5.

1500 1500

13,500

15,000

1

2

3

3

4

5

4

GLAZING
HEADQUARTERS OF FRANCE TÉLÉVISION, PARIS, FRANCE
Jean Paul Viguier Architecte

1

2

3

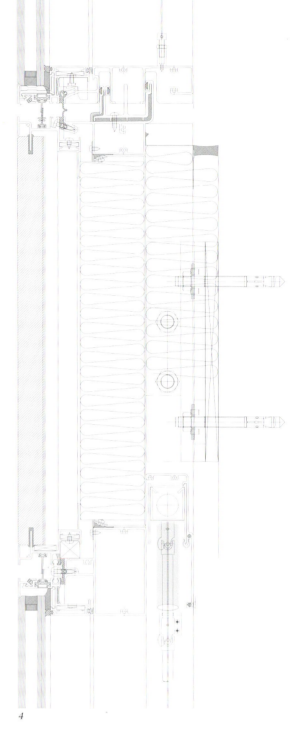

4

1 Plane exterior skin
2 General view
3 Glazed angle of bow
4 Architectural detail of plan exterior skin
5 Architectural detail of glazed angle of bow
6 Plane exterior skin at angle of bow
Photography: Georges Fessy

Located along the River Seine into ZAC CITROEN, Paris XVe, surrounded by the Boulevard Martial Valin and the street of Professor Delbarre. Furthermore the headquarters will be in an area with other media organisations: radio with the Maison de la Radio, television with Canal Plus, TFI and newspaper with the Group Expansion.

The building gathers the four companies, France Télévision, France 2, France 3 and France Espace, which where originally located in Paris. The front elevation of the building displays an architectural separation, disassociating the two channels France 2 and France 3. Each channel has its redaction organised around two atriums (one each); France

2 along the Boulevard Martial Valin and France 3 along the street of Professor Delbarre. These redactions are located above the studios.

The Chairman's office and France TV branches are located on the upper floor. Visitors circulate inside the building into a gallery that offers a view over the town. This gallery is parallel to the River Seine and contains the vertical circulations and lifts. The gallery is located in a volume called a 'grill' at the back of the redactions, allowing direct access to the Chairman's office. All the office rooms are located around several patios that provide natural light and visual communication between the two channels.

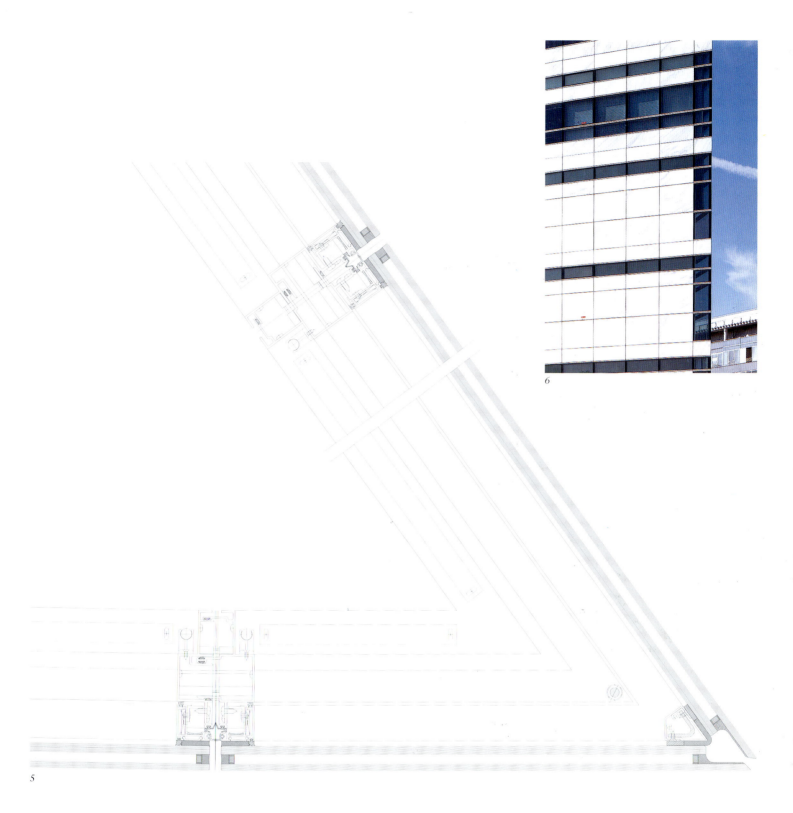

5

6

Circulations are different according to the kind of visitor or user. The public enters in a lobby shared by the channels at level 1 and is sent toward level 0. The employees utitlise the gallery and the VIP 'grill' directly via the boulevard.

Three materials were employed for this building: clear glass, ground glass and white marble. The objective was to incorporate in the building's façade three different materials on the same vertical plane to obtain a completely smooth exterior skin. The three materials are: double glazing (SKN 172 by Saint-Gobain); a white lacquered aluminum glazing stop, 4 centimetre thick marble slabs (white Tassos from Greece). To achieve the objective, the marble was notched along the middle of the entire length of the slab within which an aluminium T was introduced to hold the exterior plane of the stone at exactly the same plane as the other materials. The exterior sheet of the double glazing is at a 45 degree angle, in such a way that the glazing stop could be fixed, allowing the exterior plane to be perfectly aligned with the exterior plane of the glass.

The result is an exterior skin that is perfectly smooth giving the building's architecture an aspect of surface tension.

The detail is situated at the extremity of the building: the triangular point. Here the sought-after effect was to terminate the building with a completely glazed angle without any vertical mullion. The double glazing is composed of two sheets of glass; the exterior sheet is staggered. The weatherproofing is assured by a recessed vertical silicon joint that liberates the point and allows for total transparency. A stainless steel cable within the glazed angle carries the vertical structural charge.

PANEL AND WALL
LIBRARY, MONASH UNIVERSITY, PENINSULA CAMPUS, FRANKSTON, VICTORIA, AUSTRALIA
Williams & Boag Pty Ltd Architects

1

2

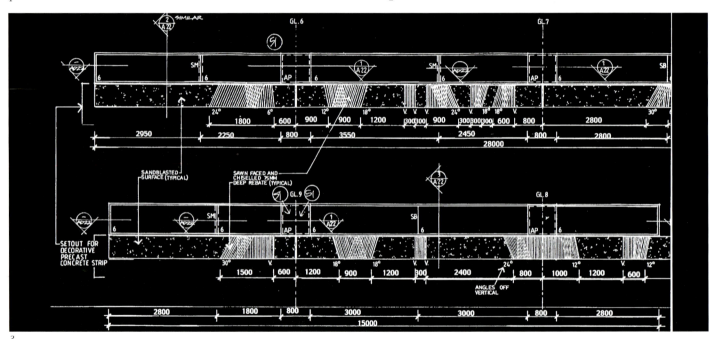

3

1 *General view from east towards entry*
2 *Detail view of precast panel with sawn and chiselled sill panels*
3 *Detailed elevational setout for decorative precast sill panels*
4 *View up main circulation stair with skylight*
5 *Cross section through wall with precast panel cladding and decorative sill panel*
Photography: Tony Miller

This purpose-built facility, completed in 1998, is the first stage of the university's program to revitalise a campus inherited by their absorption of the Chisolm Institute, which in its earliest guise was the Frankston Teachers College.

The library will provide the focus for the development of a new central pedestrian-orientated landscaped space and hence the building's entry is located to the northeast, away from the nearby intersection of the campus' main vehicular entry point, and a major urban arterial road and its associated noise.

The building comprises 3,500 square metres over two levels and consists of ground-floor administration and staff areas, archive storage, training rooms, resource areas and associated book stacks. The first floor contains further staff offices and a conference room along with group meeting rooms but predominantly contains the main book stacks and student study areas.

The concrete-framed building has external walls comprising brickwork, precast concrete panels, rendered blockwork, enamelled cement sheet and a mix of areas of expansive glazing and slot

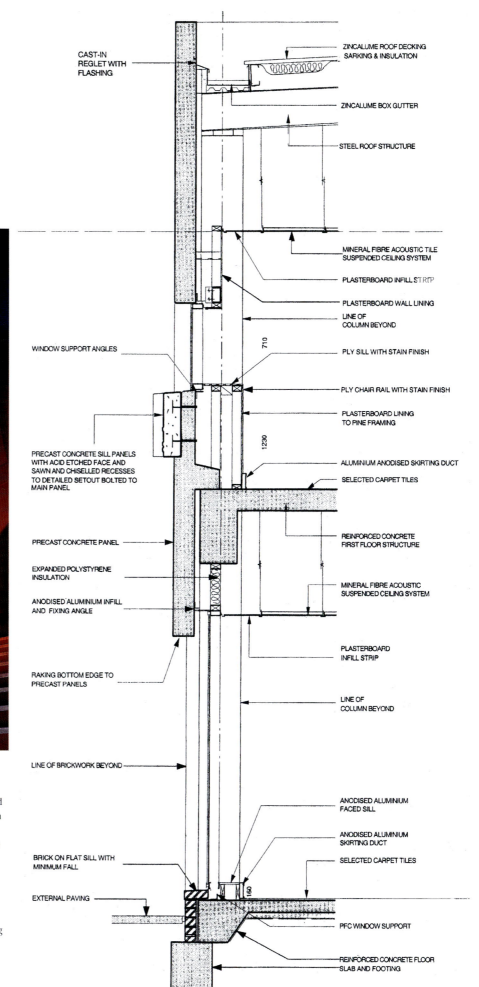

CAST-IN
REGLET WITH
FLASHING

ZINCALUME ROOF DECKING
SARKING & INSULATION

ZINCALUME BOX GUTTER

STEEL ROOF STRUCTURE

MINERAL FIBRE ACOUSTIC TILE
SUSPENDED CEILING SYSTEM

PLASTERBOARD INFILL STRIP

PLASTERBOARD WALL LINING

LINE OF
COLUMN BEYOND

WINDOW SUPPORT ANGLES

710

PLY SILL WITH STAIN FINISH

PLY CHAIR RAIL WITH STAIN FINISH

PLASTERBOARD LINING
TO PINE FRAMING

PRECAST CONCRETE SILL PANELS
WITH ACID ETCHED FACE AND
SAWN AND CHISELLED RECESSES
TO DETAILED SETOUT BOLTED TO
MAIN PANEL

1230

ALUMINIUM ANODISED SKIRTING DUCT

SELECTED CARPET TILES

REINFORCED CONCRETE
FIRST FLOOR STRUCTURE

PRECAST CONCRETE PANEL

EXPANDED POLYSTYRENE
INSULATION

MINERAL FIBRE ACOUSTIC
SUSPENDED CEILING SYSTEM

ANODISED ALUMINIUM INFILL
AND FIXING ANGLE

PLASTERBOARD
INFILL STRIP

RAKING BOTTOM EDGE TO
PRECAST PANELS

LINE OF
COLUMN BEYOND

LINE OF BRICKWORK BEYOND

ANODISED ALUMINIUM
FACED SILL

ANODISED ALUMINIUM
SKIRTING DUCT

SELECTED CARPET TILES

BRICK ON FLAT SILL WITH
MINIMUM FALL

160

EXTERNAL PAVING

PFC WINDOW SUPPORT

REINFORCED CONCRETE FLOOR
SLAB AND FOOTING

4

windows, which were designed to permit outward views yet minimise deterioration of the collection from excesssive natural light. Although airconditioned, particular attention was therefore paid to shading north and west glazing utilising large roof overhangs and horizontal and vertical sunscreens. The dark-toned brickwork provides some linkage with earlier campus buildings, however the building was envisaged to form a strong presence in its semi-open landscape setting and form a key signature building for the university clearly visible to the passing public.

5

SCREEN AND SUSPENDED BULKHEAD
McCLELLAND GALLERY, LANGWARRIN, VICTORIA, AUSTRALIA
Williams & Boag Pty Ltd Architects

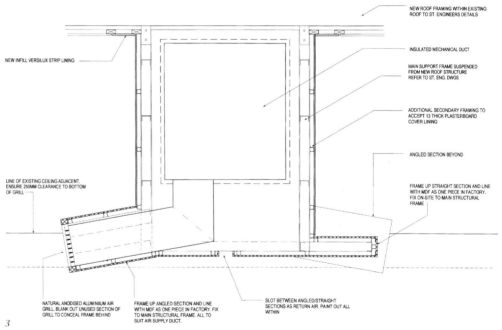

1

2

3

The McClelland Gallery is situated in Langwarrin on the outskirts of Melbourne. It is set in 8.7 hectares of natural and landscaped garden. As well as the gallery, it is the home of the Elisabeth Murdoch Sculpture Foundation.

The original (1969) gallery building has been refurbished and extended. The altered entrance area provides a new central meeting point. Each of the three main gallery spaces is entered separately from the foyer. Each gallery has its own connected external sculpture court providing a transition between the gallery and the landscape beyond. A link connects to the new storage wing.

A new gallery overlooks the front of the building. This 'glass box' is carefully screened from sun by a series of large sliding weathered steel screens.

A paved plaza space to the east provides an external gallery, looking out over the natural amphitheatre.

The refurbishment has provided a 'state-of-the-art' institution with new environmental and security controls carefully secreted into the new and existing spaces. The result is a seamless addition, which provides a new 'whole' building.

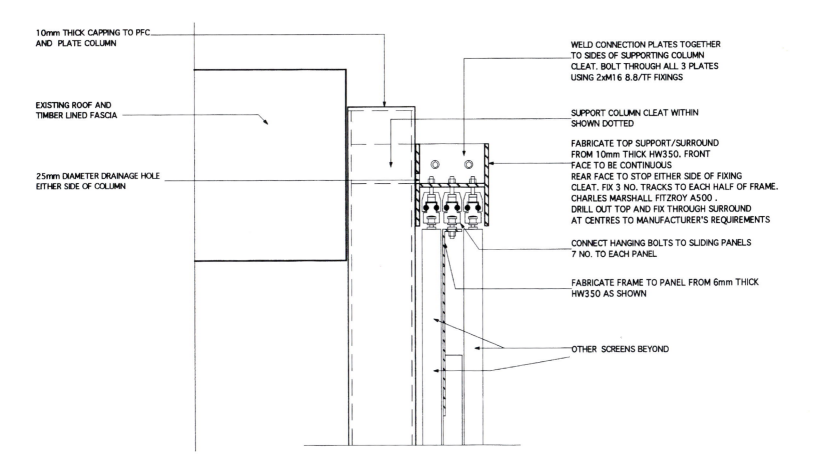

10mm THICK CAPPING TO PFC AND PLATE COLUMN

EXISTING ROOF AND TIMBER LINED FASCIA

25mm DIAMETER DRAINAGE HOLE EITHER SIDE OF COLUMN

WELD CONNECTION PLATES TOGETHER TO SIDES OF SUPPORTING COLUMN CLEAT. BOLT THROUGH ALL 3 PLATES USING 2xM16 8.8/TF FIXINGS

SUPPORT COLUMN CLEAT WITHIN SHOWN DOTTED

FABRICATE TOP SUPPORT/SURROUND FROM 10mm THICK HW350. FRONT FACE TO BE CONTINUOUS REAR FACE TO STOP EITHER SIDE OF FIXING CLEAT. FIX 3 NO. TRACKS TO EACH HALF OF FRAME. CHARLES MARSHALL FITZROY A500 . DRILL OUT TOP AND FIX THROUGH SURROUND AT CENTRES TO MANUFACTURER'S REQUIREMENTS

CONNECT HANGING BOLTS TO SLIDING PANELS 7 NO. TO EACH PANEL

FABRICATE FRAME TO PANEL FROM 6mm THICK HW350 AS SHOWN

OTHER SCREENS BEYOND

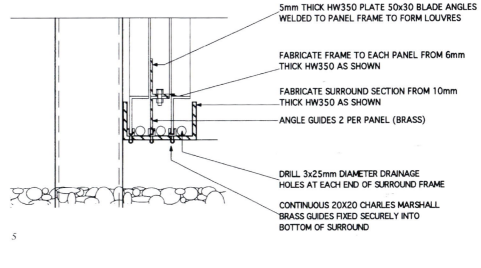

5mm THICK HW350 PLATE 50x30 BLADE ANGLES WELDED TO PANEL FRAME TO FORM LOUVRES

FABRICATE FRAME TO EACH PANEL FROM 6mm THICK HW350 AS SHOWN

FABRICATE SURROUND SECTION FROM 10mm THICK HW350 AS SHOWN

ANGLE GUIDES 2 PER PANEL (BRASS)

DRILL 3x25mm DIAMETER DRAINAGE HOLES AT EACH END OF SURROUND FRAME

CONTINUOUS 20X20 CHARLES MARSHALL BRASS GUIDES FIXED SECURELY INTO BOTTOM OF SURROUND

5

4

1   Shading screen for glazed gallery; a series of six sliding screens fabricated from HW350 steel; screen louvres are angled to deflect sun penetration to room beyond
2   View to glazed gallery from front entry court
3   A new hung bulkhead containing environmental services within existing gallery; documented detail of suspended bulkhead; supply air sections are angled to ensure minimum airflow under the adjacent ceiling
4   A new hung bulkhead containing environmental services within existing gallery; as no ceiling space exists to contain serving, the bulkhead is positioned within a higher space framed by existing verendehl trusses window and to complement the rhythm of existing ceiling bulkheads
5   Shading screen for glazed gallery; documented detail showing support and detail of screens
Photography: Tony Miller

WALL

LA CASA, COLORADO, USA
Elizabeth Wright Ingraham and Associates

1

1 Northwest elevation
2 Wall section
3 Interior north wall as seen from dining
   room; windows provide selected views to
   Colorado front range and eastern plain
Photography: J. Spencer Lake, AIA (3), Thorney
Lieberman (1)

La Casa is located on a magnificent but environ-
mentally hostile 3 acre site with a south-facing cliff
on one side, a steep ravine to the north and a
desert-type ecology. Environmental extremes and
the use of low-maintenance materials drove the
design that includes protection against the
relentless pressures of heavy winds, wide
temperature differentials and lightening.

Reinforced foundation stem walls rest on solid
limestone rock. The top of the architectural
concrete wall holds its elevation around the entire
house. Glazed structural concrete block units rise

above the plinth to form all exterior walls. Their
limestone colour ties the structure to the natural
landscape.

The limestone cliff face is subjected to continuous
failure from gravitational pull. In a symbolic
countering of the force, a 58 foot steel truss pierces
the house and provides a 27 foot cantilevered
skywalk towards the cliff. The elevated walk
affords a spectacular experiences – one where the
observer floats above a reservoir, a park with
passing freight trains in the valley below, a city
panorama to the east, mountain ranges to the west
and the daily sunrises and sunsets.

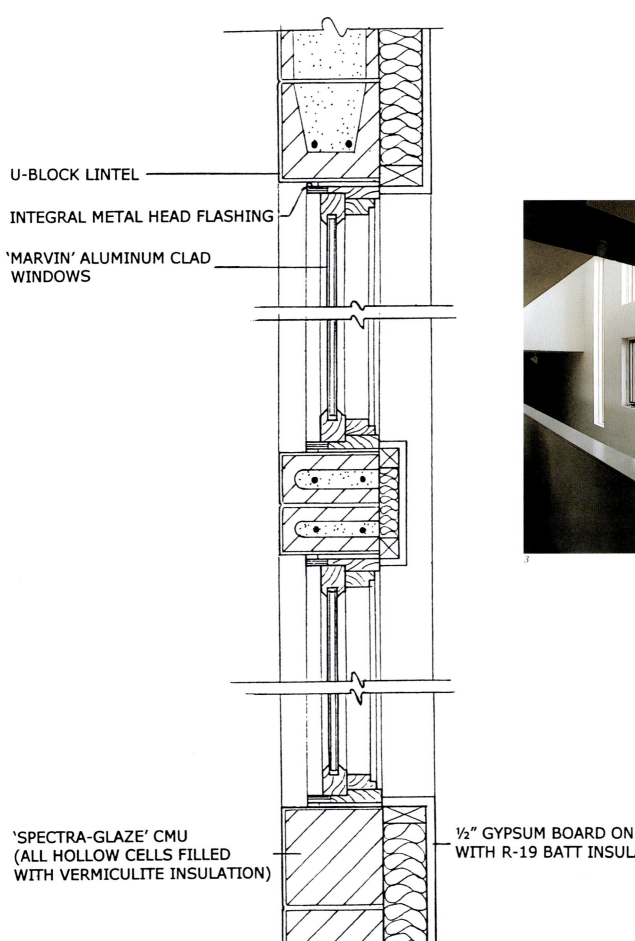

U-BLOCK LINTEL

INTEGRAL METAL HEAD FLASHING

'MARVIN' ALUMINUM CLAD
WINDOWS

'SPECTRA-GLAZE' CMU
(ALL HOLLOW CELLS FILLED
WITH VERMICULITE INSULATION)

½" GYPSUM BOARD ON 2X4 FURRING
WITH R-19 BATT INSULATION

3

2

WALL AND CANOPY

SOLAZ, COLORADO, USA
Elizabeth Wright Ingraham and Associates

5   B. WALL SECTION

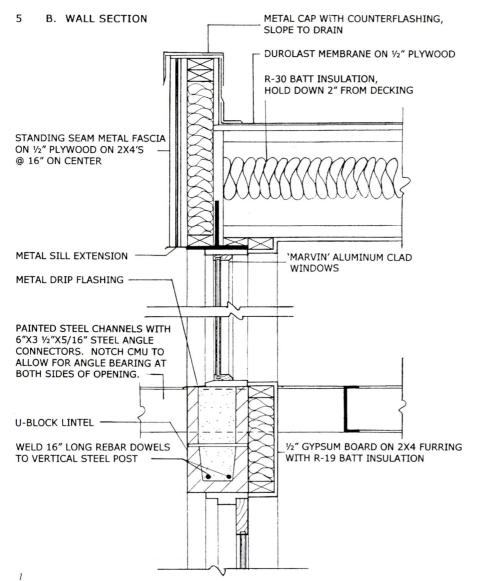

METAL CAP WITH COUNTERFLASHING, SLOPE TO DRAIN

DUROLAST MEMBRANE ON ½" PLYWOOD

R-30 BATT INSULATION, HOLD DOWN 2" FROM DECKING

STANDING SEAM METAL FASCIA ON ½" PLYWOOD ON 2X4'S @ 16" ON CENTER

METAL SILL EXTENSION

METAL DRIP FLASHING

'MARVIN' ALUMINUM CLAD WINDOWS

PAINTED STEEL CHANNELS WITH 6"X3 ½"X5/16" STEEL ANGLE CONNECTORS. NOTCH CMU TO ALLOW FOR ANGLE BEARING AT BOTH SIDES OF OPENING.

U-BLOCK LINTEL

WELD 16" LONG REBAR DOWELS TO VERTICAL STEEL POST

½" GYPSUM BOARD ON 2X4 FURRING WITH R-19 BATT INSULATION

1

2

1   *Wall section*
2   *South-west elevation of house and front terrace to pool*
3   Brise-soleil *defining entry*
4   *Steel* brise-soleil *canopy plan*
Photography: Ron Pollard (2), Joseph Oliver Church (3)

Solaz is a house and studio compound designed for a retired engineer and a distinguished artist/painter. They wanted a house with natural materials, an abundance of natural light, and ample wall space for the display of art/paintings. The design resolution responds to the clients' desire for a light-filled sanctuary interacting with the environment.

Primary living, artist's studio and garage are on the same level. The courtyard between the studio and house provides year-round outdoor living space. The guestroom and office enter out onto a lower

terrace. An integral pool at the end of the upper concrete terrace provides the sound of water.

High-density concrete block was used to insure easy maintenance. Deep-raked joints every 4 feet mock the module pattern that encompasses every part of the design. Narrow opening sash for all peripheral doors provide natural cross-ventilation. Overhead-glass garage doors provide natural light for a workshop. The program emphasises natural materials, light and space for the display of art.

3

Same-size clerestory windows around three sides of the house float the roof to create the feeling of a larger space with vertical views. The outside-inside steel *brise-soleil* was introduced to fracture direct sunlight and support interior indirect lighting. In addition, it visually defines the activities in the living, dining and kitchen space. Thermal transfer is minimal in the steel *brise-soleil* due to the thinness of the web.

4   A. STEEL BRISE-SOLEIL CANOPY PLAN

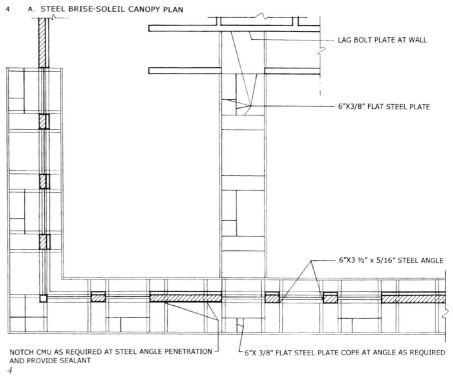

LAG BOLT PLATE AT WALL

6"X3/8" FLAT STEEL PLATE

6"X3 ½" x 5/16" STEEL ANGLE

NOTCH CMU AS REQUIRED AT STEEL ANGLE PENETRATION
AND PROVIDE SEALANT

6"X 3/8" FLAT STEEL PLATE COPE AT ANGLE AS REQUIRED

4

Index

INDEX

ACKNOWLEDGMENTS

IMAGES is pleased to present *Details in Architecture, Creative Detailing by Some of the World's Leading Architects, Volume 2* to its compendium of design and architectural publications.

We wish to thank all participating firms for their valuable contribution to this publication.